RATIONAL EPISODES

RATIONAL EPISODES

Logic for the Intermittently Reasonable

KEITH M. PARSONS

Prometheus Books

59 John Glenn Drive
Amherst, New York 14228-2119

Published 2010 by Prometheus Books

Inquiries should be addressed to
Prometheus Books
59 John Glenn Drive
Amherst, New York 14228–2119
VOICE: 716–691–0133
FAX: 716–691–0137
WWW.PROMETHEUSBOOKS.COM

14 13 12 11 10   5 4 3 2 1

Library of Congress Cataloging-in-Publication Data

Parsons, Keith M., 1952–
    Rational episodes : logic for the intermittently reasonable / by Keith M. Parsons.
        p. cm.
    Includes index.
    ISBN 978–1–59102–730–0 (pbk. : alk. paper)
    1. Logic. I. Title.

BC71.P378 2010
160—dc22

                                                                    2009019522

Printed in the United States of America on acid-free paper

CONTENTS

ACKNOWLEDGMENTS

As always, my wife, Carol, is to be thanked for patience when I had to spend many weekend days at my office, laboring to finish this book. The families of authors always have to put up with a lot, and Carol has always borne it all with grace and encouragement. Once again, I have had the pleasure of working with Steven L. Mitchell and the fine staff at Prometheus Books. Their professionalism always makes the arduous process of completing a book less rocky and exasperating. You are asking a big favor when you ask colleagues to read drafts of chapters for a textbook. However, since this text covers many subjects, and no one person can have expertise in all of them, I very much needed colleagues who were willing to impart their knowledge and experience to lead me in the right direction. Fortunately, a number of my colleagues here at the University of Houston, Clear Lake, responded to my importunities. I would like to thank Professors Frank Matthews, Dorothea Lerman, Stephanie Hart, and Hunter Stephenson for reading drafts of various chapters and for their very helpful suggestions for improvement. I would also like to thank my friend and fellow philosopher John Beversluis for saving me from committing a number of errors of form and content. Naturally, any errors or faults remaining with the text are due to me and not to my colleagues. I would also like to thank students of my introductory logic class in spring term of 2007, who greatly helped me improve the content and form of the chapters dealing with sentential and predicate logic.

PREFACE FOR INSTRUCTORS

This text was created with a certain kind of student in mind—students like those who have taken my introductory logic courses. These students tend to be brighter and more intellectually confident than the generality of students, or they would never have taken logic as an elective. Yet very few have a mathematical background, and some are afflicted with the "mathphobia" all too common among university students. For most of these students—typically majors in the humanities, the social sciences, and the human sciences—my logic course will very likely be the only one they will ever take. Many colleges and universities offer introductory courses in symbolic logic, usually covering sentential logic and predicate logic through the topics of identity and definite descriptions. While such courses are extremely valuable, they lack coverage of many important topics encompassed by the term "logic," broadly construed, namely, informal and inductive logic and scientific reasoning. A student who takes only a single logic course in an academic career really should have some exposure to formal deductive inference, but also, I think, to some of those other important topics. This text therefore encompasses the fundamentals of sentential and predicate logic, the basics of probability and inductive logic, inference to the best explanation, and topics in informal logic, such as fallacy detection and learning how to penetrate the fog of political rhetoric and spin.

Introductory logic textbooks tend to be massive and expensive. One of the leading sellers is six hundred pages, and texts in excess of four hundred pages are common. With a standard six-hundred-page logic book, the instructor has to be highly selective in choosing what to cover. Inevitably, much of the text will be wasted. My initial aim in writing this book was to produce a text that could be covered in its entirety in a single fifteen-week term. My experience teaching with drafts of these chapters shows that this goal is not really feasible. Some selection among the chapters will probably be necessary. Still, I think that much less of this book will go to waste than with the typically huge, and hugely expensive, logic textbook.

In addition to being long, logic texts, even some of the best, are often long-winded. Subsequent editions tend to get wordier and wordier. Authors succumb to creeping verbosity because they realize that many introductory logic students have liberal arts backgrounds and are intimidated by formal disciplines. The authors therefore try to explain every point meticulously and walk students through all of the steps. The aim is admirable, but often it is taken too far and results in a text that is turgid and tedious. A few texts go to the opposite extreme and restrict their expository content so severely that they become cryptic. A text needs to explain clearly and completely but also to trust in an intelligent student's ability to understand without spoon-feeding or hand-holding.

The broad scope of the text means that I cannot go into as much detail as in courses with a narrower focus. Again, though, for the kinds of liberal arts, social studies, and human sciences students I and many others get in our logic classes, I think a text that covers more topics, without being cursory or simplistic, is a better approach. Instructors who devote their courses exclusively to teaching sentential and predicate logic will find the treatment here rather limited and sketchy. There is not much on truth tables, no proofs of invalidity, relatively little on translating from ordinary speech into logical expression (too little, some will think), nothing on truth trees, and nothing on identity in the chapter on predicate logic.

My aim in giving a more succinct and selective treatment of sentential and predicate logic, besides leaving room in the term for other topics, is to get students to doing proofs as quickly as possible. Based on my experience, both as a student and as a teacher, it seems to me that doing proofs is *the* crucial activity for learning the basic concepts of logic and for improving one's logical skills. Logic, of course, is both a body of knowledge and a skill, and an introductory course should aim both to teach the basic concepts and to enhance logical thinking. One leading text has five long chapters before it gets to propositional logic and then makes the students wade through another sixty pages before they even get to the topic of natural deduction. In this text, chapters are short and students start doing proofs in the third chapter.

In writing this book I have tried to adopt an informal, lively, and conversational style. Such a style seems to offend some logic teachers, who apparently think that the dignity of the subject matter is compromised if expressed in any idiom other than deadpan. In reply, I can only say that over twenty-five years of teaching in higher education has shown me that it works to give a lighter expression to heavy subjects. Also, in the opening paragraph of my third chapter I advise students to view doing proofs as a sort of game or puzzle. One reader of a draft of the third chapter objected that logic is not a game and thought that I was disparaging logic by presenting it as such. However, I do not say that logic is nothing but a game, but that, by looking at it as a game, students might come to enjoy doing proofs as they would enjoy a game or puzzle.

Symbolic logic can, of course, be taught simply as a branch of mathematics and with all of the rigor and formalism of any mathematical subject. A rigorous first course in mathematical logic is probably best for students entering the appropriate fields, such as computer science or mathematics. However, out of consideration for the sort of student I am addressing in this book, I have chosen to employ a more intuitive and less formal approach than some texts use. Also, I continue to use the traditional basic valid argument forms such as *modus ponens, modus tollens,* and disjunctive syllogism rather than the currently more popular introduction and elimination rules. Using introduction and elimination rules for each of the logical connectives is neater and simpler, but here I want to employ argument forms that more closely model the forms of reasoning a student is likely to encounter in writings in his or her field. Even philosophers usually express their arguments informally and in natural languages, and the arguments they generally use can be more naturally modeled with the traditional basic argument forms than with the introduction and elimination rules. I also employ only natural deduction techniques of proof and do not mention truth trees.

Some instructors may object to the fact that I have changed some of the time-honored logical symbols and ways of marking assumptions. Material implication is often represented with the traditional "horseshoe," but I use the symbol "→." Assumptions are usually marked with arrows drawn in and with lines running down the side of the page until the assumption is discharged. I do not use arrows or lines to mark assumptions and their scope. The reason for the innovations is that students now generally do their work with keyboards, and I wanted to employ only symbols that are found on a normal keyboard or that can be easily set up with the options offered by Microsoft Word. Horseshoes are not on normal keyboards, and I didn't want students to have to draw in such symbols by hand or have to employ specialized software. Instructors who wish may, of course, tell their students to use the horseshoe symbols and the arrows and lines to mark assumptions.

Other readers may object that I have not taken a sufficiently "detached" or "objective" tone in my treatment of some of the topics in the last several chapters. There I deal with controversial issues such as political spin, propaganda, and pseudoscience. Although I have made every effort not to indulge in *ad hominem* abuse or mischaracterization, I have not attempted to hide my disdain for sleazy political tricks or irrational doctrines that pervert scientific and scholarly ideals for the sake of grinding an ideological ax. I feel that such disdain is both appropriate and justified, even in a logic text. Also, some readers may object to the "liberal bias" of some of my examples of fallacies and subterfuge. I do refer to fallacies committed by some on the political Left, such as radical feminists. However, the George W. Bush administration does get a disproportionate share of attention in the chapter on political spin. While all politicians employ spin and other deceptive tactics, I think it is fair and not overly partisan to say that these tactics were perfected and very widely used by the Bush White House. This book was written in the final months of the Bush administration, and for the author of a text dealing with issues such as spin, rhetoric, and fallacy, the record of that administration was just too rich a vein not to mine.

I have included exercises for the first ten chapters. The last five chapters are more "philosophical" in content, and the instructor may wish to assign short papers or essays dealing with these topics. I have included suggestions for further reading for the last seven chapters.

PREFACE FOR STUDENTS

(You Really Should Read It)

The title of this book is *Rational Episodes: Logic for Intermittently Reasonable Beings.* I gave the book this title to make a point. If we humans had been "hardwired" for logical thinking, there would be no need for a book like this. We would reason logically just as automatically and effortlessly as we blink or breathe. On the other hand, if we had never developed the capacity for logical thinking, trying to teach logic to humans would be like conducting etiquette classes for pigs. The fact is that humans are intermittently logical. Nobody is logical all the time, and, though some people might tempt us to think so, nobody is illogical all the time either. It would have been nice if we had just been born knowing everything we needed to know to make it through life. But in fact there are many important things we have to learn by inference, by *reasoning* that they are so. Reasoning from what we already know to what we don't yet know is what we mean by logical thinking. Life—or at least anything remotely like *human* life—would be impossible if we lacked the ability to reason logically. So we need logic to live as human beings; it is a necessary skill, like our complex skills of social interaction. Just as we need instruction in skills of effective social interaction, so do we need guidance in logical thinking.

Odd thing, though: Pretty much everybody sees the need for developing at least rudimentary social skills. A kindergarten kid who hits another kid and takes her toy clearly needs to be taught a lesson about sharing. Everyone can see that autistics, who suffer a dysfunction in the ability to acquire basic social skills, are placed at a considerable disadvantage. Yet, when people are offered help in developing their skills of logical thinking, they often shun the offer. Logic and logical thinking seem dubious to many people if not downright pernicious. Poets, artists, and "free spirits" of all sorts have often derided logic as a stifling impediment to their originality, spontaneity, and individuality. Walt Whitman in "Song of Myself" famously rejected the law of noncontradiction, the most basic rule of logic:

> Do I contradict myself?
> Very well then I contradict myself,
> (I am large, I contain multitudes.)
> 　　—Walt Witman, "Song of Myself," Stanza 51

Proponents of logic are often regarded as dried-out killjoys, prudes who smother creativity with stifling rules and requirements. Indeed, in the present day cadres of "advanced thinkers" have made their academic careers claiming that objective reasoning and logic are tools powerful elites use to oppress women, minorities, or the poor.

Why? How did logical thinking, without which human life would be impossible, come to be regarded as opposed to human life? Maybe because logic *looks* hard. Perhaps, with a growing sense of trepidation, you have looked at the first few chapters of this book. This stuff looks like *math*. Many of us, myself included, have had bad educational experiences relating to mathematics. I still seem to recall my algebra teacher rasping menacingly, like the heavy in an old war movie: "You vill now tell us zee quadratic formula. Vee haf vays of makink you talk." Seriously, it seemed to me in high school that mathematics, where you would hope to find the best teachers, in fact had the worst. By contrast, the "fun" subjects that practically taught themselves, like history and literature, had wonderful, inspiring, and engaging teachers. Math teachers came across as harsh, humorless, rigid, authoritarian, condescending, and ruthlessly intolerant of anyone who did not instantly comprehend.

We could do logic with no symbols or anything math-like at all. In fact, that is the way it used to be done. Logic for medieval students was a nonmathematical liberal art and was learned mainly by rote memory and drill. The problem is that you cannot learn much logic that way, and the learning process is incredibly dull and tedious. In fact, using symbols makes studying logic easier and much more interesting. So the first several chapters deal with symbolic logic. I think every educated person should be logically literate. That is, he or she should have a grasp of the basic terminology of logic, an understanding of some of the basic principles of good reasoning, and some firsthand experience with actually deriving conclusions from stated assumptions or premises. The most efficient way to gain such logical literacy is by studying symbolic logic.

Though it employs symbols to create an artificial language and has much stricter rules than ordinary language, symbolic logic grew out of our ordinary ways of speaking and reasoning. The basic argument forms I use in this book are forms of reasoning that have been recognized for centuries and that can be used to model many of the real-life arguments that people make. Also, I employ what are called "natural deduction" techniques when it comes to doing proofs; that is, the way we do proofs resembles to some extent the sort of thinking people spontaneously do when reasoning things out. Besides, if nothing else, symbolic logic is terrific mental exercise. Doing symbolic logic makes you think carefully and precisely. It is a mental workout and, like physical exercise, it requires effort, discipline, and exertion. But you will soon see that you are developing strong new mental muscles.

As this book moves from earlier to later chapters, it moves from more abstract to more practical material. In the second section of the book we look at reasoning about probabilities and the ways that scientists confirm hypotheses and figure out the explanations of things. We live in a scientific age, but, paradoxically, while many people enjoy the benefits of science, few nonscientists have any idea *how* scientists reason. This ignorance has serious consequences because you cannot understand many public issues without a considerable degree of scientific literacy. Ideologues and vested interests often oppose the findings of science and try to manipulate public opinion in the arrogant (and, alas, justified) confidence that the public is ignorant of the results and methods of science. For instance, creationists try to sow bogus doubts about evolution and businesses that profit from pollution have tried to undermine the findings of climatologists about global climate change. If you don't want to be manipulated, you need to know something about how scientists think.

Concerning probability, few things in life are certain, but, if you know how, you can make good estimates about what is likely. The problem is that without training, and too often even with it, we have an almost perverse tendency to reason badly about probabilities. Yet, thinking rightly about probabilities is a vital skill and necessary in many disciplines and in daily life.

Construed broadly, "science" includes medicine and the human and social sciences. These fields frequently employ "studies" that attempt to employ scientific methods to study the complexities of the human body, psyche, or behavior. Clearly, these results are of interest to just about everybody. The problem is that such studies so often seem to contradict each other so as to give conflicting advice. How often have we all heard that coffee, or eggs, or video games are bad for us . . . or not? Why does the advice from "experts" so often change and contradict that from other "experts?" We need to see what is going on here, and why reputedly scientific studies so often get contradictory results.

The final section of this book deals with informal reasoning and critical thinking. Thinking critically means listening more closely when people are trying to persuade you and evaluating their claims more carefully. It means being less gullible and learning not to have knee-jerk responses. Why is this important? Because there are many people out there—politicians, pundits, preachers, and, alas, professors—who have a vested interest in selling you an ideological bill of goods. They want you to believe what is in *their* interest for you to believe, and they have highly developed rhetorical skills to manipulate you. And these people are amateurs compared to the really expert manipulators, the advertisers. We live in what is called the "information age," but it really should be called the "propaganda age." Learning to protect yourself from predatory ideologues and superslick shills, like any marital art, takes study and practice. This book provides you with some of the weapons for intellectual self-defense.

So why study logic? Because it is interesting and useful. Learning logic will not make you a less creative or interesting person. On the contrary, many of the most creative people are also some of the most logical. Consider Lewis Carroll, expert logician and author of *Alice in Wonderland* and *Through the Looking-Glass.* Neither will logic make you humorless or boring. Consider the late, great Kurt Vonnegut Jr., who passed away just as this preface was being written. His novels are full of fantasy and fun, but they also make you think hard about serious questions. Like his hero Mark Twain, Vonnegut used humor and imagination to blast hypocrisy, cruelty, stupidity, and fanaticism. When you mix logic and humor you get satire, perhaps the deadliest enemy of inflated nonsense and self-serving claptrap.

So don't be afraid of logic. It takes some effort, but so does everything worth doing. Logic might not make you rich—ask any philosophy professor. Learning to think logically might also lead you away from comforting illusions, and so leave you sadder but wiser. But if you want to respect yourself, you have to know how to think for yourself, and this is where studying logic can help.

Chapter One

WHAT IS LOGIC?

W hy do we believe the things we do? We hold many of our beliefs because we were taught them at an early age and never thought to question them. We believe many things, even important things, for the slightest of reasons. A TV commercial we heard twenty years ago, which has long since faded from conscious memory, may still prompt us to prefer brand "X" over brand "Y." We believe many things because they flatter our vanity, soothe our fears, or pander to our biases. Politicians know this and that is why they are so good at pushing our buttons. Occasionally, though, we live up to our reputations as rational creatures and try to find out whether something is really so. That is, we try to think clearly and objectively about things and strive to base our beliefs on the best evidence available and not infer more than the evidence authorizes us to believe. In other words, we try to be like the wise man, who, as David Hume says, "proportions his belief to the evidence."[1]

Also, we frequently try to influence other people's beliefs. Since humans are social creatures, and we have to act collectively to get important things done, and since actions depend on beliefs, we have to be interested in other people's beliefs. Another reason to be interested in other people's beliefs is that beliefs have consequences, often serious ones. If someone believes that people like you are evil, and that anyone who dies in the act of killing people like you will receive rich rewards in paradise, then you had better be on guard. Because beliefs matter, many people exert considerable effort to influence others' opinions.

Politicians, pundits, and advertisers often try to influence people's beliefs by manipulating them in various ways—by playing on their fears or prejudices, for instance. Sometimes, though, we try to influence other people's beliefs by reasoning with them rather than merely manipulating them. When we attempt to persuade people rationally we offer them **arguments**. When we draw conclusions from arguments or evidence we make an **inference**. Logic is about argument and inference. We study logic to learn how to distinguish good arguments from bad ones and to learn how to construct good arguments. Concomitantly, logic teaches us which inferences we should or should not draw from given arguments or evidence.

When we offer an argument to someone, we are trying to get that person to accept some **conclusion**. The reasons we offer in support of those conclusions are called **premises** by logicians. Since we communicate with language, and since language is organized into sentences, our arguments will be groups of sentences. In particular, our arguments will consist only of declarative sentences, that is, sentences that assert that something is either so or not so. Other types of sentences, those that ask questions or express commands, cannot constitute arguments (though they might sometimes suggest or imply arguments, e.g., when somebody asks "Do you really plan to wear *that?*" he or she signals willingness to argue that you shouldn't wear that). So an argument consists of a set of declarative sentences, one of which is the conclusion, and with one or more premises. The following is an argument; the premises are marked by the letter "P" and a number indicating which premise it is, and the conclusion is marked by the letter "C":

P-1: Few good people enter politics, and those who do soon cease to be good.

P-2: Joan Smith has decided to enter the mayor's race.

C: Either Joan Smith is not a good person, or she will soon cease to be one.

You may agree with the conclusion of this argument, or you may find it overly cynical. The point is that anyone offering you such an argument intends that the premises give you *reasons* for accepting the conclusion. You also often hear people saying that premises *support* a conclusion, or give *grounds* for the conclusion, or *justify* the conclusion. These are just different ways of saying that the premises are supposed to give us good reason to think that the conclusion is true.

Sometimes the premises of an argument really do support the conclusion, and sometimes they do not. A good argument is one where the premises support the conclusion; a bad argument is one where the premises fail to support the conclusion. Another way of putting it is that a good argument is one where the conclusion *follows from* the premises, but a bad argument is one where the conclusion does not follow from the premises. Logic gives us norms for distinguishing good arguments from bad.

Here is a good argument:

P-1: All firemen are employees of the Department of Public Safety.
P-2: Jarrod is a fireman.

C: Jarrod is an employee of the Department of Public Safety.

Here is a bad argument:

P-1: All tenured faculty members of the History Department are PhDs in history.
P-2: Erin is a PhD in history.

C: Erin is a tenured faculty member in the History Department.

What makes the first argument good and the second one bad? In the first argument, the premises support the conclusion in the strongest possible way, namely, *if* the premises of the first argument are true, *then* the conclusion has got to be true. So if you accept the two premises as true, you have to accept the conclusion also. Why? Well, it is just *impossible* for Jarrod to be a fireman, and for *all* firemen to be employees of the Department of Public Safety, and for Jarrod not to be an employee of the Department of Public Safety. But what do we mean by "impossible" here? Lots of things are impossible. It is impossible for a cow to jump over the moon. It is impossible for me to believe that a congressman can receive lavish gifts and favors from a lobbyist and not be influenced. When we say that it is impossible for the premises of an argument to be true and the conclusion false, do we mean "impossible" in any of these senses?

When we speak of impossibility in logic, that is, when we talk of **logical impossibility**, we mean impossibility in the strongest sense. We don't mean psychologically impossible, like believing that congressmen can be impartial when they have lived like royalty on a lobbyist's tab. We don't even mean physically impossible, that is, forbidden by the laws of nature, like a cow jumping with sufficient force to achieve escape velocity from the earth's gravity. We mean absolutely and strictly impossible in the sense that you cannot even coherently *suppose* that something logically impossible is true. Try to suppose that all firemen—including Jarrod, of course—are employees of the Department of Public Safety *and* that some fireman—Jarrod, in this case—is not an employee of the Department of Public Safety. Clearly, you cannot even coherently ask somebody to *suppose* that Jarrod both is and is not an employee of the Department of Public Safety.

Put more explicitly, the kind of impossibility we are talking about here, logical impossibility, is the impossibility involved when you assert a contradiction. You assert a contradiction when you say that both a statement and its denial are true. Yet perhaps the most basic law of logic is the **Law of Noncontradiction**, the law that a statement and its denial cannot both be true. Thus, by the law of noncontradiction, it cannot be true both that Jarrod *is* an employee of the Department of Public Safety and that Jarrod *is not* an employee of the Department of Public Safety. Yet, if you accept the two premises of the argument about Jarrod as true but reject the conclusion as false, you seem to be forced into saying precisely this. This means that it is logically impossible for the premises of the argument about Jarrod to be true and the conclusion false. *When an argument is such that it is logically impossible for the premises to be true and the conclusion false, logicians say that the premises **entail** the conclusion.* The entailment relationship is one of the most important ones in logic (more will be said about entailment in chapter 4).

Getting back to our sample argument from a few paragraphs ago, the one about Erin the history PhD, this argument is very different from the argument about Jarrod the fireman. With the argument about Erin it is entirely possible for the premises to be true and the conclusion false. It is possible—that is, there is no contradiction in supposing—that all the tenured faculty in the History Department have PhDs in history, and that Erin has a PhD in history, but is not a tenured member of the History Department. Maybe she was just hired as a tenure-track assistant professor but has not gotten tenure yet. Or maybe she is employed at another university, or maybe she works as a museum curator and does not hold a faculty appointment at all. The point is, quite simply, that the premises, even if they are both true, don't guarantee the conclusion.

Logicians call arguments of the first type **valid** arguments. Valid arguments are those where the premises entail their conclusions, that is, it is logically impossible for the premises all to be true and the conclusion false. In other words, **validity** is the property, which some arguments have, that *IF* their premises are all true, *THEN* their conclusion must be true. Notice carefully what the previous sentence just said: "Validity is the property, which some arguments have, that *IF* their premises are all true, *THEN* their conclusion must be true." This definition of "validity" does not say that valid arguments actually have true premises, and it doesn't say that valid arguments must have true conclusions. Actually, validity has nothing to do with whether the premises of a valid argument *are* in fact true. Validity says that *IF* all the premises are true, *THEN* the conclusion has got to be true. Otherwise, all bets are off. If one or more of the premises turns out not to be true, the conclusion need not be true, *but that doesn't mean that the argument is not valid.* Validity is about a specific kind of *conditional (if . . . then) relationship* between an argument's premises and its conclusion. The relationship is that it is impossible for all the premises of a valid argument to be true and the conclusion false—and that's *all* it is. In logic, what a definition does *not* say is often just as important as what it does say.

The upshot is that you can have valid arguments with true premises and a true conclusion, or false premises and a false conclusion, or false premises and a true conclusion. The only thing you cannot have is a valid argument with true premises and a false conclusion. With invalid arguments, all combinations are possible. Invalid arguments *can* have true premises and a false conclusion. A valid argument therefore serves as what we might call a "truth preserver." That is, if we have a valid argument with true premises, we can be completely confident that the conclusion is true also. With the argument about Jarrod the fireman, if the premises are true, we can be assured that the conclusion is also. But with the argument about Erin, even if the premises are true, they do not tell us whether the conclusion is true or not. So if you care about truth, validity matters.

How can we tell if an argument is valid? Do we have to examine each one on a case-by-case basis and see if it seems valid to us? That would be an impossibly tedious task. Fortunately, logicians have identified a number of **argument forms** such that *any* argument having that form must be valid. However, not every valid argument has an easily identifiable form. Consider the following argument:

Pretzels are salty
_____
Pretzels have flavor.

This example is obviously valid. The premise could not possibly be true and the conclusion false since saltiness is a kind of flavor, but logicians have a hard time identifying a general form for this argument. In this text we shall just ignore arguments that are obviously valid but have no easily identifiable form. We shall focus exclusively on arguments that are valid because they have the right argument forms.

What, then, is an argument form? The best way to answer at this point is with examples. Recall the argument about Jarrod the fireman:

P-1: All firemen are employees of the Department of Public Safety.
P-2: Jarrod is a fireman.
_____
C: Jarrod is an employee of the Department of Public Safety.

Now consider another argument:

P-1: All sauropods were dinosaurs.
P-2 *Apatosaurus* was a sauropod.
_____
C: *Apatosaurus* was a dinosaur.

Though these arguments are about entirely different things—one is about Jarrod the fireman and the other is about *Apatosaurus* the sauropod—they share a common form. This is the form they share (I'm allowing "was" and "were" in the argument about dinosaurs to be variants of "are" and "is"):

P-1: All Ss are Ps.
P-2: x is an S.
_____
C: x is a P.

This is a **valid argument form,** that is, every argument that has this form is valid. If all Ss are Ps, and if x is an S, x is absolutely guaranteed to be a P also, no matter what S, P, and x refer to.

The form of an argument therefore can be thought of as the argument's "logical skeleton." Roughly speaking, it is what is left of an argument when we take away the terms that make reference to specific things or kinds of things and replace them with placeholders (like letters). We also leave in place the terms that do the logical work—terms like "all," "some," "and," "not," "or," and "if." We shall give a more precise characterization of logical form in the next chapter, but I think enough has been said to impart a rough, intuitive sense of what logical form is.

Contrast the argument about Jarrod the fireman with the argument about Erin the history PhD:

P-1: All tenured faculty members of the History Department are PhDs in history.
P-2: Erin is a PhD in History.

C: Erin is a tenured faculty member of the History Department.

Here is another argument.

P-1: All humans are mortal.
P-2: Socrates is mortal.

C: Socrates is human.

This argument is invalid. A friend of mine once had a dog she named Socrates. Socrates the dog was mortal, but he was not human. So even if all humans are mortal, and Socrates the dog is mortal, it doesn't follow that Socrates is human. Notice that this argument has the same form as the argument about Erin. The form of both arguments is this:

P-1: All Ss are Ps.
P-2: x is a P.

C: x is an S.

This is not a valid argument form. We cannot say that every valid argument has a valid argument form. The argument about pretzels we considered earlier does not have a valid form, yet it is intuitively valid. What we can say is that every argument that *does* have a valid argument form is valid, and that is what we shall be interested in.

Once the idea of logical form is grasped, we can talk about **substitution instances**. A substitution instance of an argument form is just any argument that has that form. For instance, the argument about Jarrod the fireman and *Apatosaurus* the sauropod dinosaur are both substitution instances for this argument form:

P-1: All Ss are Ps.
P-2: x is an S.
_____

C: x is a P.

Any argument that is a substitution instance of a valid argument form will be a valid argument. In doing proofs, which we shall be doing soon, it is essential to be able to recognize substitution instances of valid argument forms.

Chapters 2 through 6 have to do with proving that arguments are valid. Why do we have to prove anything? Well, if we want people to accept our arguments, and they aren't *obviously* valid, then we have to show that they are valid. Unless an argument form is obviously a valid one, we have to construct a **proof** that it is. A proof begins with the given premises and shows, step by step, that the conclusion really follows from those premises. We do that either by showing that the next step in the argument is logically equivalent to an earlier step, or by showing how the next step follows as the conclusion of a valid argument from one or more previous steps. In short, a proof *demonstrates* that a certain conclusion follows from certain premises. Each step of the proof has to either be an *obviously valid* inference from an earlier step or steps or something that is *equivalent* to something already given in an earlier step.

So, if we are going to construct proofs, we have to start by identifying some basic equivalences and some basic valid argument forms so we can move from step to step in our proofs. We get into that in the third chapter. First, we need to settle another issue. So far we have been talking as though the support that premises give a conclusion is an all-or-nothing matter. With the kind of arguments we have considered up to now, it is all-or-nothing. So far, all of the examples of arguments have been **deductive arguments**. A deductive argument is one that is intended to *prove* or *demonstrate* its conclusion. A deductive argument aims to show that the conclusion *must* be true if all the premises are. A good deductive argument—a valid argument—accomplishes that aim. A bad deductive argument—an invalid argument—proves nothing at all. So validity doesn't come in degrees; it is all or nothing.

However, there are other kinds of arguments called **inductive arguments** where the premises can offer various degrees of support for the conclusion. Consider the following argument:

P: All known species of snake are carnivorous.

C: If we discover a new species of snake, it will be carnivorous.

Clearly, the fact that all known species of snake, without exception (and we know quite a few of them), have been carnivorous, gives us good reason to expect that if we discover a new species, it will be carnivorous also. Being carnivorous just seems to be a general characteristic of snakes, like having feathers is for birds. However, you cannot be sure. Nature has surprised us many times before with things we did not expect at all. So we should probably say that the premises make us quite certain, say 99 percent certain, that any new species of snake will be carnivorous, but we cannot be 100 percent sure. Now consider another argument:

P: This coin was tossed 10,000 times and came up heads 5,536 times.

C: This coin will come up heads on the next toss.

There is reason to think that the coin is slightly biased towards heads, so there is a slightly better than even chance it will come up heads on the next toss. So the premise gives us some but not very strong grounds for saying that the conclusion is true and that we will get heads. The logic of deductive arguments is very different from the logic of inductive arguments, so we shall examine them in different sections of the book.

Some logicians make a distinction between deductive validity, which is the sort of validity we discussed previously where the premises entail the conclusions, and inductive validity, where the conclusion is not entailed by the premises but follows by the principles of good inductive reasoning. In this text only deductive arguments will be called valid (and not all of those, since some are invalid!). So if we call an argument "valid" we will mean that it is a deductive argument whose premises entail its conclusions.

Logicians sometimes identify a third type of argument called an **abductive argument**. An abductive argument is also called an **inference to the best explanation**. Here is an abductive argument:

P1: The cookie jar is empty.

P2: A trail of crumbs leads to little Johnny's room.

P3: Little Johnny looked very guilty when we asked him about the missing cookies.

_____

C: Little Johnny took the cookies from the cookie jar.

We accept the conclusion because it is the most reasonable explanation of the facts. Of course, as with inductive arguments, the premise could be true and the conclusion false. Maybe little Susie took the cookies and spread the crumbs to make it look like little Johnny took them. Maybe little Johnny looks guilty because he didn't do his homework. Still, unless we get more facts, the most plausible hypothesis is that little Johnny took the cookies.

What is the difference between an inductive argument and an abductive one? The distinction is a bit fuzzy, but logicians usually call an argument "inductive" if the conclusion is about the same properties or relations mentioned in the premises. Thus, the above arguments about snakes and coin tosses are inductive because the premises are about snakes or coin tosses and the conclusions are about the same thing. The conclusion just postulates a new fact about the same topic mentioned in the premises. With an abductive argument, however, the conclusion does not just postulate a new fact about the topic of the premises, but proposes a *cause* or an *explanation* of facts stated in the premises.

In general, logicians classify inductive and abductive arguments together as **ampliative arguments**. They call them "ampliative" because the conclusion of such an argument, if true, gives us *more* information than was contained in the argument's premises (and so the conclusion, if true, *amplifies* the information we have). Nothing in the premises of the argument about little Johnny tells us that he took the cookies. If he did, then that adds to our information about the world. With a deductive argument, on the other hand, the conclusion only spells out explicitly information that was there all along. If I know that Jarrod is a firefighter and that all firefighters are employees of the Department of Public Safety, I already have the information that he is an employee of the Department of Public Safety. The conclusion "Jarrod is an employee of the Department of Public Safety" just spells out explicitly information I already have in the premises. So, deductive arguments are nonampliative.

To summarize, a good (i.e., a valid) deductive argument gives maximum support to its conclusion. The truth of the premises *guarantees* the truth of the conclusion. However, deductive arguments pay a price for their power to grant guarantees. The price is that the conclusion cannot really give us any genuinely new information about the world. Now some of the conclusions we arrive at by deductive argument may surprise us, even shock us. We would probably all be astonished if we realized the conclusions we are logically committed to by some of our beliefs. Ampliative arguments, on the other hand, promise us new information about the world, that is, they aim to teach us things we did not know, even implicitly, before. However, they pay a price also. Their price is that we can never be sure that the conclusion is true just because the premises are. It is always possible that we will discover the herbivorous snake or that, despite the evidence, little Johnny did not take the cookies. The best an ampliative argument can give us is practical certainty, never proof. However, in this world, practical certainty is a lot.

But being rational is more than just using correct deductive and ampliative arguments. Some of the most logical people in the world use their logic to support schemes of howling lunacy. Given a paranoid schizophrenic's insane premises, he can give flawless arguments in defense of the most outrageous claims. But those claims are still insane. Hence, there is need for logic in a broader sense, logic that goes beyond just the correct construction of arguments.

To see that there is more to being logical than just using correct arguments, consider the following "argument":

P: Abortion is murder.

C: Abortion is murder.

Now this certainly meets the standards of valid deductive argument. Since the premise and the conclusion say the same thing, it is clearly impossible for the premise to be true and the conclusion false. The obvious problem is that such an "argument" will convince no one. If someone doesn't accept the conclusion that abortion is murder, he or she will certainly reject the premise, since it says the same thing. An argument that is totally unpersuasive is a bad argument, even if it formally meets all the requirements to be a valid argument. There is, therefore, a practical side of logic where the concern is not with formal rules but with the art of rational persuasion. The study of the practical side of argument was traditionally called "rhetoric," but the word "rhetoric" now has unfortunate connotations. When someone attempts to persuade by making emotional appeals, spinning the facts, and calling names, he or she is accused of resorting to "mere rhetoric." To avoid the unfortunate associations with the word "rhetoric," I shall use the term "practical logic" to refer to the art of rational persuasion.

Practical logic really has two parts: rational persuasion and baloney detection. Since, as the subtitle of this book implies, humans are only intermittently reasonable, and often, alas, resort to careless or even dishonest means of persuasion, you have to learn to be on your guard. Make no mistake about it: Many people have a vested interest in getting you to believe things that aren't so, and they will sometimes resort to underhanded tactics to get you to believe what they want. As we said earlier, lots of people are in the business of shaping people's opinions. They have an agenda. They want to get elected, or they want to get rich, or they have an emotional need to believe something and can't stand it if you don't believe it too. They know what they want you to believe and they know how to get you to believe it. They are very good at what they do. Sometimes they make perfectly honest and reasonable arguments, but not always. Sometimes those in the business of persuasion resort to manipulation. That is, they will use dishonest and deceptive tactics to try to get you to believe things.

Often the easiest and most effective way to fool people is just to lie. When the president of the United States looks you in the eye—through the medium of the TV camera—and earnestly assures you that something is so while wearing a facial expression of utter sincerity—it is hard not to at least give him the benefit of the doubt. But presidents—liberal and conservative, Democrat and Republican—have often looked right at the camera and, without a blink or a blush, lied right through their teeth. More interesting than outright lies, however, are some of the very clever ways that people can say what is—technically—the truth but tell it in such a way that it intentionally creates an entirely misleading impression. Any blockhead can lie, but it takes a really smart person to come up with a masterpiece of subterfuge. Unfortunately, it often also requires real cleverness not to be fooled by such tricks. One of the aims of practical logic is to learn how not to get tricked into believing something by people who are very skilled at such trickery.

Chapters 2–6 will deal with deductive logic. Specifically they will introduce **symbolic logic**. Elementary symbolic logic has two parts, **sentential logic** (SL) and **predicate logic** (PL). SL uses symbols to represent sentences and other symbols to represent ways that sentences can be put together. PL uses symbols to represent things and the predicates—properties or relationships—that those things have. PL also uses symbols to tell us whether "all" or "some" of a given kind of thing has a particular predicate. Symbols terrify many people, which is not surprising given the fact that "mathphobia" is a common syndrome, even among the educated and highly intelligent. But symbols really simplify things enormously. They remove distractions and allow us to concentrate on the essential matters. Once you get used to them you will see them as old friends, not intimidating strangers.

Chapters 7–11 will deal with inductive logic and scientific reasoning. The chapters and their topics are as follows:

7. Probability: The Basic Rules of Life

This chapter will introduce the basic and simplest rules of probability.

8. The Theorem of Dr. Bayes

This chapter will gently introduce a simple but profound theorem and show how it can be used to explain rational belief change.

9. Probability Illusions: Why We Are So Bad at Inductive Reasoning

This chapter will deal with the issue of why, in our spontaneous judgments of probability, we so often go so wrong (as psychologists have amply demonstrated) and how we can avoid these "inevitable illusions."

10. "Studies Have Shown" . . . Or Have They?

Every news broadcast claims that studies show something or other. How much trust should we put in these reports, and how do we tell a good study from a bad one?

11. Inference to the Best Explanation

This chapter will deal with inference to the best explanation, with illustrations about how scientists and historians come up with the best accounts of known data.

Chapters 12–15 will deal with practical logic and critical thinking, that is, how to present your argument effectively and how to detect and debunk nonsense:

12. Rhetoric: The Art of Persuasion

Since the Greeks, philosophers have examined the issue of how to make an argument that is not only valid but persuasive. By going back to the fountainhead—Aristotle—this chapter explains how to make an argument that is appropriate for given circumstances and persuasive to particular audiences.

13. Won't Get Fooled Again

This chapter deals with fallacies and dirty tricks that are used to fool people into accepting conclusions that they shouldn't. It is about identifying these underhanded ploys.

14. Spin, Spin, Spin (Or How Not to Be a Sucker)

This is a continuation of the previous chapter that shows how public opinion can be manipulated by "spin." The techniques and tricks used here are exposed with reference to real-life examples.

15. Everything You Know Is Wrong! Pseudoscience and Bogus Scholarship

Various pseudosciences, from creationism to crackpot archaeology, continue to flourish. This chapter will show how these misuses of scientific reasoning can be confronted. Also, from Holocaust deniers on the Far Right to goddess worshippers on the Left, historical scholarship has often been distorted for ideological purposes. This chapter discusses how to identify bogus scholarship.

NOTES

1. David Hume, *An Enquiry Concerning Human Understanding* (Mineola, NY: Dover, 2004), part I, section X.

EXERCISES FOR CHAPTER 1

1) Are the following statements true or false?

   (a) Valid arguments can have true premises and false conclusions.
   (b) Valid arguments can have false premises and true conclusions.
   (c) Invalid arguments cannot have true premises and true conclusions.
   (d) Invalid arguments must have false conclusions.
   (e) Valid arguments must have true conclusions.
   (f) If all the premises of a valid argument are true, the conclusion will be true.
   (g) If the conclusion of a valid argument is false, one or more premises must be false.

2) For each of the following arguments say—"yes" or "no"—whether the conclusion MUST be true IF the premises are both true. If your answer is "no," give another argument that has the same form where the premises are both obviously true and the conclusion obviously false. The form is given below the argument.

(a) All Catholics are Protestants
Richard Dawkins is a Catholic.

Richard Dawkins is a Protestant.

Form:
All Ps are Qs.
X is a P.

X is a Q.

(b) All Protestants are Christians.
Rev. Jerry Falwell is a Christian.

Rev. Jerry Falwell is a Protestant.

Form:
All Ps are Qs.
X is a Q.

X is a P.

(c) All whales are mammals.
All Orcas are whales.

All Orcas are mammals.

Form:
All Ps are Qs.
All Rs are P's.

All Rs are Qs.

(d) Some presidents of the United States were impeached.
Bill Clinton was impeached.

Bill Clinton was president of the United States.

Form:
Some Ps are (were) Qs.
X is (was) a Q.

_____

X is (was) a P.

3) Logicians lay arguments out in neat numbered lines with premises clearly distinguished from conclusions. In real-life arguments, premises and conclusions are almost never presented in such a neat, orderly fashion, but are often mixed together in confusing ways. Conclusions can be at the beginning, end, or in the middle of an argument. Worse, sometimes conclusions are left unstated and only implied, whereas premises are sometimes merely assumed (perhaps because they are considered "obvious") rather than stated outright. One thing that helps is that there are certain words and phrases that indicate premises and others that indicate conclusions. Words and phrases like "because," "for," "since," or "for the reason that" indicate that the following assertions are premises. Words and phrases like "therefore," "hence," "so," "it follows that," or "it must be that" indicate that the following statement is a conclusion. A lot of times, though, such words are not used, and you just have to figure out what the author wants you to conclude and what reasons he or she is giving for that conclusion. Consider the following arguments, which are written to be like those you are likely to encounter in real life, maybe as letters to the editor of the local newspaper. Underline premises and write a "P" under the line. Underline conclusions and put a "C" under the line. By the way, before sending me nasty messages, please note that I don't necessarily endorse any of these arguments and I don't even know if all of the premises are true. They are merely meant to illustrate some of the arguments I have actually heard.

(a) It doesn't really matter how we got into Iraq or how the terrorists got there. The fact is that we are there now and the terrorists are there now. We can either fight them there or we can fight them when they come over here, and it is far better to fight them over there instead of in our backyard. So, you have a simple choice: You can grouse all day about how we were "lied into war" and all the "bad intelligence," or you can suck it up and decide to fight the battle we are already in.

(b) Since the inflation-adjusted cost of basic goods and services, especially medical care, has increased significantly over the last thirty years, and because, again adjusted for inflation, the cost of a new house is significantly higher than it was for our parents' generation, most households now must have two incomes just to make ends meet.

(c) Keeping a gun in your home won't make you safer. How do we know this? Because statistics show that you or a family member are fifty times more likely to be injured or killed by a gun kept in your home than that the gun will be used to injure or kill an intruder.

(d) The "glass ceiling" is a myth. The percentage of women who occupy the highest management positions is not low because of bias, but because of the choices women make. A much higher percentage of women than men leave the workforce to devote themselves to their families. By the time they return to the work-force—if they ever do—their seniority has been lost. Also, a smaller percentage of women opt for "fast track" positions that hone them for corporate leadership. In general, women opt for more "nurturing" professions, like teaching or nursing, than for the dog-eat-dog competition of the business world.

(e) No one should have the right to pollute my air with stinking, dangerous tobacco smoke. The evidence is now clear that "sec-ondhand" smoke is deadly. Also, it is just plain rude to spread acrid clouds of eye-burning, choking smoke, especially in restau-rants where it keeps nonsmokers from enjoying their dinners. How would a smoker like it if, just as he sat down to eat, I set a burning tire on his table? Therefore, smokers have no grounds for complaint if city ordinances make them go outside to indulge their filthy, disgusting habits.

(f) Just because some "experts" say that corporal punishment—spanking—is bad for children is no reason for parents to stop punishing their children in the manner they find most effective. "Spare the rod and spoil the child" is a time-tested proverb that has been proven true by parents over many generations, despite what some so-called experts claim. When your child deliberately and willfully does something wrong, he or she should be physically chastised. A parent who is too timid to impose such punishment, or who is overly influenced by what the "experts" think, is not doing his or her duty to God or to the community.

4) Identify the following arguments as valid (i.e., a deductive argument whose premises entail its conclusion), inductive, or abductive. Remember that if the conclusion *cannot* be false when the premises are all true, it is a valid argument. If it *is* possible for the conclusion to be false even when the premises are all true, the argument is ampliative, that is, it is either inductive or abductive. If the argument is ampliative, and the conclusion just postulates some new fact about the properties or relations mentioned in the premises, it is inductive. If, on the other hand, the conclusion proposes a *cause* or an *explanation* of the facts mentioned in the premises, it is abductive.

(a) There was no sign of forced entrance or a struggle.
Neighbors in adjacent apartments heard no cries or commotion.
The dog did not bark, though it normally barked at strangers.

Therefore, the murder must have been committed by someone well known to the victim.

(b) Out of each production run of 10,000 widgets, 2 percent (200), were selected at random for testing.
Of the 200, 29 proved defective.

Therefore, approximately 14.5 percent of the widgets are defective.

(c) A strong cold front is moving in from the northwest.
An offshore high is pumping very warm and moist tropical air up from the south.
These conditions usually precede heavy rain events.

We will have heavy rain tomorrow.

(d) An economic slowdown will mean an increase in layoffs and a decrease in capital gains.

The only thing that will prevent a slowdown is if the Fed lowers the prime rate.

The Fed has indicated that it will not lower the prime rate at this time.

Therefore, there will be an increase in layoffs and a decrease in capital gains.

(e) All dinosaurs are classified as members of the class *reptilia* (reptiles).

Some dinosaurs had very birdlike features.

Some reptiles had very birdlike features.

(f) Paleoclimatologists (scientists who specialize in the study of ancient climates) say that there was a worldwide, catastrophic cold spell between 536 and 541 CE. Massive volcanic eruptions,such as the eruption of Tambora in 1815 and Krakatoa in 1883, lead to dramatic climatic cooling.

Ice cores from Greenland dating from the years 536–541 CE show a very abnormally high concentration of atmospheric sulphates, symptomatic of the occurrence of a major eruption.

Contemporary records from China and Indonesia report major explosive eruptions at that time.

The catastrophic cold spell of the sixth century CE was caused by a massive volcanic eruption.

Chapter Two

SENTENTIAL LOGIC BASICS

Sentential logic (SL) is the most basic part of symbolic logic. It is called "sentential" because it deals with whole sentences. It starts with **simple sentences.** A simple sentence is a declarative sentence that cannot be broken down into simpler declarative sentences. "It is raining," "The cat is on the mat," and "Mr. Smith is on vacation" are examples of simple sentences. **Compound sentences** are sentences that you get by using **sentence connectives** with one or more simple sentences. "It is not raining," "The cat is on the mat and the dog is at the door," "If Mr. Smith is on vacation, then the billing will not get done," and "We are going to the movies or to the beach" are compound sentences in which simple sentences are used with sentence connectives like "not," "and, "or," and "if . . . then." So a compound sentence can always be broken down into one or more simple sentences and one or more sentence connectives. Even if a compound sentence is made by putting together other compound sentences, those constituent sentences can be ultimately broken down into simple sentences. By analogy, just as molecules, however complex, can be ultimately broken down into atoms, so compound sentences can be ultimately resolved into simple sentences and connectives. Later in the chapter we will give rules that spell out more precisely what is to count as a sentence in SL.

Sentence connectives get their name from the fact that, except for "not," they are always used to connect two sentences. For instance, "We are going to the movies or to the beach" uses "or" to connect the simple sentences "We are going to the movies" and "[We are going] to the beach." (Notice that the conventions of ordinary English usage may leave part of a simple sentence implicit when it is combined into a compound sentence.) By convention we still call "not" a connective, even though it is not used to connect sentences. To be precise (and we have to be in logic), "not" is a **unary connective**, that is, it applies only to the sentence to its immediate right. The other connectives are **binary connectives** because they always connect two sentences.

So that we do not have to write out sentences like "the cat is on the mat" every time we talk about arguments, we use uppercase letters like A, B, or C, which we call **sentence constants**, to stand for simple sentences. So whenever you see a sentence constant like A, B, or C, think of it as a proxy for a simple declarative sentence. When we use sentence constants like A, B, or C, therefore, we will simply speak of them as sentences.

We recognize five sentence connectives in SL: "not," "and," "or," "if . . . then," and "if and only if." Rather than write these out every time, we shall use the following symbols for our sentence connectives:

"~" will stand for "not." "~A" should be read as "not A," or, with phrasing that is clumsier but sometimes clearer, "It is not the case that A."

"&" will stand for "and." "A & B" should be read as "A and B."

"v" will stand for "or." "A v B" should be read as "A or B."

"→" will stand for "if . . . then." "A → B" can be read as "If A, then B" or, equivalently, "B if A" or "A only if B."

Finally, "⇔" will stand for "if and only if." "A ⇔ B" should be read as "A if and only if B."

As you can see, each connective symbol is given with an English "translation," but the connective in SL is more precisely defined than its ordinary language "translation," so you might sometimes read more into the meaning of a connective than you should (more on this below). In the exercises at the end of the chapter you will get practice in relating these connectives to their everyday language correlates.

An essential feature of SL is that it is **truth functional**. That is, when we make compound sentences out of simple sentences and connectives, the **truth-value** (that is, its truth or falsity) of a compound sentence is *strictly* *determined* by the truth-values of its constituent simple sentences and the particular connectives. Suppose that "A" is a true simple sentence and "B" is a false simple sentence. "A & B" will be a compound sentence. Is "A & B" true or false? That depends on the truth values of A and B (true and false respectively in this case), and how we define "and." In logic, "and" simply denotes the operation of putting two sentences together in such a way that the compound is true when *both* components are true and false when one component is false or when both are. Hence, if "A" is true and "B" is false, as in our example, the compound sentence "A & B" will be false since one of the two component simple sentences is false.

The clearest way to define our connectives is with **truth tables.** A truth table is just a simple way to present all possible combinations of truth-values when we combine sentences with our connectives. We do it like this: We take a compound sentence, say A & B, and we first list all of the possible combinations of truth values for its component, A and B:

A B

T T

T F

F T

F F

If you have two sentences, A and B, the only possible combinations of truth values are: A is true and B is true, or A is true and B is false, or A is false and B is true, or A is false and B is false. These combinations of truth values are listed under A and B in the truth table. Next we list the resulting truth values we get from putting together sentences with each of these combinations of truth values:

A B A & B

T T   T

T F   F

F T   F

F F   F

That is, when A and B are both true, A & B will be true. With every other combination, A & B will be false.

From now on when we do truth tables in this text we will use lower-case letters like p and q in the truth tables, not our uppercase sentence constants like A and B. Why? Recall that whenever we use sentence constants, like A, B, or C, we are regarding them as proxies for particular sentences. But the truth tables give general rules that apply not just to particular sentences but to any sentence whatsoever. So we have to use symbols of greater generality. We call lowercase letters like p and q **sentence variables**, because, just like the x's and y's we use in algebra, they are mere placeholders that allow us to state rules that are good for *any* sentences, whether simple or compound, that we substitute for the variables. Whenever we give general rules, therefore, we use sentence variables, not sentence constants (this sounds like hair-splitting, but if you don't keep these things straight in logic, you wind up horribly confused).

The truth table defining "and" is as follows:

p	q	p & q
T	T	T
T	F	F
F	T	F
F	F	F

The above truth table shows that for *any* two sentences, which we represent with the variables p and q, both sentences can be true, the first true and the second false, the first false and the second true, or both can be false. The table stipulates that any compound sentence, represented by p & q, is true when p is true and q is true, and false otherwise. A sentence formed by putting two other sentences together with "and" is called a **conjunction**. Each of the two sentences joined by the "and" is called a **conjunct**. Again, this truth table *defines* the logical connective "and."

The truth table defining "not" is even simpler:

p ~ p

T   F

F   T

The sentence formed by putting "not" in front of another sentence is called a **negation**. When you negate a sentence, the negation has the opposite truth-value of the original sentence. If the original sentence was true, the negation is false; if the original sentence was false, the negation is true, as the above truth table shows.

The sentence you get from putting two sentences together with "or" is called a **disjunction**. Each of the two sentences that you join with an "or" is called a **disjunct**. The truth table defining "or" is as follows:

p q p ∨ q

T T   T

T F   T

F T   T

F F   F

So a disjunction is true whenever one, the other, or both of the original sentences is true, and false only when both the original sentences are false. This may seem a bit odd to you. Often in ordinary conversation we will say that one thing *or* another is so, meaning that only one can be true but not both. In logic we find it convenient to have a looser sense of "or" where we can say "p or q" is true even when "p" and "q" are both true.

The sentence you get from putting two sentences together with the "if . . . then" connective is called a **conditional**. We read p → q as "if p, then q." The sentence that comes just after the "if" in a conditional is called the **antecedent** and the sentence that comes after the "then" is called the **consequent**. Pay careful attention to its truth table:

p	q	p → q
T	T	T
T	F	F
F	T	T
F	F	T

The sentence p → q is true when p is true and q is true, or whenever p is false. The only time it is false is when p is true and q is false. Any "if . . . then" sentence with a false antecedent, no matter what, is true. This seems odd, to say the least. In SL, the sentence "If pigs have wings, then North Dakota has a tropical climate" is true because the antecedent "pigs have wings" is false. The apparent weirdness is due to the fact that logicians give a particular meaning to "if . . . then." In logic, the relationship defined by "→" is called **material implication**, and it is important not to read too much into it. In logic, when we say that a sentence that has the form p → q is true, we mean that it is not the case that the antecedent (p) is true and the consequent (q) false—and that is *all* that we mean. In other words, p → q is false *only* when p is true and q is false, and it is true otherwise. Using the symbols we have just learned, p → q is equivalent to ~(p & ~q), which is how we symbolize "it is not the case that both p and not-q." Consider the truth table for ~(p & ~q):

p	q	~q	(p & ~q)	~(p & ~q)	p → q
T	T	F	F	T	T
T	F	T	T	F	F
F	T	F	F	T	T
F	F	T	F	T	T

The truth table for ~(p & ~q) is the same as for p → q, so in logic p → q is equivalent to ~(p & ~q), no more and no less. So when we use the "if . . . then" of material implication, when we say "If p, then q," we mean only "It is not the case that p is so and q is not," and this is all we mean.

Finally, the sentence you get from putting two sentences together with "if and only if" is called the **biconditional**. It is called the biconditional ("bi" means "two"), because "p if and only if q" is equivalent to "if p, then q and if q, then p," as the truth table shows:

p q	p → q	q → p	(p → q) & (q → p)	p ⇔ q
T T	T	T	T	T
T F	F	T	F	F
F T	T	F	F	F
F F	T	T	T	T

So the biconditional is true when the two component sentences have the same truth-value and false when they have different values.

At the beginning of this chapter we spoke of sentences in an informal and intuitive way that made reference to ordinary sentences in English. Now that we have the necessary symbols for SL we can state somewhat more rigorously and clearly the grammatical rules for forming sentences in SL. The three kinds of symbols we use in SL are sentence constants, connective symbols, and sentence variables. I shall use the neutral term **expression** to signify any symbol of SL or any combination of such symbols. Some expressions are not sentences. For instance, the expression A~B& is not a sentence. The following seven rules tell us what counts as a sentence in SL:

(1) A single sentence constant by itself (e.g., A, B, or C, etc., standing by itself) is a sentence of SL. Such a sentence is called a simple sentence.

(2) An expression consisting only of a "~" immediately to the left of a sentence is a sentence. Such a sentence is called a negation.

(3) An expression consisting only of two sentences connected with "&" is a sentence. Such a sentence is called a conjunction.

(4) An expression consisting only of two sentences connected with "v" is a sentence. Such a sentence is called a disjunction.

(5) An expression consisting only of two sentences connected with "→" is a sentence. Such a sentence is called a conditional.

(6) An expression consisting only of two sentences connected with "⇔" is a sentence. Such a sentence is called a biconditional.

And equally importantly:

(7) Only expressions of the types specified in rules (1)–(6) are sentences in SL. In other words, the only types of sentences we have in SL are simple sentences, negations, conjunctions, disjunctions, conditionals, and biconditionals.

From these rules we can generate compound sentences of any degree of complexity, with sentences nested inside of sentences, nested inside of sentences, and so on. For instance, by rule (1) A is a sentence. By rule (2) ~A is a sentence, so by rule (2) again ~~A is also a sentence (you can keep this up *ad nauseam*; ~~~~~~A is also a sentence). By rule (3) ~~A & B is a sentence, since it uses "&" to connect the sentence ~~A with the sentence B. By rule (4) (~~A & B) v C is a sentence since it uses "v" to connect the sentence ~~A & B with the sentence C. By rule (5) [(~~A & B) v C] → ~D is a sentence, since it uses "→" to connect the sentence (~~A & B) v C to the sentence ~D. By rule (6) {[(~~A & B) v C] → ~D} ⇔ (~D v ~C) is a sentence (though almost certainly we would never utter a sentence like this in English) because it uses "⇔" to connect sentence [(~~A & B) v C] → ~D to sentence (~D v ~C). Finally, rule (7) tells us why expressions like A~B& are not sentences in SL. A~B& is not a sentence of SL because it is not one of the types of expressions specified in rules (1)–(6).

You probably noted that we used parentheses—( ), brackets—[ ], and braces—{ } to punctuate the compound sentences in the above paragraph. Parentheses, brackets, and braces are not really symbols of SL; they are merely punctuation marks used to make the meaning of compound sentences clear. Like correct sentences in ordinary language, we require that sentences in SL be properly punctuated. Consider the following expression:

(1) A v B → C

This expression is **ambiguous**. An ambiguous expression is one that could have either (any) of two or more meanings, that is, by adding parentheses, brackets, or braces to it, we could turn it into either (any) of two or more different sentences. Expression (1) could mean that we take A, put together with B by disjunction, and then make the whole disjunction the antecedent in a conditional with C as the consequent. Or it could mean that we have a conditional with B as the antecedent and C as the consequent, and then we attach A to the conditional by disjunction. In other words, the above expression could mean either of these two sentences:

(2) $(A \lor B) \rightarrow C$

(3) $A \lor (B \rightarrow C)$

These two sentences are *not* equivalent, any more than $(2 + 5) \times 4$ and $2 + (5 \times 4)$ are. If A is true, B is false, and C is false, then (2) is false and (3) is true. So we use parentheses to indicate to which sentence constants or variables a connective applies. The parentheses in the first expression indicate that the "v" applies only to the A and the B. For more complicated expressions, we use brackets, [ ], as well as parentheses. For instance:

(4) $[(A \lor B) \rightarrow C] \& \sim D$

This tells us that we first put A and B together by disjunction, then make the disjunction the antecedent of a conditional with C as the consequent, and then take that whole expression and make it half of a conjunction with ~D. With even more complicated expressions we add braces, { }, to brackets and parentheses. For instance:

(5) $A \rightarrow \{(B \lor \sim D) \lor [\sim(H \& \sim G) \Leftrightarrow (K \lor \sim D)]\}$

This is a conditional sentence with A as the antecedent and everything in the braces as the consequent.

So long as an expression remains ambiguous, we cannot tell *which* sentence it is supposed to represent. We therefore stipulate that, where necessary, we shall use parentheses, brackets, and braces to remove ambiguity from expressions in SL.

In keeping clear on what kind of sentence we have—whether it is a conditional, disjunction, conjunction, and so forth—it is often useful to be able to identify the **main connective**, that is, the connective that joins everything into a whole complex sentence. For instance, in the following expression

[(A v B) → C] & ~D

the main connective is the "&" because it brings the sentence [(A v B) → C] together with the sentence ~D to make a whole new sentence [(A v B) → C] & ~D. Another way to put it is that the **scope** of the main connective is the *entire* sentence. The scope of a connective is the connective itself and whatever it connects. The main connective connects together the entire sentence, so the whole sentence is within its scope. Every other connective has a limited scope that does not extend to the whole sentence. The "v" only connects the A and the B, the "→" connects (A v B) with C, and the "~" only applies to D. Only the "&" connects the whole thing. The main connective determines what kind of sentence a compound sentence is. If the main connective is a "~," the sentence is a negation; if the main connective is a "&," it is a conjunction; if the main connective is a "v," the sentence is a disjunction; if the main connective is a "→," it is a conditional; finally, if the main connective is a "⇔," it is a biconditional.

Now that we know what a sentence is in SL, we can define a **sentence form**. Further, since sentence forms can constitute **argument forms**, we can give a more precise statement of that notion than we did in the previous chapter. An expression of SL is a sentence form if and only if: (a) it consists of one or more sentence variables and any connectives, if present, and (b) when you replace each variable by a simple or compound sentence, making sure that each occurrence of a given variable is replaced by the same simple or compound sentence, and leaving all connectives unchanged, the result is a simple or compound sentence according to our seven rules.

This sounds rather complicated, but the idea is really quite simple. Consider the expression

(1) p → (q & ~r)

this is a sentence form because if we replace p with the sentence A, q with the sentence B & C, and r with the sentence D v ~C, we get

(2) A → [(B & C) & ~(D v ~C)]

which is a sentence according to our seven rules. The sentence you get from a sentence form by replacing each of its sentence variables with a properly punctuated sentence is called a **substitution instance** of that form. Thus, sentence (2) above is a substitution instance of the sentence form (1). It is important to realize that quite complex sentences can be substitution instances of very simple sentence forms. For instance,

{[A & ~(~C v ~~D)]→[(D v ~~C) & ~E]} ⇔ [B → (D v E)]

still has the simple sentence form p ⇔ q because p can stand for

[A & ~(~C v ~~D)] → [(D v ~~C) & ~E]

and q can stand for

B → (D v E).

Note that when we substitute a sentence for a sentence variable in a sentence form, we have to be sure to use proper punctuation with parentheses, brackets, or braces. If we don't respect correct punctuation, we might create a sentence that is not a substitution instance of the given form. For instance, consider the sentence form ~p. Now suppose we try to substitute the sentence A v B for p, but we forget to properly punctuate A v B by enclosing it in parentheses. The result will be the disjunction ~A v B, which is not a substitution instance of the sentence form ~p. To make the negation apply to the whole expression A v B, you have to enclose it in parentheses. ~(A v B) is correct.

Note also that each occurrence of a given variable has to be replaced by the same sentence. If your argument form is, for instance, p v (p & q) you cannot substitute the sentence A for the first instance of p and B for the second instance of p. A v (B & C) is not a substitution instance of p v (p & q).

Finally, note that a compound sentence *always* is a substitution instance of two or more sentence forms. For instance:

~[A v (C → D)]

is a substitution instance of the following forms:

p (substitute the sentence ~[A v (C → D)] for p)
~p (substitute the sentence A v (C → D) for p)
~(p v q) (substitute the sentence A for p and the sentence C → D
    for q)
and ~[p v (q → r)] (substitute A for p, C for q, and D for r)

You can put sentence forms together to make argument forms. For instance, this is an argument form (let's call it "f"):

(f)
   p → (r & s)
   ~r v ~s
   _____

   ~p

The two sentence forms above the line are the premises and the sentence form below the line is the conclusion. If we replace each of the sentence variables in the above argument form with particular sentences, making sure that each instance of each variable in the argument form is replaced by the same sentence, the result will be an argument that has that form. For instance,

(a)
   A → (B & C)
   ~B v ~C
   _____

   ~A

This is an argument that has the specified form. We substituted A for p, B for r, and C for s. Likewise, if we substitute different sentences for the sentence variables in the argument form we get a different argument of that same form. For instance,

(a*)

$(D \& H) \rightarrow [(E v F) \& \sim H]$
$\sim (E v F) v \sim\sim H$

_____

$\sim (D \& H)$

Here we substituted D & H for p, E v F for r, and ~H for s. (a*) is therefore a different argument than (a) but it has the same form, namely, both arguments (a) and (a*) have the form (f). Put another way, like sentence forms, argument forms can have substitution instances. Arguments (a) and (a*) are different substitution instances of the argument form (f).

Why are we going to all this trouble to define sentence forms and argument forms? Because the most important thing students do in introductory logic is to construct proofs, and to construct proofs in SL you have to start with some simple, basic, valid argument forms. These will be given at the beginning of the next chapter. Being able to recognize that an argument, even a rather complex one, can have one of these simple forms is an essential skill for doing proofs. You have to be able to see the simple form in the confusing mass of symbols. To do this you need to know what an argument form is and what it means for an argument to be a substitution instance of a form.

EXERCISES FOR CHAPTER 2

1) As always, ordinary language is both richer and vaguer than the special languages logicians create. It is not always easy to see how to "translate" from ordinary language into the formal and more rigorous idiom of logic. However, there are some useful guidelines.

"If p then q" can be expressed as "if p, q," "q, if p" or "p only if q." This may seem confusing, since "if" and "only if" sound so much alike, but really their meaning is quite different. Consider the following two sentences: (a) "You can win the lottery only if you buy a lottery ticket" and (b) "You can buy a lottery ticket if you have $1." Sentence (a) does not say that you will win the lottery *if* you buy a ticket; buying a ticket only gives you a (very small) chance of winning. But you *cannot* win if you don't buy a ticket. Sentence (b) says that you *can* buy a ticket if you have $1. That is, having a dollar is all you need to get a ticket. For right now, just remember that when you see "if" right before a sentence, that sentence is the antecedent in your "if . . . then" sentence, and when you see "only if" right before a sentence, that sentence is the consequent in the "if . . . then" sentence.

Another problem is "unless." When you see a sentence that has the form "p unless q," take "unless" to mean "if not." In other words, take the sentence that follows the "unless," negate it, and make it the antecedent in your "if . . . then" sentence. For instance, if we have the sentence "We will have a picnic tomorrow unless it rains," symbolize this (using R for "it rains" and P for "We will have a picnic") as ~R → P.

Finally, ordinary language often has sentences like "This restaurant does not have much atmosphere, but the food is good." We will just translate "but" as "and." So, "This restaurant does not have much atmosphere, but the food is good" would be translated (using the obvious sentence constants) as ~A & G. All the other translations will probably be pretty obvious.

Translate the following sentences from ordinary language to SL. Use the indicated letters for sentence constants. Then, when you have finished the translation, indicate the main connective.

(a) The Democrats will carry the election only if they don't commit a major blunder before election day.
D = The Democrats will carry the election.
B = They commit a major blunder before election day.

(b) Harry will not visit the dentist unless he has an excruciating toothache.
H = Harry will visit the dentist
T = He has an excruciating toothache.

(c) The mill will remain open only if the workers back off from their demands or the owners have a change of heart.

M = The mill will remain open.

W = The workers back off from their demands.

O = The owners have a change of heart.

(d) If Route 69 is jammed, you take the Baker Street exit and go left until you get to Shorter Avenue.

R = Route 69 is jammed.

B = You take the Baker Street exit.

S = You go left until you get to Shorter Avenue.

(e) A cover sheet must accompany all TPS reports unless you have previously filled out a PZQ/az form and filed it in triplicate with the director of marketing.

C = A cover sheet must accompany all TPS reports.

P = You have previously filled out a PZQ/az form.

F = You have filed it in triplicate with the director of marketing.

(f) A major league team plays in the World Series if and only if it wins the pennant of the National League or the American League.

M = A major league team plays in the World Series.

N = It wins the pennant of the National League.

A = It wins the pennant of the American League.

(g) You can adopt a child from a third world country, but it helps to be rich and to be a pop star.

A = You can adopt a child from a third world country

R = It helps to be rich.

P = It helps to be a pop star.

(h) You can't always get what you want, but if you try sometimes, you just might get what you need.

W = You always get what you want.

T = You try sometimes.

N = You just might get what you need.

2) Show how parentheses, brackets, and braces can be used to punctuate the following ambiguous expression and turn it into five different non-ambiguous sentences (more than five are possible, but just do five).

A v B → C & D v E

3) Indicate which of the following are sentences of SL according to the seven rules. If it is a sentence of SL, indicate whether it is a simple sentence, a negation, a conjunction, a disjunction, a conditional, or a biconditional.

> (a) B & ~D
> (b) ~~H
> (c) B v H & C
> (d) A &
> (e) ~[C v ~(F → D)]
> (f) v H
> (g) ~H ~M
> (h) ~L → (M v ~D)
> (i) (M & R) ⇔ (L v ~L)
> (j) @##*^!!!

4) For each of the following argument forms, indicate—"yes" or "no"—whether the following sentences are substitution instances of that form. Here is how you tell:
Consider the argument form

p v ~r

Is A v ~(B & C) a substitution instance of p v ~r? Yes it is, and you can tell by showing which sentence you substitute for which sentence variable. Thus:

p : A

r : B & C

That is, if you substitute A for p and B & C (properly punctuated with parentheses) for r, you get A v ~(B & C) from the sentence form p v ~r.

Is the sentence A v (~B & C) a substitution instance of p v ~r? No it isn't, and you can tell by the fact that there is no sentence you can substitute for r that will give you A v (~B & C):

p : A

r: ???

If you tried to substitute ~B & C for r you would get A v ~(~B &C), not A v (~B & C).

So, say which sentences are substitution instances of the following forms, and for each one that is a substitution instance, show which sentence replaces which variable.

(a) p v q
    (1) A v (B v C)
    (2) (B & C) v ~A
    (3) (D v F) → (G v E)
    (4) ~E v ~(F ⇔ G)
    (5) [D v (F v G)] v ~E

(b) ~p & ~q
    (1) B v ~(F & G)
    (2) C & ~(H & I)
    (3) ~(L v F) & ~~H
    (4) ~M & ~[F v (H v G)]
    (5) ~H & B

(c) p → (r & s)
    (1 A → B
    (2) (H v J) → {L & [M & (A v B)]}
    (3) D v (H & N)
    (4) E → ~(B & A)
    (5) (B v D) → (~J & ~K)

5) For each of the following argument forms, say, "yes" or "no," whether the following arguments have that form:

(a) **p → q**
p
———
q

(1) ~A → ~B
~A
———
~B

(2) (A v B) → (C & ~D)
A v B
——————————
C & ~D

(3) H → (J & K)
J & K
————————
H

(b) **p v q**
~ p
———
q

(1) ~A v ~B
~A
———
~B

(2) (A v B) v C
~(A v B)
————————
C

(3) [H v (J & ~C)] v ~L
   ~[H v (J & ~C)]

―――――――――――

~L

(c) p → q
    q → r

――――

p → r

(1) M → (R v S)
   (R v S) → ~H

―――――――――

M → ~H

(2) H → A
   (M & L) → A

―――――――――

H → (M & L)

(3) [H & (J v K)] → ~B
   ~B → (F & C)

―――――――――――――

[H & (J v K)] → (F & C)

(d) p → q
    ~q

――――

~p

(1) ~H → (B v C)
   ~(B v C)

―――――――――

~~H

(2) $M \rightarrow (L \ \& \ B)$
~M
_____

~(L & B)

(3) $[(H \ v \ M) \ v \ J] \rightarrow \ \sim K$
~~K
_____

~[(H v M) v J]

Chapter Three

SENTENTIAL LOGIC PROOFS

Okay. Everything up to now has been preliminary to doing proofs, and we can finally start with the business of proofs. Doing proofs in sentential logic may be thought of as like a puzzle or game. It is like doing a crossword puzzle, a chess problem, or a "brain teaser." What this means is that doing proofs in logic can actually be fun—even if you are not a geek. As Aristotle realized long ago, all humans, by nature, enjoy using their minds. It only becomes burdensome if you are frustrated by failure or incomprehension. This book aims to minimize those problems.

Rules of the game: Like any game, SL has rules. When you play chess, you can't simply grab your opponent's king and yell "checkmate!" You have to do it by the rules, or there just isn't any point. In SL, the rules are that certain types of basic valid argument forms, and only those, will be allowed. The rules also permit you to substitute certain strings of symbols for their equivalent forms whenever you want to. Let's begin with the basic valid argument forms.

Basic valid argument forms: These are basic *forms* of valid arguments. They will be presented in the simplest way. It is essential to remember, though, that *any* argument, *however* complicated it might be, that takes this form (i.e., is a substitution instance of this form) will be a valid argument. I'll give you the simplest version of these forms, but you will need to learn to recognize their more complex substitution instances.

(1) *Modus Ponens* (MP):

$$p \to q$$
$$p$$
$$\overline{}$$
$$q$$

57

(2) *Modus Tollens* (MT):

$$p \rightarrow q$$
$$\sim q$$

_____

$$\sim p$$

(3) *Hypothetical Syllogism* (HS):

$$p \rightarrow q$$
$$q \rightarrow r$$

_____

$$p \rightarrow r$$

(4) *Disjunctive Syllogism* (DS): (there are four acceptable forms)

p ∨ q	p ∨ q	p ∨ ~q	~p ∨ q
~p	~q	q	p
q	p	p	q

(5) *Addition* (Add):

$$p$$

_____

$$p \vee q$$

(6) *Conjunction* (Conj):

$$p$$
$$q$$

_____

$$p \ \& \ q$$

(7) *Simplification* (Simp): (there are two acceptable forms)

p & q	p & q
p	q

So that's it! These are all the valid argument forms you need to do proofs. Why do we use just these forms, since alternative sets are possible (and, indeed, an alternative set of basic valid argument forms is given in the first appendix)? I picked these because they are like many of the actual arguments you hear people use in real conversations. Consider the following hypothetical dialogue between the participants on an imaginary sports program on college football:

> Chris: OK, guys, here is the scenario: On January fourth, West Coast State plays Big Texas University for the BCS national championship. Who wins?
>
> Kirk: West Coast, no question about it. WCS has last year's Heisman winner playing quarterback and their star running back won the Heisman this year. If you have two Heisman winners on your team, you won't lose in a championship game.
>
> Lee: Not so fast my friend! BTU has the finest defense in the country, limiting opponents to a measly 7.6 points per game this year. WCS's great offense will have to wear down BTU's great defense or BTU hangs on to win. But, hey, great defense always outlasts great offense.

Kirk's argument can be modeled as a *modus ponens:*

If (p) WCS has two Heisman winners, then (q) it will win the championship game.

(p) WCS has two Heisman winners.
(q) It will win the game.

Lee's argument can be modeled as a disjunctive syllogism:

(p) WCS's offense will beat BTU's defense or (q) BTU hangs on to win the game.
(~p) WCS's offense will not beat BTU's defense.
(q) BTU hangs on to win the game.

As an exercise you should try to come up with real-sounding arguments that can be modeled as hypothetical syllogism and *modus tollens.*

The last three of the above argument forms are harder to find in real conversation, but only because they are so obvious that we usually never bother to make them explicit. However, in logic, we have to spell out our rules, and not just assume that everybody will automatically follow them. If I say of some student, "He's smart, but lazy." This can be modeled as giving the premise "He is smart and he is lazy" from which anyone could immediately conclude "he is smart," or anyone could conclude "he is lazy." So the inference here could be modeled as simplification, that is, from p & q you can infer either p or q. Again, though, the inference would be so automatic that we would just take it for granted. Likewise, suppose I said to you "He is smart" and later on added "He is lazy." You could conclude "He is smart and he is lazy" and you would be unconsciously employing the conjunction inference, that is, if you have p on one line, and q on another, you can infer p & q. The one that probably never occurred to anybody except logicians is addition, that is, from any p you can infer p v q. Recall that a disjunction is true if at least one disjunct is. So if you take anything as true, say, "Paris is the capital of France," then you can add anything—anything at all—to that statement by disjunction and the disjunction will still be true. For instance, "Paris is the capital of France or the moon is made of green cheese" is true because one disjunct is true. This no doubt sounds very odd, but it is a valid form of inference and it comes in handy in proofs, so we list it.

Now for the equivalences. Equivalences are simply expressions that always take the same truth-value as other expressions. Here is an example of two equivalent expressions—~(p v q) and ~p & ~q—with a truth table to demonstrate their equivalence:

p	q	p v q	~(p v q)		p	q	~p	~q	~p & ~q
T	T	T	F		T	T	F	F	F
T	F	T	F		T	F	F	T	F
F	T	T	F		F	T	T	F	F
F	F	F	T		F	F	T	T	T

As the truth table shows, ~(p v q) and ~p & ~q have the same truth-value in every situation, whatever truth p and q are given. Both expressions are always false except when p and q are both false. This shows that the expressions ~(p v q) and ~p & ~q are equivalent. Since equivalents always have the same truth-value, and since SL is truth functional, you can always replace an expression with its equivalent without changing the truth-value of the whole. So you may substitute an equivalent expression *wherever* you want to. Here I symbolize this equivalence relation by a double colon sign (::). Wherever an expression with the form on one side of the double colon occurs, it can be replaced by the equivalent expression with the form on the other side of the double colon.

(1) *Commutation* (Comm):
$$(p \lor q) :: (q \lor p)$$
$$(p \,\&\, q) :: (q \,\&\, p)$$

(2) *Association* (Asso):
$$(p \lor q) \lor r :: p \lor (q \lor r)$$
$$(p \,\&\, q) \,\&\, r :: p \,\&\, (q \,\&\, r)$$

(3) *Distribution* (Dist): (There are two forms)
$$p \lor (q \,\&\, r) :: (p \lor q) \,\&\, (p \lor r)$$
$$p \,\&\, (q \lor r) :: (p \,\&\, q) \lor (p \,\&\, r)$$

Commutation, association, and distribution should be familiar from elementary algebra. For instance, addition and multiplication obey commutative and associative laws, that is, $x + y = y + x$ and $ab = ba$. Also, $(x + y) + z = x + (y + z)$ and $(ab)c = a(bc)$. Also, there are distributive laws in algebra: $a(b + c) = ab + ac$.

(4) *Exportation* (Exp):
$$(p \,\&\, q) \rightarrow r :: p \rightarrow (q \rightarrow r)$$

This one may seem a bit strange, but think of a commonsense example. Here is a sentence with the form $(p \,\&\, q) \rightarrow r$: "If the relative humidity is 100 percent and the temperature drops, then it will rain." If this is so, then this sentence also must be true: "If the relative humidity is 100 percent, then, if the temperature drops, it will rain." This last sentence has the form $p \rightarrow (q \rightarrow r)$.

(5) *Implication* (Impl):

$$p \to q :: \sim p \vee q$$

This one is a bit harder to see in common language. "If it rains, it pours" is not too obviously equivalent to "It does not rain or it pours." Maybe the best thing here is just to look at the truth table to be sure they are equivalent:

p	q	~p	p → q	~p v q
T	T	F	T	T
T	F	F	F	F
F	T	T	T	T
F	F	T	T	T

So, we see that $p \to q$ and $\sim p \vee q$ are equivalent in truth, whatever the values of p and q.

(6) *Contrapositive* (Contra):

$$p \to q :: \sim q \to \sim p$$

I think this one is also clear to common sense. Suppose I say "If he's alive, then he's got a pulse." Anyone who says this would also say "If he doesn't have a pulse, then he isn't alive." The first sentence has the form $p \to q$ and the second one has the form $\sim q \to \sim p$.

(7) *De Morgan's Rules* (DeM):

$$\sim(p \& q) :: \sim p \vee \sim q$$
$$\sim(p \vee q) :: \sim p \& \sim q$$

We gave a truth table for one of these above, but I think common sense also supports these equivalences (named after famous logician Augustus De Morgan). If I say that Art is neither handsome nor rich, which we might symbolize as $\sim(H \vee R)$, then it follows pretty obviously that Art is not handsome and Art is not rich, which we symbolize as ~H & ~R. Likewise, if we say that Senator Phogbound is either misinformed or dishonest, which we symbolize as $\sim I \vee \sim H$, then it is pretty clear that Senator Phogbound is not both informed and honest, that is, $\sim(I \& H)$.

(8) *Biconditional* (Bicon):
$$p \Leftrightarrow q :: (p \rightarrow q) \& (q \rightarrow p)$$

This rule just spells out the nature of the biconditional. If we say "p if and only if q," which is what $p \Leftrightarrow q$ means, we are saying "p if q," which is $q \rightarrow p$, and "p only if q," which is $p \rightarrow q$.

(9) *Double Negation* (DN):
$$p :: {\sim}{\sim}p$$

This is pretty obvious, as your English teacher pointed out to you if you ever used a double negative. If someone says, ungrammatically, "I haven't got no money," then the pedantic English teacher will point out "If you HAVEN'T got NO money, then you must have some." In other words, if M is "I have money" then ${\sim}{\sim}$M, "I haven't got no money," is logically equivalent to M (unfortunately, though, being both logically and grammatically correct still doesn't get you any money).

(10) *Tautology* (Taut):
$$p :: p \vee p$$
$$p :: p \& p$$

In everyday contexts nobody would say something with the form p v p, like "Spam is delicious or Spam is delicious." But in doing proofs it is sometimes helpful to recognize that p is equivalent to p v p and p & p.

So that's it! With these seven argument forms and ten equivalences (plus the quantifier stuff in a later chapter), you can do all the proofs you need to in this course. Note: Don't forget that equivalences work "both ways." The one on the right of the "::" may be substituted for the one on the left just as the one on the left can substitute for the one on the right. For some reason, people have a psychological block with seeing that they go from right to left and not just left to right (maybe it is because English reads from left to right, and maybe readers of Arabic or Hebrew would have the opposite problem). So be sure to keep in mind that equivalences work "both ways."

Warning! Whereas the equivalences can be put in *wherever* you wish, the basic valid argument forms must be applied to *whole lines*. For instance, you cannot perform *modus ponens* on part of a line. Suppose one line of a proof is this:

$$(A \ \& \ B) \rightarrow (C \rightarrow D)$$

and elsewhere in the proof you get the line:

$$C$$

You *cannot* put the C with the part of the previous line that reads $C \rightarrow D$ to get $(A \ \& \ B) \rightarrow D$ by *modus ponens*. This is an *illegitimate* application of *modus ponens*, because it only applies to *part* of a line. Equivalences, though, can be stuck in anywhere, even in part of a line, because equivalent expressions always have the same truth-value. For instance, since the contrapositive is one of our equivalences, we can substitute $(\sim D \rightarrow \sim C)$ for $(C \rightarrow D)$ in the line $(A \ \& \ B) \rightarrow (C \rightarrow D)$ to get $(A \ \& \ B) \rightarrow (\sim D \rightarrow \sim C)$. This is a very important point, so make sure you understand it. If you don't, you will go badly wrong when you try to do proofs.

Doing proofs: Now that you have all the tools you need to start doing proofs, you just need practice doing them. We'll start with very simple proofs and explain every step. Suppose you are given A v B and ~A & C as premises and the conclusion you are asked to prove is B. You do it like this:

(1) A v B   p

(2) ~A & C /: B   p

First, you list the premises as steps (1) and (2) of the proof; we mark the premises with the letter p. The symbol "/:" indicates that given these two premises, your job is to prove B. Now we proceed like this:

(3) ~A   2, Simp

Step (3) applies the basic valid argument form simplification (simp) to line (2), so it puts down "2" for line (2) and "simp" to indicate that the justification for line (3) is that simp was performed on line (2).

(4) B   1, 3 DS

We use lines (1) and (3) to form a disjunctive syllogism argument with the conclusion B. Since B is what we wanted to prove, this ends our proof.

   This is the way all proofs will be done. Each line after the given premises must be justified by referring to a previous line or lines and citing the valid argument form or equivalence that was used to get that line. Here's another one:

   (1) A → B   p

   (2) ~B v C /: A → C   p

   (3) B→ C   2, Impl

We apply implication, equivalence (5), to line (2).

   (4) A → C   1, 3 HS

We use lines (1) and (3) to make a hypothetical syllogism argument; the conclusion is **A → C**, which is what we wanted to prove.

   Here is a slightly more complicated one:

   (1) (A & B) ⇔ C   p

   (2) A   p

   (3) B /: C   p

Cover up the solution below and try it yourself first.

   (4) [(A & B) → C] & [C → (A & B)]   1,Bicon

   (5) (A & B) → C   4,Simp

   (6) A & B   2,3 Conj

   (7) C   3,6 MP

   This one was slightly more difficult not only because it is longer but also because it requires that you recognize that a rather complex sentence can have a simpler form. Consider the first sentence:

   (1) (A & B) ⇔ C

To see that you can apply equivalence (8), Bicon, to (1), you have to see that sentence (1) has the sentence form p ⇔ q, even though it has three letters, A, B, and C, and p ⇔ q only has the two letters, p and q. Recall that sentence variables can stand for *any* sentence, simple or compound. Therefore, p can stand for the compound sentence A & B, and q can represent the simple sentence C, and therefore p ⇔ q can be the sentence form for the compound sentence (A & B) ⇔ C. So, to repeat a theme from the previous chapter, seeing the simple in the complex is one of the most important skills in logic.

Some things that look complex are therefore really instances of something simple. Several of the valid argument forms permit you to simplify by getting rid of parts of a line, which is helpful since doing proofs often requires you to get rid of unnecessary symbolic junk. For instance, suppose you get the following as a line:

[(A v B) v C] v (B & D)

This looks rather complicated. Suppose, though, you have or can get another line that says:

~(B & D)

Now you can simplify. How? Simply by applying disjunctive syllogism:

[(A v B) v C] v (B & D)
~(B & D)
_____

(A v B) v C

You do this by recognizing that the complicated argument

[(A v B) v C] v (B & D)
~(B & D)
_____

(A v B) v C

has the same *form* as the simple model of disjunctive syllogism given above:

$$p \vee q$$
$$\sim q$$
$$\overline{}$$
$$p$$

That is, the complicated argument is a substitution instance of the simple argument form Disjunctive Syllogism.

So, again, learning to recognize the simple in the complex makes things much easier. This applies to equivalences as well as to valid argument forms. For instance, ~[(A v ~D) & ~(F → ~G)] is equivalent to ~(A v ~D) v ~~(F → ~G) by equivalence (7), DeM. How? One form of the De Morgan's (DeM) equivalence is ~(p & q) :: ~p v ~q.

If p stands for (A v ~D) and q stands for ~(F → ~G), then the sentence ~[(A v~D) & ~(F → ~G)] is an instance of the sentence form ~(p & q), and the sentence ~(A v ~D) v ~~(F → ~G) is an instance of the sentence form ~p v ~q.

OK, we can finally get back to proofs. Try this one (cover up the solution):

(1) C v (~F & G)

(2) A → ~C

(3) A & ~B   /: ~F

Solution with explanation:

(4) (C v ~F) & (C v G)   1, Dist

> It probably is a good idea to do distribution whenever you can, especially if it leaves you with a conjunction, as it does here. You can then drop half of the conjunction by simplification.

(5) C v ~F   4, Simp

> I want ~F in my answer, so I get rid of the unnecessary stuff.

(6) A   3, Simp

I notice that I can apply *modus ponens* on step (2) if I have
an A, so I get the A by simp.

(7) ~C   2, 6 MP

I do the *modus ponens*.

(8) ~F   5, 7 DS

Disjunctive syllogism gives me the answer.

Here is a tough one. If you can do this one already, you move to the head
of the class:

(1) [(H & C) → B] v (D & ~H)

(2) ~D v H

(3) H & ~B   /: ~C

Solution with explanations:

(4) ~D v ~~H   2, DN

I notice that (2) looks suspiciously like the right-hand disjunct in (1). Maybe if I can get ~(D & ~H), I can just
drop the right-hand disjunct by DS and simplify
things. Maybe DeM can help me, but I need both disjuncts in (2) to have negation signs in front of them to
use DeM, so I use DN to get negation signs in front of
the right-hand disjunct. (Sometimes in logic, as in
chess, you have to think a few moves ahead.)

(5)~(D & ~H)   4, DeM

OK, I take away the negation sign in front of the D in (4)
and one of the two negation signs in front of the H,
add parentheses, add a negation sign on the outside,
and change the v to &—that's how you do DeM here.
Now I've got the negation of the right-hand disjunct
in (1) that I was looking for.

(6) (H & C) → B   1, 5 DS

Now that looks better!

(7) H → (C → B)   6, Exp

For some reason, people often forget about exportation. It
    comes in handy pretty often.

(8) H   3, Simp

With H, I can do MP on (7). Fortunately, I can get H from
    (3) by simplification.

(9) C → B   7, 8 MP

(10) ~B   3, Simp

Nearing the end.

(11) ~C   9, 10 MT

So that's how you do it. Of course, the only way to learn how to do it is
with practice, so we turn to the exercises.

EXERCISES FOR CHAPTER 3

1. Here are some solved proofs. In each line state the rule—the basic
   valid argument form or the equivalence—that justifies that line.

   (a)

   (1) (A & ~C) v B   p

   (2) (B v ~C) → H   p /: H

   (3) B v (A & ~C)   1,

   (4) (B v A) & (B v ~C)   3,

(5) B v ~C	4,
(6) H	2, 5

(b)

(1) (F & B) → H	p
(2) C → F	p
(3) C & B	p /: H
(4) F → (B → H)	1,
(5) C → (B → H)	2, 4
(6) C	3,
(7) B → H	5, 6
(8) B	3,
(9) H	7,8

(c)

(1) (D v F) & (D v G)	p
(2) A & ~D	p
(3) B v ~F	p /: B v E
(4) D v (F & G)	1,
(5) ~D	2,
(6) F & G	4, 5
(7) F	6,

(8) B   3, 7

(9) B v E   8,

(d)

(1) A → ~B   p

(2) L → (A & B)   p /: ~L

(3) ~A v ~B   1,

(4) ~(A & B)   3,

(5) ~L   2,4

(e)

(1) H v H   p

(2) (M & N) → ~(H v T)   p /: M → ~N

(3) H   1,

(4) H v T   3,

(5) ~~(H v T)   4,

(6) ~(M & N)   2, 5

(7) ~M v ~N   6,

(8) M → ~N   7,

(f)

(1) A → B   p

(2) ~A → (F v D)   p

(3) (~F → D) → ~B   p /: ~A ⇔ ~B

(4) (~~F v D) → ~B   3,

(5) (F v D) → ~B   4,

(6) ~A → ~B   2, 5

(7) ~B → ~A   1,

(8) (~A → ~B) & (~B → ~A)   6, 7

(9) ~A ⇔ ~B   8,

(g)

(1) H → (I & J)   p

(2) M & H   p /: M & I

(3) ~(I & J) → ~H   1,

(4) H   2,

(5) ~~H   4,

(6) ~~(I & J)   3, 5

(7) I & J   6,

(8) I   7,

(9) M   2,

(10) M & I   8, 9

2. Do the following proofs. The first ten are easy and can be done in a few lines. The last ten are harder.

(a)

    (1) B & ~ A

    (2) C → A   /: ~C

(b)

    (1) B v (~D v H)

    (2) ~H

    (3) D   /: B

(c)

    (1) A → ~A   /: ~A

(d)

    (1) ~H → ~C

    (2) H → L   /: C → L

(e)

    (1) ~E   /: ~(E & I)

(f)

    (1) F ⇔ (I & H)

    (2) F   /: H

(g)

    (1) A → (B → C)

    (2) ~C   /: ~A v ~B

(h)

 (1) ~H v (F & L)   /: H → F

(i)

 (1) (M v N) v A

 (2) ~M & ~N   /: A

(j)

 (1) M

 (2) N

 (3) (M & N) → J   /: J

(k)

 (1) B v (C & D)

 (2) ~B

 (3) F v ~C   /: F

(l)

 (1) ~B → M

 (2) ~F & ~D

 (3) M → (D & F)   /: B

(m)

 (1) ~H ⇔ [(B & K) → L]

 (2) B & (~H & ~H)   /: ~K v L

(n)

    (1) N & ~B

    (2) (L v S) → B   /: N & ~L

(o)

    (1) (S v ~D) & (S v ~F)

    (2) ~(D v F) → C   /: ~S → C

(p)

    (1) ~{N v [(H → ~C) v F]}

    (2) ~H   /: ~L

(q)

    (1) ~B ⇔ (C & R)

    (2) (C → I) v ~H

    (3) H & ~I   /: H & B

(r)

    (1) M → R

    (2) M v Q   /: ~Q → R

(s)

    (1) (M v ~L) v ~F

    (2) [F & (~M v ~M)] ⇔ G

    (3) G & ~A   /: ~L

(t)

    (1) (S & ~H) v (S & B)

    (2) ~L v H   /: ~B → ~L

Chapter Four

MORE SENTENTIAL LOGIC

Contradictions, Tautologies, and Assumptions

There are two kinds of sentences that are of special interest to logicians: tautologies and contradictions. Most sentences can be true or false depending on the circumstances; we call such sentences **contingent** sentences. If I say "Boston beat New York 5–4 in extra innings last night," this is a contingent sentence that is true if Boston did beat New York 5–4 in extra innings last night, and not true if they didn't. But there are some odd sentences that are true no matter what the circumstances and some sentences that are false no matter what the circumstances. "The earth is either round or not round" is true no matter what the shape of the earth. "Today is Tuesday and today is not Tuesday" is false no matter what day it is. A sentence that is true in every conceivable circumstance is called a **tautology**. A sentence that is false in every conceivable circumstance is called a **contradiction**. How can a sentence be true in every conceivable circumstance or false in every conceivable circumstance? It can when its truth or falsity is determined by its *form* alone.

Consider the sentence "The earth is round or not round," or, expressing it a little more formally, "The earth is round or it is not the case that it is round." This sentence is a substitution instance of the sentence form p v ~p. In this case, you get the sentence by substituting "The earth is round" for p. Every other sentence that is a substitution instance of the sentence form p v ~p is also true. "Haggis is delicious or it is not the case that haggis is delicious" is a substitution instance of the sentence form p v ~p, and it is true no matter what haggis tastes like. The sentence form p v ~p is an example of a **tautologous sentence form**. A tautologous sentence form is a sentence form such that every substitution instance of that form is true.

The same sort of thing can be said about contradictions. Consider the sentence "Today is Tuesday and it is not the case that today is Tuesday." This sentence is a substitution instance of the sentence form p & ~p. In this case you get the sentence by substituting "Today is Tuesday" for p. Every other substitution instance of p & ~p is also false. "Cats are mammals and it is not the case that cats are mammals" is also a substitution instance of p & ~p, and it is false no matter whether cats are mammals. The sentence form p & ~p is an example of a **contradictory sentence form**. A contradictory sentence form is a sentence form such that every substitution instance of that form is false.

We can therefore define "tautology" more precisely as a sentence that is a substitution instance of a tautologous sentence form, and we define "tautologous sentence form" as a sentence form such that every substitution instance of that form is true. Similarly, we define "contradiction" as a sentence that is a substitution instance of a contradictory sentence form, and we define "contradictory sentence form" as a sentence form such that every substitution instance of that form is false.

But *why* should every substitution instance of a tautologous sentence form be true and every substitution instance of a contradictory sentence form be false? We can see the answer best by using truth tables. Consider the truth table for the tautologous sentence form p v ~p.

p	~p	p v ~p
T	F	T
F	T	T

The only possibilities for p are to be T or F. When p is T, then, by the definition of negation, ~p is F. When p is F, then ~p is T. Since disjunction is defined so that a disjunction is true whenever at least one of the disjuncts is true, then, obviously, any sentence with the form p v ~p is going to be true since one of the disjuncts is always true. For example, the substitution instance A v ~A is true, as is the substitution instance H v ~H. Similarly, we can see that any expression of the form p & ~p will be false:

p	~p	p & ~p
T	F	F
F	T	F

The definition of conjunction requires that the conjunction be false whenever one or both conjuncts is false, and when the conjuncts are p and ~p, obviously one or the other will always be false, so the conjunction will always be false.

We can also use truth tables to show that more complicated expressions are tautologies or contradictions. Consider ~[(p → q) → (~p v q)]:

p	q	~p	p → q	~p v q	(p → q) → (~p v q)	~[(p → q) → (~p v q)]
T	T	F	T	T	T	F
T	F	F	F	F	T	F
F	T	T	T	T	T	F
F	F	T	T	T	T	F

This shows that the sentence form ~[(p → q) → (~p v q)] is false in every possible substitution instance, whatever the truth-values of its constituent simple sentences. This shows that the sentence form ~[(p → q) → (~p v q)] is a contradiction. Notice, by the way, that ~[(p → q) → (~p v q)] is the negation of (p → q) → (~p v q), which, as the truth table shows, is always true in every substitution instance, and so a tautology. In general, the negation of a tautology is a contradiction, and the negation of a contradiction is a tautology.

Since ancient times, the idea of a contradiction has given people a way of proving things called the method of *"reductio ad absurdum"*—reduction to absurdity. The basic idea is this: If you want to prove something, assume its negation and show that the negation leads to a contradiction. If you want to prove x, and you assume ~x, and this assumption leads to a contradiction, then this shows that ~x is false, so x must be true. Some of the most famous proofs in mathematics use the *reductio ad absurdum* method. The ancient Greek mathematician Euclid proved that there is no highest prime number by assuming that there *is* a highest prime and showing that this assumption leads to a contradiction.

It is easy to adapt *reductio ad absurdum* reasoning to SL. To see how we need to understand an important fact about valid arguments, namely, that if you conjoin the premises of a valid argument with the *negation* of its conclusion, you get a contradiction. We said in the first chapter that a valid argument is one where you wind up saying something illogical and absurd if you accept the premises but reject the conclusion. You can't do anything more illogical and absurd than to contradict yourself, that is, to violate the law of noncontradiction. If you conjoin the *negation* of the conclusion of a valid argument with all of the premises, the resulting sentence is a contradiction. Let's illustrate these points with the simple valid argument form *modus tollens*:

p	q	~p	~~p	~q	$p \rightarrow q$	$(p \rightarrow q)$ & ~q	$[(p \rightarrow q)$ & ~q] & ~~p
T	T	F	T	F	T	F	F
T	F	F	T	T	F	F	F
F	T	T	F	F	T	F	F
F	F	T	F	T	T	T	F

Modus tollens says that from the premises $p \rightarrow q$ and ~q we can conclude ~p. The negation of the conclusion is therefore ~~p. The truth table shows that if we conjoin the negation of the conclusion, ~~p, with the premises $p \rightarrow q$ and ~q, we get a sentence form—$[(p \rightarrow q)$ & ~q] & ~~p— that is false in every instance, and so is a contradiction.

It is pretty easy to see that these ideas make sense. Well, actually it isn't all that easy, so read the next paragraph slowly and carefully.

A conjunction is true *only* when *both* conjuncts are true; that's what the truth table for conjunction showed. When one conjunct is false, or both are, the conjunction is false. Again, that is what the truth table for "&" in chapter 2 told us. But it will *never* happen that both conjuncts are true when one conjunct is all the conjoined premises of a valid argument and the other conjunct is the *negation* of the conclusion of that valid argument. Why? Again imagine that all the premises of a valid argument are true and we conjoin all those premises to make a compound sentence P. P, since it is the conjunction of sentences, each of which is true, is itself true. Since we are presuming the argument to be valid, the conclusion C will also be true since all the premises are true. If C is true, the negation of C, ~C, will have to be false. So if we conjoin P (which we are assuming is true) with ~C (which must be false), the resulting conjunction, P & ~C, will have to be false. In *any* other circumstance, where one or more premises is false, then the conjunction of the premises, sentence P, will be false, so the conjunction P & ~C will be false also. *Therefore, in no possible circumstance will P be true and ~C true also, so* P & ~C *is a contradiction.*

So, in summary, if you have a valid argument and you conjoin the premises with the negation of the conclusion, the resulting sentence is a contradiction. On the other hand, if an argument is *in*valid, it *is* possible for the premises to all be true and the conclusion false. This means that if you conjoin the premises of an *in*valid argument with the negation of its conclusion, the resulting sentence will *not* be a contradiction. We can say, therefore, that if we conjoin the premises of an argument with the negation of the conclusion, the resulting sentence will be a contradiction *when and only when* the argument is valid. The practical value of this is that you can test an argument for validity by conjoining the premises with the negation of the conclusion. If you do this, and you get a contradiction, the argument is valid.

But how do you prove that a contradiction follows from the conjoined premises and the negation of the conclusion? We could use a truth table, but that would often be incredibly tedious, irritating, and time consuming. An easier way would be to show that when you put the premises together with the negation of the conclusion, you can derive an explicit contradiction. That is, we show that an explicit contradiction, something with the form p & ~p, follows as a valid deductive consequence from the sentence formed by conjoining the premises and the negation of the conclusion.

To see why this is so, we need to pause and explain in detail another important logical concept, the idea of **entailment**, that we introduced in chapter 1. Consider the sentence (A → B) & A. If we make this sentence the premise of an argument, then the sentence B follows as a conclusion, as we can show:

(1) (A → B) & A	p
(2) A → B	1, Simp
(3) A	1, Simp
(4) /∴ B	2, 3 MP

Since B is validly deducible from (A → B) & A, we say that (A → B) & A *entails* B. In general, if any sentence q is validly deducible from another sentence p, we say that p entails q. The symbol logicians use for entailment is "⊨." Thus, p ⊨ q reads "p entails q."

It is important not to confuse "⊨" with "→." "→" is just the sign for material implication. When we say p → q, we mean only that as a matter of fact, if p is true, q is also true, or in other words, as a matter of fact, it is not the case both that p and not q. There is no implication of necessity; the next time we check, p might be true and q false, and p → q would no longer be true. But if we say p ⊨ q, then we are saying that if p is true, q *must* be true because, by a valid deductive argument, q follows from p. For instance, as we saw above, if p is the compound sentence (A → B) & A, and q is the sentence B, then p ⊨ q because we can validly infer q from p by making p our premise and inferring q as the conclusion. So, if the sentence (A → B) & A is true, the sentence B *must* be true because it follows as a valid deductive consequence of (is entailed by) (A → B) & A.

It follows that any sentence that entails a contradiction must itself be a contradiction. That is, if p ⊨ q where q is a contradiction, p must be a contradiction also. Why? If q is a contradiction, q *must* be false always and in every circumstance; that is what being a contradiction means. Hence, since true premises cannot entail a false conclusion, if p entails q, p must also be false always and in every circumstance. In other words, p must be a contradiction. So, again, *any sentence that entails a contradiction is itself a contradiction.*

This property of valid arguments allows us to use *reductio ad absurdum* reasoning to prove them. The method of proof that uses *reductio ad absurdum* reasoning is called **indirect proof** (IP). IP works like this: You *assume* the negation of what you are trying to prove—your conclusion, that is—and stick that in as an additional premise in your argument. Now, if you can prove that a contradiction follows, you know that the conclusion is validly deducible from the premises. Why? Because in effect what you are doing is creating a compound sentence from the conjunction of the premises and the negation of the conclusion, and showing that an explicit contradiction follows. By showing that a contradiction follows, you show that the sentence created by conjoining the premises and the negation of the conclusion is a contradiction. You have thereby shown that the argument is valid. This neat trick has been used to prove some of the most important results in mathematics.

Here is how we use IP:

(1) D → E	p
(2) F → G	p
(3) D v (F & J) /∴ E v G	p

We could, of course, do this the ordinary way, just by using the basic argument forms and equivalences, but let's try it the new way. Let's assume the negation of the conclusion and put that in as a premise. This will allow us to construct a *reductio ad absurdum* proof.

(4) (~*) ~(E v G)	AIP

We mark our assumption for IP with the symbol (~*) put next to the step number. We annotate the step with "AIP" to stand for "assumption for indirect proof." What we have now done, in effect, is to conjoin the premises listed in steps (1), (2), and (3) with the negation of the conclusion, which we list in step (4). If we wanted to do this explicitly, we would put steps (1) through (4) together with successive employments of conjunction to form the sentence {[(D → E) & (F → G)] & [D v (F & J)]} & ~(E v G), but we shall assume that we have tacitly done this by listing steps (1)–(4) in the proof. We now prove that this sentence leads, by a series of valid steps, to an explicit contradiction.

(5) ~E & ~G	4, DeM
(6) ~E	5, Simp
(7) ~D	1,6 MT
(8) F & J	3, 7 DS
(9) F	8, Simp
(10) ~G	5, Simp
(11) ~F	2, 10 MT
(12) F & ~F	9,11 Conj

OK, using the rules of SL we have shown that you can derive a contradiction—F & ~F in this case—from the given premises and from the negation of the conclusion. This shows that the conjunction of the premises and the negation of the conclusion entails a contradiction, and so itself is a contradiction. Therefore, the argument is valid. So you can just write down the conclusion in the next line.

(13) (~*) /: E v G   4–12, IP

We indicate by the symbol (~*), the same symbol we used to introduce the IP assumption, that we are concluding our IP and we annotate the final step as "4–12 IP" indicating that we used steps (4)–(12) to do an indirect proof.

Another way of using assumptions in proofs is often helpful. Suppose that you are doing a proof and that at some point need to get a conditional sentence, or something you can derive from a conditional, but you are having problems getting it. Suppose you could just *assume* the antecedent of the conditional, stick it in as a premise, use that premise to derive the consequent of the conditional, and then just write down the conditional as the next step in your proof. Well you can! Suppose you want to do the following proof:

(1) A → (D v E)   p
(2) B → (H & ~E) /: (A & B) → (D & H) p

It is not obvious how to proceed given the rules you have so far (you could do it; it would just be a pain). So let's introduce a new rule, we'll call **conditional proof** (CP). Let's allow an assumption, any assumption, to be put into a proof (Of course, the assumption has to be taken out again later. You knew there would be a catch.) Here it would obviously help if we could just assume A & B, so let's do it:

(3) (→*) A & B   ACP

We mark our assumption by putting (→*) next to the number of the step of the proof and put a capital "ACP" for "Assumption for Conditional Proof" as our justification. The proof now proceeds straightforwardly:

(4) A   3, Simp
(5) B   3, Simp
(6) D v E   1, 4 MP

(7) H & ~E	2, 5 MP
(8) ~E	7, Simp
(9) D	6, 8 DS
(10) H	7, Simp
(11) D & H	9, 10 Conj

The rule of CP now allows us to put in the conclusion as the final step:

(12) (→*) /: (A &B) → (D & H)	3–11, CP

When we are finished with an assumption we have to "discharge" it. In effect, we take back our assumption and remove it from the proof. The symbol (→*) in step (12) indicates that we are discharging the assumption we marked by the same symbol (→*) earlier in the proof. We discharge the assumption by making it the antecedent of a conditional, and the previous step the consequent of the conditional, and entering the conditional as that line in the proof. In this case, the step where we discharge the assumption ends the proof. Note that we annotate the step by writing "3–11, CP." This indicates that in steps (3)–(11) we have shown that given our premises and the assumption we made in step (3) (A & B), we can validly derive the sentence in step (11) (D & H). Therefore, we can say that, given our other premises, if A & B, then D & H—and this is all that our conclusion says.

This way of proving things is called a "conditional proof"—CP for short. You can use CP more than once in a proof, either sequentially or by "nesting" one assumption inside of another. For instance:

(1) D v (E & C)	p
(2) ~(D v E) /: C → (H → E)	p
(3) (→*) C	ACP
(4) (→**) H	ACP
(5) (D v E) & (D v C)	1, Dist
(6) ~D & ~E	2, DeM
(7) ~D	6, Simp
(8) D v E	5, Simp
(9) E	7, 8 DS
(10) (→**) /: H → E	4–9, CP
(11) (→*) /: C → (H → E)	3–10, CP

In step (3) we assume C, so we mark the assumption with a (→*). Let's call the **scope of an assumption** all the steps of the proof that occur between the step where we introduce the assumption and the step where we discharge it. In step (4) we assume H, and since this is an assumption inside the scope of another assumption—assumption C, which we introduced in step (3)—we mark it with (→**). In step (9) we get E, so since we have assumed H, we can write H → E as step (10), discharging the assumption H. We indicate that H is the assumption we are discharging with the symbol (→**); this indicates that we are discharging the assumption that we marked in step (4) with the same symbol (→**). We annotate step (10) as 4–9 CP, indicating that we used steps(4)–(9) and conditional proof to get step (10). When you nest one assumption inside the scope of another assumption, you always discharge the "inside" assumption first. Since C was our first assumption, we discharge it in step (11) and annotate that step 3–9 CP, indicating that we got it from steps (3) through (10) by conditional proof. In discharging assumption C in step (11), we use the symbol (→*), the same symbol we used to introduce C as an assumption for conditional proof in step (3). You can nest as many assumptions inside of other assumptions as you need to do the proof.

Important cautions: An assumption only holds as long as it is assumed. *Once you have discharged an assumption, you cannot use it again unless you specifically assume it again.* Also, *you cannot take any step that you used within the scope of an assumed premise and use it again after the assumption has been discharged.* The reason is that any step you derive within the scope of an assumption only holds *given* that assumption. Once the assumption is discharged, you are no longer assuming it. Consider the following proof:

(1) I v K	p
(2) ~K	p
(3) M v N	p
(4) ~N /: (H → I) & (L → M)	p
(5) (→*) H	ACP
(6) I	1, 2 DS
(7) (→*) /: H → I	5–6, CP
(8) (→*) L	ACP
(9) M	3, 4 DS
(10) (→*) /: L → M	8–9 CP
(11) (H → I) & (L → M)	7, 10 Conj

Here I use CP twice, assuming H in step (5) and discharging it in step (7), and assuming L in step (8) and discharging it in step (10). [Note that when I introduce my assumption L in step (8), I use the symbol (→*), not (→ **), because assumption H has already been discharged and so L is not "nested" within the scope of H.] Step (6) is derived within the scope of the assumption H, which is discharged in the next step. Therefore, I cannot use step (6) to derive any of the steps (8)–(11) that follow the discharge of assumption H in step (7).

EXERCISES FOR CHAPTER 4

1) Use truth tables to determine whether the following sentences are contradictions or tautologies:

(a) ~(A & B) v ~(~A v ~B)
(b) [(M → G) & (M → ~G)] & M
(c) ~{[(H → F) & ~F] → ~H}
(d) [C v (D & B)] → (~C → B)
(e) [(I & ~G) → E] ⟺ [I → (G v E)]

2) Use conditional proof to prove the following:

(a)

(1) A → B
(2) C → D
(3) A v C /: ~B → D

(b)

(1) (B v C) → A
(2) ~D → B /: A v D

(c)

(1) [H → (G → I)] v K
(2) K → (M & L)

(3) I → J
(4) ~M /: H → (G → J)

(d)

(1) K v J
(2) ~J v L
(3) ~L v M
(4) ~M v ~K /: ~K ⇔ L

3) Use indirect proof to prove the following:

(a)

(1) A → B
(2) ~C → ~B
(3) (D v ~C) & (A & E) /: D

(b)

(1) H → (I → ~J)
(2) (J v J) & I /: ~H

(c)

(1) (M v P) v (E & L)
(2) H & ~P /: ~(~M & ~L)

(d)

(1) A → B
(2) C → D
(3) A v C /: ~B → D

For additional practice, you can go back to the exercises at the end of the last chapter and do the proofs there using CP and/or IP.

Chapter Five

PREDICATE LOGIC BASICS

Aristotle (384–322 BCE) was the first systematic logician. His work on logic was considered definitive and was scarcely improved upon for over two millennia. Aristotle's logic was based on the **syllogism**. A syllogism is a deductive argument form consisting of three sentences—two premises and a conclusion. The sentences he used were **categorical sentences**. Categorical sentences are so called because they state relationships between categories or classes of things. "All whales are mammals" is a categorical sentence because it states a relationship between the category of things we call "whales" and the category of things we call "mammals." The sentence says that everything that falls within the category "whale" also falls within the category "mammal."

Every categorical sentence contains a **quantifier**, a word that says how many of a given category we are talking about. In "All whales are mammals," the quantifier is "all," indicating that we are talking about all whales. Each categorical sentence also contains a **subject term** and a **predicate term** that name the two categories of things we are talking about. In "All whales are mammals," "whales" is the subject term and "mammals" is the predicate term. Aristotle recognized four types of categorical sentences, which are called A, E, I, and O sentences. These four types have the following forms, where "S" and "P" stand for subject and predicate terms:

A: All S are P.
E: No S is P.
I: Some S is P.
O: Some S is not P.

A and E sentences use the quantifiers "all" and "no," indicating that they are asserting something about all members of the subject class (if I say "No S is P," I am saying of *all* Ss that they are not Ps). I and O sentences use the quantifier "some," indicating that they are talking about some (where "some" means "at least one") member or members of the subject class. Here is an example of a syllogism:

> All mammals are air breathers.
> All whales are mammals.
> _____
> All whales are air breathers.

It is clear that this is a valid argument. If all mammals are air breathers, and all whales are mammals, it clearly must be the case that all whales are air-breathers. Yet, though this argument is obviously valid, we have no way to prove it valid in SL. How would we represent this syllogism in SL symbolism? It would have to be something like this:

> A
> B
> —
> C

None of our rules in SL permit us to prove valid an argument so symbolized.

Aristotle offered a number of rules to test syllogisms for validity. Or you could just memorize which ones were valid. Medieval students were taught to sing little Latin ditties that told them which forms of the syllogism were valid. Aristotelian logic, which for so long was the core curriculum for the study of logic, has now been absorbed within what modern logicians call **predicate logic** (PL). PL can do everything Aristotle's logic could do, and a lot more besides. Predicate logic is given that name because it deals with the logic of properties or attributes things have. Philosophers call a term a "predicate" if it names any property or attribute something possesses. For instance, if we say "Art is tall," we name someone, Art, and attribute a predicate to him, tallness in this case.

In PL we designate predicates with capital letters, and we name individuals with lowercase letters from the whole alphabet except w, x, y, and z (which we are saving for another use). So we symbolize "Art is tall" in PL as "Ta." "T" is our **predicate constant** and "a" is our **subject constant**. A subject constant is just a proper name, a name of a *particular* person, place, thing, or concept (actually, a subject constant is more like a pronoun that refers to a particular entity, like using "he" to refer to Art). We never use subject constants to designate groups, classes, or categories of things. A predicate constant signifies a property or attribute of a subject. To state that a certain subject has a given predicate, we simply take the constant signifying that subject and put it just to the right of the constant signifying its predicate. For instance, Ta says "a is T." Predicate constants like T can stand for **simple predicates** like "tall" or they can stand for **relational predicates** like "taller than." Thus, we could say "Taf" to mean "Art is taller than Fred" or Bsmb for "Springfield is between Mayberry and Bedrock." Simple predicates are **one-place predicates**, like Ta, that apply to only one subject; relational predicates, like Taf, are **multiple-place predicates** that relate two, three, or more things.

Often we attribute predicates to no one person or thing in particular, but to either some or all members of some group. For instance, when we say "Some guys prefer boxers to briefs," we are not talking about one particular guy, like Art, but some unspecified group of guys. To symbolize sentences like these, we obviously cannot use subject constants, since these name particular individuals. Instead, we use **universal quantifiers**, **existential quantifiers**, and **subject variables** along with our predicate constants. Subject variables are represented by lowercase letters from the end of the alphabet—w, x, y, and z. Universal quantifiers are represented with a pair of parentheses around a special symbol, ∀ ("upside down A"), and a variable. For instance, (∃x) is a universal quantifier and we read it as "all x's," "for every x," "for all x's," or something equivalent. Likewise, (∃y) would read "for all y's" or "for every y," and so on. Existential quantifiers are represented with parentheses and a special symbol, ∃ ("backward E"), and a variable. For instance, (∃x) is an existential quantifier and it reads "some x" or "some x's"—where "some" again means "at least one"—or "there exists an x," "there is an x," or an equivalent expression. Using an existential quantifier and the variable x, we could say "Some fashion-conscious buyers prefer Gucci to Versace." If "F" stands for the property of being a fashion-conscious buyer, and g stands for "Gucci" and v for "Versace," then we symbolize "Some fashion-conscious buyers prefer Gucci to Versace" as (∃x)(Fx & Pxgv).

Let's pause to note two things about our symbolization of "Some fashion-conscious buyers prefer Gucci to Versace," (∃x)(Fx & Pxgv). First, note that we employ the sentence connective "&" just as we did in SL. In fact, in PL we retain all of the sentence connectives we used in SL (though, technically, in PL they do not always connect sentences, but can be used on other expressions as well). We also retain all of the basic valid argument forms and all of the equivalences. These will be used in doing proofs in PL just as they were in SL. Notice also that we enclose the symbols Fx & Pxgv in parentheses. These parentheses indicate the **scope** of the preceding existential quantifier (∃x). A quantifier's scope just indicates which variables we are quantifying, that is, we specify of which x's (or y's or z's, or whatever) we are saying "some x's (or y's or z's)" or "all x's (or y's or z's)." When you have a universal or an existential quantifier, there must be parentheses, brackets, or braces surrounding the expressions that follow whenever they are needed to indicate the scope of the quantifier. When only a single predicate constant and its attached subject variables or constants immediately follow a quantifier, (∀x)Fxb, for instance, the scope of the quantifier is unambiguous and the parentheses may be dropped.

A quantifier is said to "bind" a particular variable within its scope, so we speak of some variables as **bound variables**. Thus (∃x)(Fx & Pxgv) *binds* the variable x within the subsequent parentheses, or in other words, x is the bound variable in the expression (∃x)(Fx & Pxvg). Any variable that is not bound by *any* quantifier in the particular expression in which it occurs is said to be a **free variable**. For instance, in the expression (∃x)(Bx v Rxy) v Nx, the x variable next to the predicate constant N is free with respect to the existential quantifier because it falls outside of its scope. The y variable is also free, even though it falls within the scope of the existential quantifier. The y here is free because it is not the variable specified by the quantifier. Had the expression been (∃y)(Bx v Rxy) then the y would have been bound and the two x's free.

We now have the PL tools to symbolize all the categorical sentences of Aristotelian logic—and a lot more. First consider the A-type sentence: "All S are P." Since A sentences assert that *all* members of a given class have a certain property, it is pretty clear that we use a universal quantifier. Note that "All S are P" can be rephrased, using the variable x, as "If x is an S, then x is a P." The symbolization is now straightforward: (∀x)(Sx → Px). E sentences also use a universal quantifier since to say that "No S is P" is to say of *all* Ss that they are not Ps. Using the variable x, we can rephrase "No S is P" as "For every x, if x is S, then x is not P." The symbolization would therefore be (∀x)(Sx → ~Px). E sentences say that *some* S is P, so clearly we will use the existential quantifier. Rephrasing "Some S is P" using the variable x, we get "Some x is both S and P." The translation is obvious: (∃x)(Sx & Px). Finally, the I sentence "Some S is not P" can be rephrased as "Some x is S but is not P." The translation into PL is (∃x)(Sx & ~Px).

In summary, then, the PL translations of the Aristotelian categorical sentences are as follows:

A: (∀x)(Sx → Px)

E: (∀x)(Sx → ~Px)

I: (∃x)(Sx & Px)

O: (∃x)(Sx & ~Px)

We can now translate any syllogism into PL. Consider the syllogism

> No Senator is a PhD biologist.
> Some Senators are creationists.
> _____
> Some creationists are not PhD biologists.

Let Sx = "x is a Senator," Px = "x is a PhD biologist," and Cx = "x is a creationist." We translate the above syllogism into PL as follows:

> (∀x)(Sx → ~Px)
> (∃x)(Sx & Cx)
> _____
> (∃x)(Cx & ~Px)

Here is another one:

> No mammals are feathered.
> All cats are mammals.
>
> ───────────────────────
>
> No cats are feathered.

This is symbolized as

> $(\forall x)(Mx \rightarrow \sim Fx)$
> $(\forall x)(Cx \rightarrow Mx)$
>
> ──────────────
>
> $(\forall x)(Cx \rightarrow \sim Fx)$

PL can therefore symbolize everything in syllogistic logic (and lots more, besides), and in the next chapter we shall see that PL also has the tools to prove the validity of syllogisms (and lots more, besides). Let's now look at some other sentences we can symbolize in PL:

> Everyone loves Raymond
>
> $(\forall x)(Px \rightarrow Lxr)$

Here we are letting Px mean "x is a person" and Lxr mean "x loves Raymond." Our symbolization literally reads "For every x, if x is a person, then x loves Raymond." We can express this even more simply by limiting our **universe of discourse**. The universe of discourse is just the set of objects that our subject variables and subject constants are allowed to represent. In some contexts, for instance, we might want to limit our universe of discourse to the natural numbers, so that our variables will be allowed to stand only for natural numbers. If we limit our universe of discourse to persons, so that every x or y is understood to stand for some person or persons, we could express "Everybody loves Raymond" simply as

> $(\forall x)Lxr$

Note again that we do not have to put parentheses around Lxr because it is the only thing listed after the quantifier, so the scope of the quantifier obviously extends just to Lxr.

If no universe of discourse is specified in a given case, it is understood that the universe of discourse is "everything"—whatever that means. Here are some more symbolizations (with no specified universe of discourse):

Somebody does not love Raymond:

(∃x)(Px & ~Lxr)

Literally this reads "There exists an x such that x is a person and it is not the case that x loves Raymond" or "Some x is a person and x does not love Raymond."

Nobody loves Raymond:

(∀x)(Px → ~Lxr)

Literally, this is "For every x, if x is a person, it is not the case that x loves Raymond."

Some people love Raymond and some do not:

(∃x)(Px & Lxr) & (∃x)(Px & ~Lxr)

Note that we can use the same variable, x, to symbolize those who love Raymond and those who do not. The second existential quantifier binds a different set of x's, so there is no confusion about the two quantifiers talking about the same x's (so we aren't in any danger of saying that the same people love and do not love Raymond).

Another way to symbolize "Some people love Raymond and some do not" is (∃x)(∃y)[(Px & Lxr) & (Py & ~Lyr)]

Notice here that we use *overlapping* quantifiers that have the same scope, as marked by the brackets, so, to avoid confusion, whenever we have overlapping quantifiers we make sure that they bind different variables. Here, for instance, we use different variables for those who love Raymond and for those who don't.

Raymond loves everyone:

(∀x)(Px → Lrx)

Raymond loves someone:

(∃x)(Px & Lrx)

Raymond loves himself:

Lrr

Everybody who loves Raymond watches some TV sitcom:

(∀x)[(Px & Lxr) → (∃y) (Sy & Wxy)]

This is how we symbolize it if what we mean is that everybody who loves Raymond watches some sitcom or other. That is, we have no particular sitcom in mind.

> There is a sitcom watched by everybody who loves Raymond:

(∃x){Sx & (∀y) [(Py & Lyr) → Wyx]}

This is how we would symbolize it if we meant to say that there is some particular sitcom that is watched by everyone who loves Raymond.

OK, you probably noticed that when we use an existential quantifier, we use "&" in the parentheses, and when we use a universal quantifier, we use "→." This is no accident. Think of what we are trying to say. When we say "Somebody loves Raymond," we *don't* mean (∃x)(Px → Lxr). This last expression is equivalent to (∃x)(~Px v Lxr) (by Impl), and this only says "There is something which is either not a person or it loves Raymond," which is clearly not the same thing as saying that there is a person who loves Raymond. In fact, it is hard to imagine any context (besides writing logic books) where you would be tempted to say something like "There is something which either is not a person or it loves Raymond." Similarly, if you want to say "Everybody loves Raymond," you would *not* symbolize it as (∀x)(Px & Lxr). This last expression says "*Everything* is a person and loves Raymond," and clearly this is not what you meant to say. Even if every person loves Raymond, it is clearly false that everything is a person and loves Raymond. A duck, for instance, is not a person and (presumably) doesn't love Raymond either.

Finally, just as in chapter 2 we gave formal grammatical rules for what constitutes a sentence in SL, so we need formal rules for what counts as a grammatically correct logical expression in PL. Grammatically correct expressions in PL are called "formulas of PL," or just "formulas." We speak of "formulas" in PL, instead of sentences, because PL lets us use expressions that are not complete sentences whereas in SL we had to use whole sentences. The following rules specify what counts as a formula in PL. Other formulations of these rules are possible, and some of the others might be preferred by some logicians, but this set of rules seems clearest and most intuitive to me. The symbols we use in PL are the five symbols for connectives that we used in SL, predicate constants, subject constants, subject variables, and the symbols for universal and existential generalization. As with SL, we require that parentheses, brackets, and braces be used where needed to prevent ambiguity. I use Old English font and Greek letters for the symbols to indicate that they stand for *any* predicate constants, subject constants, subject variables, or formulas. "𝔓" will stand for any predicate constant, "α . . . κ" will stand for one or more, not necessarily distinct, subject constants or subject variables, "𝔄" and "𝔅" will stand for any formulas, and α will stand for any subject variable.

(1) Any expression of the form 𝔓 α . . . κ is a formula.

Note: This rule just means that any predicate constant with any combination of attached subject variables or subject constants—like Px, Py, Pxy, Pxx, Pax, Pab, Paa, Psmb, and so on—is a formula.

(2) If 𝔄 is a formula, then ~𝔄 is a formula.

(3) If 𝔄 and 𝔅 are formulas, then 𝔄 v 𝔅 is a formula.

(4) If 𝔄 and 𝔅 are formulas, then 𝔄 & 𝔅 is a formula.

(5) If 𝔄 and 𝔅 are formulas, then 𝔄 → 𝔅 is a formula.

(6) If 𝔄 and 𝔅 are formulas, then A ⇔ 𝔅 is a formula.

(7) If 𝔄 is a formula, then (∀α)𝔄 is a formula, provided that 𝔄 contains at least one free instance of α, and there are no quantifiers binding α in 𝔄.

(8) If 𝔄 is a formula, then (∃α)𝔄 is a formula, provided that 𝔄 contains at least one free instance of α, and there are no quantifiers binding α in 𝔄.

(9) Only expressions resulting from one or more applications of rules 1–8 are formulas.

Note: The restrictions following "provided" in rules 7 and 8 keep us from having vacuous quantifications like $(\forall x)Cy$, where the quantifier doesn't bind anything, and from having formulas like $(\exists x)[Px \mathbin{\&} (\forall x)(Mx \rightarrow Dx)]$, where different quantifiers bind the same variable. Such expressions are not allowed as formulas of PL according to the rules we have chosen to use.

Repeated application of the rules will allow us to build formulas of any degree of complexity. For instance, the formula $(\forall x)(\exists y)[Fx \rightarrow (Gy \mathbin{\&} Lxy)]$ can be built up from Fx, Gy, and Lxy, which are formulas by rule 1. Gy & Lxy is a formula by rule 4. $Fx \rightarrow (Gy \mathbin{\&} Lxy)$ is a formula by rule 5. $(\exists y)[Fx \rightarrow (Gy \mathbin{\&} Lxy)]$ is a formula by rule 8, and $(\forall x)(\exists x)[Fx \rightarrow (Gy \mathbin{\&} Lxy)]$ by rule 7.

EXERCISES FOR CHAPTER 5

1) Translate the following expressions from English into predicate logic using the following predicate logic symbols: Px = "x is a politician" and Lx = "x is a liar."

   (a) Some politicians are liars.
   (b) Some politicians are not liars.
   (c) All politicians are liars.
   (d) No politicians are liars.
   (e) Some liars are politicians.
   (f) Some nonliars are not politicians.
   (g) Some nonpoliticians are not liars
   (h) Some politicians are liars and some nonpoliticians are liars.
   (i) All nonliars are nonpoliticians but some nonpoliticians are liars.
   (j) All politicians are liars but not all liars are politicians.

2) Translate the following expressions in English into predicate logic using the following predicate symbols: Kx = "x is a kid," Vx = "x is a video game," Px = "is a parent," Lxy = "x loves y," and Hx = "x hates y."

(a) Every kid loves some video game.
(b) There is a video game that every kid loves.
(c) Some kid loves every video game.
(d) Some parents hate every video game.
(e) Every parent hates some video game.
(f) There is a video game that every kid loves and that every parent hates.
(g) Every video game is loved by some kids and hated by some parents.
(h) There is a video game that some parents do not hate but every kid hates.
(i) Every video game that some kids love is hated by some parents.
(j) Some video game is hated by all parents and some kids.

3) State, "yes" or "no," whether each of the following expressions is a formula of PL.

(a) (x)Fx
(b) (∀x)
(c) Fx
(d) Faa
(e) ~Faa
(f) ~&(∃y)
(g) (∀x)(Mx → Bxb)
(h) ~(∃y)[My & (∀x) (Gx → Fxy)]
(i) (∀x)(∃y) G
(j) (∀x)Mxg & ~(∃y)(Py & Ry)

Chapter Six

PROOFS IN PREDICATE LOGIC

O ur proofs in PL will be very much like those in SL. We shall use the same basic valid argument forms and the same equivalences. We also shall use the two forms of proof with assumptions, CP and IP. Consider one of the syllogisms we symbolized in PL in the last chapter:

> No senator is a PhD biologist.
> Some senators are creationists.
> _____
> Some creationists are not PhD biologists.

We symbolized this syllogism as:

> $(\forall x)(Sx \rightarrow {\sim}Px)$
> $(\exists x)(Sx \,\&\, Cx)$
> _____
> $(\exists x)(Cx \,\&\, {\sim}Px)$

This argument would be easy to prove if we could find a way to get rid of the quantifiers in the premises and just deal with the material in the parentheses and then add the quantifier back on when we got the conclusion. Without the quantifiers, we would just have

> (1) $Sx \rightarrow {\sim}Px$
> (2) $Sx \,\&\, Cx$ /: $Cx \,\&\, {\sim}Px$

This we can prove very easily:

(3) Sx	1, Simp
(4) ~Px	1,3 MP
(5) Cx	2, Simp
(6) Cx & ~Px	4,5 Conj

If we could add the existential quantifier to line 6, we would have our conclusion. So the main things we need to do proofs in PL are rules for the elimination and addition of quantifiers. We therefore have four rules: Universal Elimination (UE) for the elimination of universal quantifiers, Existential Elimination (EE) for the elimination of existential quantifiers, Universal Addition (UA) for the addition of universal quantifiers, and Existential Addition (EA) for the addition of existential quantifiers.

Warning: These rules will sound *very* forbidding and complicated. They have to be, because they have to be designed to permit every legitimate inference in PL and to outlaw every illegitimate one, even ones you are very unlikely to try. Don't despair! You really do not have to remember all that much to use them correctly, and, with a bit of practice, their use will soon be second nature to you. After stating the formal rules and their informal explanations, I list the six simple rules that are probably the only ones you will need to remember to do proofs.

All the rules involve adding or dropping a quantifier and replacing one variable with another variable or (in one case only) with a constant. In stating these rules, I'll give a formal statement of the rule and follow it with an informal explanation. Once again I use Old English font and Greek letters to indicate that I am talking about *any* formulas, subject variables, or subject constants. The symbols $\mathfrak{A}$ and $\mathfrak{B}$ can stand for any formulas of PL. Also, α and β can stand for any particular subject variables (*not* subject constants, though), and κ can stand for any particular subject constant.

Universal elimination (UE): Formal Statement: You perform UE
on any formula of the form $(\forall \alpha)\mathfrak{A}$ by either

(1) replacing $(\forall\alpha)$ 𝔄 with 𝔅, where 𝔅 results from eliminating the universal quantifier $(\forall\alpha)$ from $(\forall\alpha)$𝔄, leaving 𝔄, and then uniformly replacing each freed occurrence of α in 𝔄 with an occurrence of any subject constant κ,

or

(2) replacing $(\forall\alpha)$𝔄 with 𝔅, where 𝔅 results from eliminating the universal quantifier $(\forall\alpha)$ from $(\forall\alpha)$𝔄, leaving 𝔄, and then uniformly replacing each freed occurrence of α in 𝔄 with an occurrence of any variable β, provided that each freed occurrence of α in 𝔄 is replaced by an occurrence of β free in 𝔅.

Informal Explanation: This is really a very easy rule to use. What it basically says is that when you want to get rid of a universal quantifier you just drop it. Then you can replace the variable that had been bound by that quantifier with practically any variable or with any constant you please. You only have to make sure that you replace *every* occurrence of the variable you have freed by dropping the universal quantifier with the *same* constant or the same *free* variable.

For an example of the correct use of UE, consider the first line of our above symbolized syllogism: $(\forall x)(Sx \rightarrow {\sim}Px)$. We perform UE on this line by first removing the universal quantifier, leaving $(Sx \rightarrow {\sim}Px)$. This frees both occurrences of the variable x, the one next to the S and the one next to the ~P. We next replace each occurrence of the variable x with another occurrence of a particular free variable (*and don't forget that we can always "replace" x with itself*) or with any particular constant. Therefore, $Sx \rightarrow {\sim}Px$ would be correct, as would $Sy \rightarrow {\sim}Py$ or $Sa \rightarrow {\sim}Pa$. It would *not* be correct to replace one occurrence of x with one variable or constant and the other instance with some other variable or constant. Thus, we could not perform UE on $(\forall x)(Sx \rightarrow {\sim}Px)$ and get $Sx \rightarrow {\sim}Py$.

The "provided that" rule keeps you from freeing a variable in a formula by removing the quantifier and then replacing the freed variable with a new variable that is bound in the resulting formula. Such accidental binding of the replacement variable might lead to an invalid inference. For instance, suppose we have $(\forall x)(\exists y)Hyx$, where we limit our universe of discourse to counting numbers, so that H means "higher than" and $(\forall x)(\exists y)Hyx$ means "For every counting number x, there exists a higher number y," which is true. If we could apply UE to $(\exists y)Hyy$, removing the universal quantifier and replacing x with y, then the newly introduced y would be bound in the resulting formula $(\exists y)Hyy$. This would be bad because $(\exists y)Hyy$ says that there is a counting number higher than itself, which is nonsense.

Note that the "provided that" rule requires only that *newly introduced* occurrences of the replacement variable be free in the formula resulting from removing the universal quantifier and substituting the replacement variable for the original variable. Suppose you have the formula $(\forall x)[(\exists y) Gy \& Bx]$. You could UE to $(\exists y)Gy \& By$, where the instance of y after the G is not free in the resulting formula because the instance of y after the G did not get there by replacing the x freed when we removed the universal quantifier.

> Existential elimination (EE): Formal Statement: You perform EE
> on any formula of the form $(\exists \alpha)\mathcal{A}$ by replacing $(\exists \alpha)\mathcal{A}$ with
> $\mathcal{B}$, where $\mathcal{B}$ results from eliminating the existential quantifier
> $(\exists \alpha)$ from $(\exists \alpha)\mathcal{A}$, leaving $\mathcal{A}$, and then uniformly replacing
> each freed occurrence of α in $\mathcal{A}$ with an occurrence of any
> variable β, provided that
>
> (1) β is not free in any previous line of the proof.
>
> (2) Each freed occurrence of α in $\mathcal{A}$ should be replaced by
> an occurrence of β free in $\mathcal{B}$.

Informal Explanation: This rule is just slightly more complex than UE. As with UE, you basically just drop the quantifier and replace the freed variable with another. The only two additional things you have to remember are (1) unlike UE, you can *never* replace your freed variable with a constant—the rule says that you can replace variables *only* with variables, *never* constants—and (2) your replacement variable cannot have been free in a previous line of the proof.

For an example of EE, take the second line of our symbolized syllogism: $(\exists x)(Sx \& Cx)$. We do EE by taking away the existential quantifier leaving $Sx \& Cx$. We complete EE by replacing each of the x's with a variable that has not been free previously in the proof. If, for instance, the variable y is free on a previous line of the proof, you cannot use y when you perform EE. Also, when you do EE, unlike UE, you cannot use constants, so you *cannot* go, for instance, from (∃x)(Sx & Cx) to Sa & Ca.

The reason why EE has more restrictions than UE is easy to understand. A universally quantified formula states that something is so in every case; for instance, that every x that is S is also P. If it is so in every case, it will be so in any particular case—if *everything* that is S is P, then *any particular thing* that is S is P— so we can replace our variable when we do UE with any constant we please. An existentially quantified formula, however, only says that *some* things are so; for instance, that for some x, it is both S and P. If only *some* things are so, we cannot assume that it is so of *any particular thing*. Therefore, when we do EE, we cannot replace our variables with constants.

So when we apply UE, it does not matter whether that variable we use was already free in the proof, but if we allowed EE to use variables already free in the proof, we could get invalid arguments. For instance, let (∃x)Px mean "Some x is a politician" and (∃x)Hx to mean "Some x is honest," both of which are true. We could then perform EE on (∃x)Px and get Px. If we then let ourselves do EE on (∃x)Hx to get Hx, we could put Px and Hx together with conjunction on a later line of the proof to get Px & Hx. If we then added the existential quantifier back to this formula, which we can do by rule EA (explained below), we would get (∃x)(Px & Hx), which would say "There exists something that is both a politician and is honest," which could very well be untrue.

Note once again that when we introduce a replacement variable, no newly introduced occurrence of that variable can be bound in the resulting formula. Suppose "Mx" means "x is a mammal" and "Fx" means "x has feathers." (∃x)(∃y)(Mx & Fy) means "Something is a mammal and something has feathers," which is true. If we could apply EE to (∃y)(My & Fy), this would mean "Something is a mammal and has feathers," which is false. The reason why you are not allowed to introduce a constant with EE is easy to see. You cannot, for instance, go from (∃x) Fx to Fa, because a names a particular thing. From the fact that something is F, we cannot conclude that a particular thing is F.

We now consider the rules for adding quantifiers. Basically, these are just the reverse of the elimination rules. Instead of dropping quantifiers and then substituting variables (or constants with UE), we change the variables and then add a quantifier in the addition rules. The first is Universal Addition (UA) which has the most restrictions of any of these rules.

> Universal addition (UA): Formal Statement: You perform UA on $\mathfrak{A}$, where $\mathfrak{A}$ contains at least one free occurrence of α, by replacing $\mathfrak{A}$ with $(\forall\beta)\mathfrak{B}$, where $(\forall\beta)\mathfrak{B}$ results from uniformly replacing each free occurrence of α in $\mathfrak{A}$ with any variable β, yielding $\mathfrak{B}$, and then adding the universal quantifier $(\forall\beta)$ to $\mathfrak{B}$ to produce $(\forall\beta)\mathfrak{B}$, provided that
>
> (1) the variable α in $\mathfrak{A}$ does not occur free in any previous line obtained by EE,
>
> (2) the variable α in $\mathfrak{A}$ does not occur free in any undischarged assumed premise on a previous line, and
>
> (3) every occurrence of β in $\mathfrak{B}$ is obtained by replacing an occurrence of α free in $\mathfrak{A}$ with an occurrence of β free in $\mathfrak{B}$.

Informal explanation: Basically, you replace a variable (*never* a constant) with a variable and add a universal quantifier, so long as the stated conditions are met. The reason that UA has so many restrictions is that it works only if the variable α is *arbitrary*, that is, there are no special conditions or restrictions that limit its universalizability. In mathematics we often prove things by saying things like "Let n be any real number" or "Let ABC be any triangle." Whatever is true of *any* arbitrary real number or *any* arbitrary triangle must be true of *all* real numbers or triangles. Clearly, then, we *cannot* universally generalize from a constant with UA because, by definition, a constant is not arbitrary but names a particular thing. So, you cannot go from, for example, Ta to $(\forall x)Tx$ because a is a constant that names a particular thing that is T, and we cannot conclude from the fact that a is T that everything is T.

Further, if α is a variable freed by an application of EE, then α exists on a previous line quantified by an existential quantifier. But an existential quantifier only says that *some* α's have a given predicate, not that *all* do. If we could then perform UA on α, we might then falsely conclude something about all α's. For instance, suppose we have (∃x)Tx, meaning that something is a turtle (or turtles exist), which is obviously true. We could perform EE on (∃x) Tx and get Tx. If we now could perform UA on Tx, we would get (∀x)Tx, which makes the ridiculously false statement that everything is a turtle. By the way, *any* variable free in a line obtained by EE is off limits for UA, whether or not that variable was the one freed by the use of EE. For instance, if you have (∃x)(Fx & Gy) in a line and then use EE to get Fx & Gy, you cannot use y as your variable for UA on a later line, even though x was the variable freed by EE, not y.

Likewise, any α introduced free in an assumed premise will not be universalizable within the scope of that assumption, for the simple reason that we are *assuming* the expression in which α occurs free, and so we are assuming that some predicate applies to α. For instance, if we assume Tα, we are assuming that α is whatever T stands for. But making such an assumption means that α cannot be arbitrary; for it to be arbitrary, we cannot assume anything about it. Once the assumption is discharged, however, then our assumption about α is eliminated from the proof, and α might be universalizable if all other conditions of UA are met.

The reason for condition (3) on UA is to make sure that when we replace one variable with another in UA, there are not already bound or unbound occurrences of the replacement variable in the formula we are going to quantify. For instance, if we had Txy and we tried to do UA on it to get (∀y)Tyy, this could be false. From "x is taller than y" we cannot infer "Everything is taller than itself," which is nonsense. If the replacement variable is already present as a bound variable in the formula we are quantifying, we could use UA to get a formula with the same variable bound by two different quantifiers, which is not even a formula according to our rules. For instance, if we had Fx → (∃y)Py and we could do UA with the replacement variable y, we would get (∀y)[Fy → (∃y)Py], which isn't even a formula by our rules because it has two quantifiers binding the same variable. We avoid both these problems if we don't permit any occurrence of the replacement variable in our quantified formula unless it got there by replacing an occurrence of our original variable that is free in the original formula.

Existential addition (EA): Formal Statement: You perform EA on 𝒜, where A contains at least one free occurrence of any variable α, or at least one occurrence of any subject constant κ, by either

(1) replacing 𝔄 with (∃β)𝔅, where (∃β)𝔅 results from replacing at least one free occurrence α in 𝔄 with any variable β, yielding 𝔅, and then adding the existential quantifier (∃β) to 𝔅 to produce (∃β)𝔅, provided that every occurrence of β in (∃β)𝔅 results from replacing an occurrence of α free in 𝔄 with an occurrence of β free in 𝔅,

   or

(2) replacing 𝔄 with (∃β)𝔅, where (∃β)𝔅 results from replacing at least one occurrence of κ in 𝔄 with any variable β, yielding 𝔅, and then adding the existential quantifier (∃β) to 𝔅 to produce (∃β)𝔅, provided that every occurrence of β in (∃β)𝔅 results from replacing an occurrence of κ in 𝔄 with an occurrence of β free in 𝔅.

Informal Explanation: Note that you can perform EA from a variable or a constant. For instance, from Fx you can infer (∃x)Fx by EE. Also, from Fa you can infer (∃x)Fx. The latter is clearly a valid inference. From the fact that some individual, say, Art, is F, it follows that something is F, which is what (∃x)Fx says. The only odd thing about EA is that we do not have to replace *every* instance of a variable free in the original formula or *every* instance of a constant in the original formula. We only have to replace *at least one* occurrence of the variable or constant. For instance, if we have Px & Gx, you could then get (∃y)(Py & Gx) by applying EA to Px & Gx. You could also get (∃y)(Px & Gy) or (∃y)(Py & Gy). If you take into consideration this peculiarity of EA, you don't have much to worry about in using it. Also, as with UA, we have to make sure that there are no bound or unbound occurrences of the replacement variable already present in the formula we are going to quantify. If we did not prohibit this, we could have, for instance, Txy on a line and then get (∃y)Tyy by EE. But, we cannot infer from "x is taller than y" on one line that "something is taller than itself," on a subsequent line.

Caution: One very important thing all these quantifier elimination and addition rules have in common is that they can only be applied to *whole* *lines.* For instance, if we have the line (∀x) Gx → (∃y) (My & Qy). We *cannot* apply UE to drop the universal quantifier and get Gx → (∃y) (My & Qy) because the scope of the universal quantifier here only encompasses Gx and does not include the whole line. If the quantifier's scope had included the whole line, that is, if the line had been (∀x) [Gx → (∃y) (My & Qy)], then we *could* have used UE to get Gx → (∃y) (My & Qy). The same restriction applies to EE: it can be used only on *whole lines.*

Now, all these conditions, caveats, and restrictions on the elimination and addition rules probably sound horribly complex and confusing, like the fine print on a credit card contract or an IRS form, but practically speaking, there are not that many things to remember. The rules you really need to remember can be summarized as follows:

(1) Never try to use EE to introduce a constant or a variable free previously in the proof.

(2) Never attempt to do UA *from* a constant or *from* a variable free on a line obtained by EE or *from* a variable free in an undischarged assumed premise on a previous line.

(3) When you eliminate a quantifier (using UE or EE), *every* variable freed by dropping the quantifier must be replaced by a free variable (or a constant with UE).

(4) When you apply UA to a line, you must bind *every* occurrence of the free variable you are binding in that line.

(5) When you apply EA to a line, you must bind *at least one* occurrence of the free variable you are binding in that line.

(6) Only use UE, EE, UA, and EA on *whole* lines.

Still think this is too complicated? Well here is the dirty little secret about PL: If you employ the indirect proof strategy we talked about in chapter 4, you can prove everything with just the two simple rules UE and EE. If you use IP, you do not have to worry at all about UA and all of its horrendous conditions and restrictions. Why the hell didn't I tell you this several pages back!? Because some proofs are actually easier and feel more "natural" if you don't use IP, but prove it directly with the quantifier addition rules.

As with the IP proofs in chapter 4, you do it here by assuming the negation of what we are trying to prove, stick that in as an assumed premise, and see if we can derive a contradiction. If we can, we know that the argument is valid. Here is an example:

(1) $(\forall x)(\exists y)[Hx \rightarrow (By \& Cy)]$ p

(2) $(\exists x)(Hx \& Dxa)$ /: $(\exists y)\ Cy$ p

(3) $(\sim^*) \sim(\exists y)\ Cy$ AIP

So we negate the conclusion and stick it in as an assumed premise, marking it as our assumption for *reductio*. Let's do UE on the first premise of the above argument.

From

(1) $(\forall x)(\exists y)[Hx \rightarrow (By \& Cy)]$

we can get

(4) $(\exists y)[Hx \rightarrow (By \& Cy)]$ UE

Here we "replace" x with itself. Likewise, we could have written:

$(\exists y)[Hz \rightarrow (By \& Cy)]$ or $(\exists y)[Ha \rightarrow (By \& Cy)]$. Note carefully that, as the rules say, we can substitute *any* free variable or *any* constant for the variable x when we do UE. On the other hand, we *cannot* get $(\exists y)\ [Hy \rightarrow (By \& Cy)]$ by UE. Why? Because the variable y is not free in the expression; it is bound by the existential quantifier $(\exists y)$.

Now let's do EE on the remaining expression $(\exists y)[Hx \rightarrow (By \& Cy)]$:

(5) $Hx \rightarrow (By \& Cy)$ EE

Here, we drop the existential quantifier and "replace" the bound variable y with the free variable y. Note that we *cannot* go from (∃y) [Hx→ (By & Cy)] to Hx → (Bx & Cx) by EE. Why? Because the rule says that the variable you introduce by EE cannot be free previously in the proof, and x is already a free variable, in line (4).

Note: Though it is perfectly "legal" to perform UE first in a proof and EE next, as we have done here for purposes of illustration, it is generally better to do EE first, as we explain below.

OK, we now have a way of getting rid of the quantifiers, but we are not free to start proving yet. We don't yet know what to do with expressions involving the negation of quantifiers, like ~(∃y) Cy. So let's introduce the simple rule of QN, quantifier negation. QN has two forms. I use A to represent any formula:

> QN (first form): Any formula of the form ~(∀α)A can be replaced by a formula of the form (∃α)~A.

Informally, the negation of a universally quantified expression can be replaced by an existentially quantified expression with the negation sign "passed through" the quantifier and placed just to the right of the existential quantifier.

For instance, from ~(∀x)(Hx → Rx) you can write (∃x)~(Hx → Rx) by QN.

> QN (second form): Any formula of the form ~(∃α)A can be replaced by a formula of the form (∀α)~A.

Informally, the negation of an existentially quantified expression can be replaced by a universally quantified expression with the negation sign "passed through" the quantifier and placed just to the right of the quantifier and just to the left of the quantified expression.

For instance, from ~(∃x)(Cx & Dx), you can write (∀x)~(Cx & Dx) by QN.

OK, let's get back to our proof and start over, now that we finally have all the rules we need:

(1) $(\forall x)(\exists y)[Hx \rightarrow (By \, \& \, Cy)]$ p

(2) $(\exists x)(Hx \, \& \, Dxa)$ /: $(\exists y)Cy$ p

(3) $(\sim\!*) \sim(\exists y)Cy$ AIP

(4) $(\forall y) \sim Cy$ 3, QN

We "pass through" the negation sign and replace the existential quantifier with a universal one.

Note: When we do quantifier negation, we will just give our justification for the line as "QN," whether it is the first form of QN or the second form.

(5) $Hx \, \& \, Dxa$ 2, EE

Big Hint: Whenever you can, *always* do your EE before you do your UE. Why? Because if you do UE first and you get a free variable, then you cannot EE to that same free variable—that's what the rule for EE says. But, if you EE first, you can always UE to the same variable you introduced by EE (nothing in the rule for UE says you can't).

(6) $(\exists y)[Hx \rightarrow (By \, \& \, Cy)]$ 1, UE

(7) $Hx \rightarrow (By \, \& \, Cy)$ 6, EE

Note again that when you do EE here, you cannot use the variable x because it is already free in the proof.

(8) Hx 5, Simp

(9) $By \, \& \, Cy$ 7, 8 MP

(10) Cy 9, Simp

(11) $\sim Cy$ 4, UE

You UE to the variable y so that you can have a contradiction to Cy.

(12) $Cy \, \& \sim Cy$ 11, 12 Conj

(13) (~*) /: (∃y) Cy   3–12 IP

Let's try another one:

(1) (∀x)(∃y) [(Px → Gxy) & (Rx → Hxy)]

(2) Pa & Ra /: (∃x)(∃y)(Gxy & Hxy)

(3) (~*) ~(∃x)(∃y)(Gxy & Hxy)   AIP

We assume the negation of the conclusion to do IP.

(4) (∀x)~(∃y) (Gxy & Hxy)   3, QN

We "pass through" the negation sign and place it next to the (∃y), changing the existential quantifier (∃x) to a universal quantifier (∀x). The next step, of course, is to use QN again and pass it through the (∃y).

(5) (∀x)(∀y) ~(Gxy & Hxy)   4, QN

(6) (∀x)(∀y)(~Gxy v ~Hxy)   5, DeM

We can use the equivalences here just as we did in SL.

(7) (∀x)(∀y) (Gxy → ~Hxy)   6, Impl

(8) (∃y) [(Pa → Gay) & (Ra → Hay)]   1, UE

Remember, you can UE to a constant—"a" in this case.

(9) (Pa → Gay) & (Ra →Hay)   8, EE

You can EE to the variable y because y is not free previously in the proof.

(10) (∀y) (Gay → ~Hay)   7, UE

(11) Gay → ~Hay   10, UE

(12) Pa   2, Simp

(13) Pa → Gay   9, Simp

(14) Pa → ~Hay   11, 13, HS

(15) ~Hay   12, 14, MP

(16) Ra   2, Simp

(17) Ra → Hay   8, Simp

(18) Hay   16, 17 MP

(19) Hay & ~Hay   15, 18, Conj

(20) (~*) /: (∃x)(∃y) (Gxy & Hxy)   3–19 IP

Really, once you use UE, EE, and QN to get rid of quantifiers and the negations of quantifiers, PL is done just like SL.

Note: You can also use IP to get *any line you need*, not just the conclusion. Consider the following problem:

(1) (∃x) Fx → (∀x)(∀y) (Fx → Gxy)

(2) Fa /: Gab

You now put in the negation of the conclusion for your IP proof:

(3) (~*) ~Gab   AIP

But where do you go from here? You cannot do EE or UE on line (1), because these can only be applied to *whole* lines. It would help, of course, if we had (∃x) Fx, because we could just use MP to get rid of it and then we would have (∀x)(∀y)(Fx → Gxy) by itself, which looks promising. Well, let's assume ~(∃x) Fx and see if we can derive a contradiction. If we can, we will then have (∃x) Fx, and we can put it in as a premise.

(4) (~**) ~(∃x) Fx   AIP

(5) (∀x) ~Fx   4, QN

(6) ~Fa   5, UE

(7) Fa & ~Fa	2,6 Conj
(8) (~**) /: ~~(∃x) Fx	4–7 IP

OK. Now DN gives us what we need.

(9) (∃x) Fx	8, DN
(10) (∀x)(∀y)(Fx → Gxy)	1, 9 MP

The rest of the proof is simple.

(11) (∀y) (Fa → Gay)	10, UE
(12) Fa → Gab	11UE
(13) Gab	2, 12, MP
(14) Gab & ~ Gab	3,13 Conj
(15) (~*) /: Gab	3–14 IP

All proofs in PL can be done with the IP method, if you just cannot face using UA and EA. However, as I said, some proofs are easier with these additional rules. Consider the first proof we did above:

(1) (∀x)(∃y)[Hx → (By & Cy)]	p
(2) (∃x)(Hx & Dxa) /: (∃y)Cy	p

Let's do it directly, and not with IP.

(3) Hx & Dxa	2, EE
(4) (∃y)[Hx → (By & Cy)	1, UE
(5) Hx → (By & Cy	4, EE
(6) Hx	3, Simp
(7) By & Cy	5,6 MP
(8) Cy	7, Simp
(9) (∃y)Cy	8, EA

So you can do it directly in fewer steps, and it really is an easy proof once you eliminate the quantifiers.

Finally, let's do one using the dreaded UA rule:

(1) ~(∃x)(Ax & Px)   p

(2) (∃y)My → (∀x)(Gx → Ax)   p

(3) (∃x)Mx /: ∀x)(Gx → ~Px)

Let's first do QN to get the first premise into something we can work with.

(4) (∀x)~(Ax & Px)   1, QN

(5) (∀x)(~Ax v ~Px)   4, DeM

(6) (∀x)(Ax → ~Px)   5, Impl

OK, let's now deal with the premise in line (2). We cannot perform any elimination rules on it because no quantifier applies to the whole line. However, line (3) has something we might work with.

(7) Mx   3, EE

Note that you have introduced x free in a line obtained by EE. This means that you cannot use UA to bind x.

(8) (∃y)My   7, EA

(9) (∀x)(Gx → Ax)   2, 8 MP

(10) Ay → ~Py   6, UE

Why do you apply UE to the variable y, here? Why not use x? Because we introduced x as a free variable in a line obtained by EE, so we will need to use a new variable if we are going to apply UA.

(11) Gy → Ay   9, UE

(12) Gy → ~Py   10, 11 HS

This is everything we need except for the universal quantifier. We check and make sure that y is not free in a line introduced by EE (no, we used x), and there are no assumed premises, so we are free to proceed.

(13) (∀x)(Gx → Px)   12, UA

Note: Don't get confused here. The rules permit you to do UA *to* x here even though it was introduced free in a line obtained by EE [line (7)]. What the rule forbids you to do is to do UA *from* a variable free in a line introduced by EE. The x in line (13) was obtained by applying UA to line (12), which uses the variable y, which is not free in a line obtained by EE.

And one more:

(1) (∃x)[Sx & ~(∃y)(Gy & My)] → ~(∃x)(Rx & Lx)   p

(2) Ry   p

(3) Ly /: (∀x)[Sx → (∃z)Mz]   p

We can't really do anything until we turn the first line into something useful. Lines (2) and (3) look promising if we put them together.

(4) Ry & Ly   2,3 Conj

Now we use EA to get something that looks even more useful.

(5) (∃x)(Rx & Lx)   4, EA

If we use DN on (5) we can use it to do MT on (1) and maybe break (1) down into something we can use. In doing PL proofs, as with SL, a good strategy is to break down complex expressions into simple ones.

(6) ~~(∃x)(Rx & Lx)   5, DN

(7) ~(∃x)[Sx & ~(∃y)(Gy & My)]   1,6 MT

(8) (∀x)~[Sx & ~(∃y)(Gy & My)]   7, QN

(9) (∀x)[~Sx v ~~(∃y)(Gy & My)]   8, DeM

(10) (∀x)[~Sx v (∃y)(Gy & My)]	9, DN
(11) (∀x)[Sx → (∃y)(Gy & My)]	10, Impl

Now we are ready to eliminate.

(12) Sx → (∃y)(Gy & My)	11, UE
(13) (→*) Sx	ACP

Of course, we can use CP in PL like SL.

(14) (∃y)(Gy & My)	12, 13 MP
(15) Gz & Mz	14, EE

We can't EE to y, because y is free earlier in the proof, on lines (2), (3) and (4), and we can't EE to x, since it is also free earlier in the proof, on line (12), so let's use z.

(16) Mz	15, Simp
(17) (∃z)Mz	16, EA
(18) (→*)\: Sx → (∃z)Mz	13–17 CP

The variable x is free in the assumed premise, line (13), but since it is discharged in line (18), and x is not free in a line obtained by EE (we used z), we can UA from that variable:

(19) (∀x)[Sx → (∃z)Mz]	18, UA

EXERCISES FOR CHAPTER 6

1) The following contain lines of PL proofs in which UE and EE are done *incorrectly*. State why the use of UE or EE is incorrect.

(a)

(1) (∀x) (Mx → Bx)

(2) Mx → By   1, UE (wrong)

(b)

(1) (∀x)(∃y) [Cx → (My & Pxy)]

(2) (∃y) [Cy → (My & Pyy)]   1, UE (wrong)

(c)

(1) (∃x)(Px & Gx) v (∃x)Nx

(2) Px & Gx   1, EE (wrong)

(d)

(1) (∃x)(Mx & Lx)

(2) Ma & La   1, EE (wrong)

(e)

(1) Gy & Tz

(2) (∃x) Mx

(3) My   2, EE (wrong)

2) The following contain lines of proof in which UA and EA are done
incorrectly. State why the use of UA or EA is incorrect here.

(a)

(1) Mx & (∀y)(Cy → Bxy)

(2) (∃y)[My & (∀y)(Cy → Byy)]   1, EA (wrong)

(b)

(1) Mx → (∃y)(By & Mxy)

(2) (∀y)(My → (∃y)(By & Myy)   1, UA (wrong)

(c)

(1) Ma → Ca	
(2) (∀x)(Mx & Cx)	1, UA (wrong)

(d)

(1) (∃x)(Mx & Bx)	
(2) Mx & Bx	1, EE
(3) Mx	2, Simp
(4) (∀x)Mx	3, UA (wrong)

(e)

(1) →* Fy & Cz	ACP
(2) Cz	1, Simp
(3) (∀z)Cz	2, UA (wrong)

3) Do the following PL proofs (some are pretty tough):

(a)

(1) (∀x) (Tx → Vx)

(2) (∀x) (Vx → Rx)

(3) Ta /: Ra

(b)

(1) ~(∃x) (Wx & Fx)

(2) Fa /: ~Wa

(c)

(1) (∀x) (Mx → Gx)

(2) (∀x) (Gx → ~Lx) /: (∀x) (Mx → ~Lx)

(d)

(1) (∃x) (Bx & Dx)

(2) (∀x) (Mx → ~Bx) /: (∃x) ~Mx

(e)

(1) (∀x)(∃y)[Px → (Gy & ~Rxy)]

(2) (∀x) Px /: ~(∀y) Ray

(f)

(1) ~(∃x)(Mx & Nx)

(2) ~(∀x)(Mx → Qx) /: (∃x) ~Nx

(g)

(1) (∀x)(∃y) [Gyx → (Ax & Fy)]

(2) (∀x)(∀y) Gxy /: (∃x) Fx

(h)

(1) ~(∃x)(Qx & Lx) → ~(∃x)(~Lx & Rx)

(2) (∀x)(Qx → ~Lx) /: (∀x)(~Lx→~Rx)

(i)

(1) (∃x) ~Hx → (∀y) (Py →Gy)

(2) ~(∀x) Hx

(3) Pa /: Ga

(j)

(1) ~(∀x)(∀y) [Fx → (Jx → Lxy)]

(2) (∀x)(∀y) (Bx → Lxy) /: (∃x) ~Bx

(k)

(1) (∃x)(∃y) Cxy

(2) (∀x)(∀y) (Cyx → Byx) /: (∃x)(∃y) Byx

(l)

(1)(∃x)(∃y)(Fxy) → (∀x)(∀y) (Fxy → Gy)

(2) Fab /: Gb

(**Hint**: Remember that you can use IP to get any line you need, not just the conclusion.)

(m)

(1) (∃x)[Gx & (∀y)(Sy → Lyx)] /: (∀x)[Sx → (∃y)(Gy & Lxy)]

Chapter Seven

PROBABILITY: THE BASIC RULES OF LIFE

So far in this book we have looked at deductive logic. One nice thing about deductive logic is that it gives us some certainties in an uncertain world. When we have a valid deductive argument, it tells us that if certain things are so, other things *must* be so, and this is good to know. But in life we often have to make do with less than certainty. Often, even if we know that certain things are so, we cannot conclude that other things *must* be so, only that they have some **probability** of being so. In fact, life is full of uncertainties, and if we waited until we could be *sure* before we took action, then we wouldn't get much done. We have to make decisions, sometimes crucial ones, when we are uncertain and can only project some degree of probability for various outcomes.

Here is an example. I live south of Houston, near the Gulf Ccoast. This is a hurricane zone. When a hurricane warning comes, you have to make a decision: Do you evacuate or not? If you do, you will spend many hours in a traffic jam with other exasperated drivers and a vehicle full of anxious family members and howling pets. This is a major hassle and it may be totally unnecessary. Even with banks of supercomputers, it is hard to predict just where the hurricane will hit and how strong it will be when it hits. It could miss you by two hundred miles or weaken considerably, and you would have been better off hunkering down at home. Or you could get a direct hit by a screaming category five monster, in which case you would have a much worse problem than being stuck in a traffic jam. So you have to make your best decision on the basis of a number of factors, none of which can be known with certainty.

Small wonder that probability has been called the "guide of life." Our spontaneous estimates of probability are often wrong (see chapter 8) and frequently also the values of the probabilities we have to consider do not admit of precise quantification. In this chapter we are going to introduce probability in contexts where there are only a few factors to consider and their probabilities can be precisely stated. Even simple cases like these have application to everyday life, however. For instance, the mathematical study of probability began when an aristocratic seventeenth-century dice addict asked famous mathematician Blaise Pascal a question about odds. Today, the laws of probability have made Las Vegas what it is. Even if you do not spend your vacations in Las Vegas (and a study of probability just might give you pause in your choice of recreations), you, in effect, make bets all the time. When you get life insurance, your insurance company is betting that you will live long enough to pay them more in premiums than they will ever have to pay your beneficiaries.

So what sorts of things have probabilities? Is there a probability that our universe would be the one that exists out of all the possible universes that conceivably could have existed? Is it probable or improbable that God exists? Philosophers debate these points endlessly and not particularly fruitfully. In this chapter we will restrict our attention to events in the physical world and forgo attempting to apply probability to questions of metaphysics or the supernatural. That is, in this chapter we shall restrict attention to the calculation of the probabilities of physical occurrences. In the next chapter we shall expand our study of probability to ask how strongly we should believe or disbelieve that something is so.

Let's say that an **event** is something that occurs in some definite way so that we can say, with no vagueness or ambiguity, that it either did or did not happen. This keeps us from falling into the trap of trying to determine probabilities in situations where we are not really sure what we are talking about. Thus, tossing a coin and having it land heads is an event. A rocket booster that fails to fire is an event. Hitting a home run in the final at bat of your major league career (as Ted Williams did) is an event.

In this chapter we will let letters represent events, and we will symbolize the phrase "the probability that event a occurs" as p(a). Likewise, p(~a) means the probability that event a will not occur; p(b) means the probability of event b; p(a v b) means the probability of the occurrence of event a or event b; p(a & b) means the probability of both events a and b.

= the probability that event ~a will occur?

Some events are certain. Unsupported massive objects near the earth's surface do fall down. Count on it. On the other hand, some things are impossible. Despite the nursery rhyme, a cow cannot jump over the moon. When an event is certain, we say it has a probability of one. So the probability that an unsupported 10-kg dumbbell will fall down when you drop it in the gym is, effectively, one. Symbolically, if a is the event of the unsupported dumbbell falling, $p(a) = 1$. When something is impossible, we say that it has a probability of zero. When something is neither certain nor impossible, we give it a fractional value (also expressed as a decimal or percentage) somewhere between zero and one. Thus, the weatherperson on the TV says that there is a 40 percent (or .4 or 2/5) chance of rain tomorrow. This means that it is neither certain nor impossible that it will rain. It is somewhat unlikely that it will, but you shouldn't be too surprised if it does. To be on the safe side, pack an umbrella. So our first rule of probability is this:

PR-1: Every event has a probability from zero to one inclusive.

That is, an event is either impossible, certain, or somewhere in between.

Notice that in the above paragraph we said that an event with a 40 percent chance of occurrence probably will not occur. If there is a 40 percent chance of rain tomorrow, what is the probability that it will *not* rain? Pretty obviously there is a 60 percent chance it will not rain. So our second rule of probability is our rule for determining the probability that a given event e will *not* happen. If the probability of e happening is x, then the probability of e not happening is one minus x:

PR-2: If $p(e) = x$, then $p(\sim e) = 1 - x$.

How do we determine the probability of a single occurrence of some kind of event? Practically speaking, we do that in a number of ways. Basically, we can do it either empirically, by observing many instances of that sort of event to see if the frequency of its occurrence converges on a particular value, or theoretically, by learning the values of all of the relevant causal factors that influence the outcome. Science writer Timothy Ferris has a nice passage explaining this in his book *Coming of Age in the Milky Way* (New York: William Morrow, 1988):

One cannot reliably calculate the odds of a particular thing having happened unless one either understands the process— that is, can properly identify and quantify all the variables involved—or has an adequate experimental data base from which to draw phenomenological information about it. If, for instance, we want to predict how close an intercontinental ballistic missile will land to its intended target, we can calculate all the variables—the flight characteristics of the missile, the influences of the environment on its navigational system, etc.—or we can test real missiles, as often as possible, in order to generate a database about how they perform. In practice one does both, since both approaches may err. (p. 373)

So determining the probability of particular events is often rather complex, and the hard work is done by scientists and engineers. We have an easier job. We shall just assume that we have some way of deciding on the probabilities of particular events. What we want to know now is this: Given that event a has a probability of x and that event b has a probability of y, how do we figure the probability of the joint occurrence of both a *and* b? What about the occurrence of a *or* b?

Sometimes, in order for something to happen, lots of other things have to all happen first. Consider NASA launching a rocket. Launching a rocket into space is no easy task; this is why the rocket scientists who do it *do* have to be really smart. Many, many things all have to work properly and in the right order for a launch to be successful. *All* systems have to be "go," and multiple redundancies are built in to provide backups for many systems. Still, though, to the great frustration of observers and sometimes the astronauts themselves, planned launches are often delayed. What is the chance that a planned launch will go as scheduled? It is the combined probability that *everything* will work right. That is, if L is the launch of rocket r at time t, and L depends on the occurrence of all of the events a, b, c, d, e . . . , then the probability of L is equal to the probability of a & b & c & d & e & . . . . Since the occurrence of none of the events a, b, c, d, e, and so on is certain, then, even if each event has individually a very high degree of probability, if there are enough events a, b, c, d, e . . . , something is likely to go wrong somewhere.

If rocket science isn't your thing, consider this: What is the chance that a given healthy nineteen-year-old college student will be dead in six months? Pretty low, actually. In other words (by rule 2), the chance that a healthy nineteen-year-old will *not* die within the next six months is quite high. However, if you consider a random selection of one hundred thousand healthy nineteen-year-old college students, the chances that *all* of them will still be alive in six months is quite low (again, such morbid statistics permit insurers to make sizable profits). So, even if the probability of individual cases is quite high (the probability that a healthy nineteen-year-old college student will still be alive in six months), the joint probability of all such cases can be quite low.

The above examples suggest that the probability of the joint occurrence of two or more events, where each event is less than certain, is less than the probabilities of the individual events. Since events that are neither certain nor impossible have fractional values, what arithmetical operation on fractions results in a lower fraction? Multiplication (e.g., ½ X ½ = ¼). So it looks like the rule is going to be that if you want to know the joint probability of two or more events, you multiply the individual probabilities of the events.

Well, we are on the right track here, but there is a complication. Some events are independent, that is, the occurrence of one does not condition or affect the occurrence of the other. For instance, so far as we know, if I roll a die at the same time that a friend tosses a coin, the results (1, 2, 3, 4, 5, or 6 showing on the die and heads or tails for the coin toss) have no influence on each other. So we say that, for instance, getting a "5" on the die roll and a "heads" on the coin toss are **independent events**. If two events are independent, then we do indeed calculate their conjoint probability, the probability of a *and* b both occurring simply by multiplying their individual probabilities. Here is the rule:

PR-3 (special conjunction rule): If two events a and b are *inde-pendent*, then p(a & b) = p(a) X p(b).

Thus the probability of getting a "5" on the roll of a fair die is 1/6, and the probability of getting "heads" on the toss of a fair coin is 1/2. So the probability of getting "5" on the die and "heads" on the toss is 1/6 X 1/2, which is 1/12.

Sometimes, though, events are not independent and the occurrence or nonoccurrence of one will affect the occurrence or nonoccurrence of the other. To take an obvious case, the chance that you will get the flu this winter depends to a very considerable extent on whether or not you get a flu shot. Since flu vaccines are not 100 percent reliable, getting a shot will not *guarantee* that you will not get flu, but it will greatly reduce your chances, say, from a 25 percent (or, equivalently, ¼ in fractional form or .25 in decimal form) chance of getting flu to only a 1 percent (1/100 or .01) chance in a given flu season. This suggests that if you want to figure the joint probability of two events that are *not* independent, then you have to take into account the degree to which the probability of one event depends on the occurrence of the other event. In other words, if you want to know the probability of events a and b *both* occurring, where the probability of b is influenced by the occurrence (or nonoccurrence) of a, then the probability of a and b is a times b *given* that a occurs. Here is the rule:

> PR-4 (general conjunction rule): When two events a and b are *not* independent, then p (a & b) = p (a) X p (b | a) (the upright bar "|" will be our symbol for "given").

$$p(a \& b) = p(b \& a) \ ?$$

Suppose that there is a .8 chance that you will get a flu shot this year. What is the probability that you will get the flu shot and still get the flu? If S is the event of getting a flu shot and F is the event of getting the flu, then the probability that you'll get the flu shot and still get the flu is equal to p(S & F) = P(S) X p(F | S) = .8 X .01 = .008, or only a 0.8 percent chance. What is the probability that you will not get a flu shot and not get the flu? Since p(~S) = 1 − p(S) = 1 − .8, p(~S) = .2. Further, p(~F | ~S) = 1 − p(F | ~S) = 1 − .25 = .75. So, p(~S & ~F) = p(~S) X p(~F | ~S) = .2 X .75 = .15, or a 15 percent chance.

So we now have a way of determining the probability that *both* of two events will occur, given that we know the probabilities of each event by itself. What about when we want to know the probability of the disjunction of two events, that is, that one event *or* another will happen? Remember that in logic, when we say "a or b," we mean that we can have just a and not b, just b and not a, or both a and b. When we can have just a and not b, or just b and not a, we say that a and b are **mutually exclusive**. That is, when a and b are events, the occurrence of one excludes the occurrence of the other. For instance, exams are normally graded so that you get a definite letter grade, A, B, C, D, or F. Therefore, getting an A on an exam excludes getting a B, and vice versa. So if event a is getting an A and event b is getting a B, these events are mutually exclusive. Suppose we want to know the odds that a given student, Susie, will make an A or a B on a given exam. If her odds of getting an A are .2 and of getting a B are .3, then, pretty clearly, Susie's odds of getting an A or B are .2 + .3, which is .5. This suggests our next rule of probability:

PR-5 (special disjunction rule): When two events a and b are mutually exclusive, p(a v b) = p(a) + p(b).

But, of course, oftentimes events are not mutually exclusive, that is, the occurrence of one event does not rule out the occurrence of the other. If you treat probabilities that are not mutually exclusive as though they are, you go badly wrong in trying to calculate the probability of their disjunction. Mathematician John Allen Paulos in his entertaining book *Innumeracy* (New York: Hill and Wang, 2001) tells the story of the TV weatherman who said that there was a 50 percent chance of rain on Saturday and a 50 percent chance of rain on Sunday and concluded that there was a 100 percent chance of rain that weekend. Wrong. Actually, there is a fair chance that it will not rain at all on a weekend with a 50 percent chance of rain on Saturday and a 50 percent chance of rain on Sunday.

What went wrong here? The problem is that rain on Saturday and rain on Sunday are not mutually exclusive events. It could rain both Saturday and Sunday (or neither day). When events are not mutually exclusive, we cannot get the probability of their disjunction simply by adding their separate probabilities. The rule we need is this:

PR-6 (general disjunction rule): When two events a and b are not mutually exclusive, p(a v b) = p(a) + p(b) – p(a & b).

Why do we have to subtract out p(a & b) when a and b are not mutually exclusive? Suppose we tried to calculate p(a v b) using PR-5, the special disjunction rule, even though a and b are *not* mutually exclusive. Since a and b are not mutually exclusive, their probabilities overlap.

Event a can take place in either of two mutually exclusive ways, either a occurs by itself, (a & ~b), or it occurs with b, (a & b). So p(a) = p(a & ~b) + p(a & b). By the same reasoning, p(b) = p(~a & b) + p(a & b). So, if we tried to calculate p(a v b) using PR-5, we would get p(a v b) = p(a) + p(b) = p(a & ~b) + p(a & b) + p(~a & b) + p(a & b).

But this cannot be right because p(a & b) gets included twice for no good reason. In fact, the disjunction of event a and event b, a v b, where a and b are not mutually exclusive, can occur only in three different ways: a by itself, (a & ~ b), or b by itself, (~a & b), or a and b occurring together, (a & b). Since these are the only possibilities, and these possibilities *are* mutually exclusive, we can figure p(a v b) simply by adding up the disjunctions of the possibilities using PR-5 twice:

p(a v b) = p{[(a & ~b) v (~a & b)] v (a & b)}

p(a v b) = p[(a & ~b) v (~a &b)] + p (a & b) (by PR-5)

p(a v b) = p(a & ~b) + p(~a & b) + p(a & b) (by PR-5)

So the first calculation is wrong because the overlap in the probabilities of p(a) and p(b) made us count p(a & b) twice when we used PR-5. Hence, to get it right we have to subtract p(a & b) out once. The formula we have to use is p(a v b) = p(a) + p(b) – p(a & b), which is rule PR-6.

Using PR-6, we can now correct the innumerate weatherman's error: If a is the event of rain on Saturday, and b is the event of rain on Sunday, and there is a 50 percent chance of rain on each day, then the chance that it will rain over the weekend is the probability of the disjunction a v b. So our formula is p(a v b) = p(a) + p(b) – p(a & b). We stipulate that p(a) = .5, p(b) = .5, and, assuming that a and b are independent, we calculate p(a & b) using PR-3, the special conjunction rule: p(a & b) = .5 X .5 = .25. So, p(a v b) = .5 + .5 – (.5 X .5) = 1 – .25 = .75.

Really, then, there is a good chance, 25 percent, that it will not rain at all over the weekend, even though there is a 50 percent chance of rain for Saturday and the same chance for Sunday.

As stated, the rules tell us how to figure the probabilities of the conjunction or disjunction of two events when we know the probabilities of the individual events. However, it is easy to extend our rules to cover three or more events. The two easiest cases are when we want to figure a conjunction of three or more events that are all independent from each other. We extend our special conjunction rule and simply multiply all of the probabilities of the individual events. Thus, if a, b, and c are independent events, p(a & b & c) = p(a) X p(b) X p(c). Similarly, if we want to know the probability of the disjunction of three or more events, where they are all mutually exclusive, we just extend our special disjunction rule and add up the individual probabilities. For instance, if a, b, and c are mutually exclusive events, p(a v b v c) = p(a) + p(b) + p(c). If three or more events are *not* independent, then we have to consider this in figuring the probability of their conjunction. Thus, if a, b, and c are not independent events, p(a & b & c) = p(a) X p(b | a) X p(c | a & b). If three events, a, b, and c, are *not* mutually exclusive, we figure their disjunction with the following formula: p(a v b v c) = p(a) + p(b) + p(c) – p(a & b) – p(a & c) – p(b & c) + p (a & b & c). If we want to know the probability of the disjunction of more than three events p(a v b v c v d, . . .), the easiest way to figure it will be to figure the probability that *none* of the events occurred (since this is the only way a disjunction can be false), that is, figure p(~a & ~ b & ~c & ~d, . . .) using one of the conjunction rules. After figuring that, use rule PR-2 and subtract the probability that *none* of the events will occur from one. This will give you the probability that *some* (one or more) of the events will occur, which is what we mean by the disjunction of these events a, b, c, d, and so on.

I said at the beginning of the chapter that probability is the guide of life. Using the six simple rules given here, we can calculate events of life-and-death significance. Consider that during World War II the US Army Eighth Air Force was conducting massive bombing attacks on Hitler's Germany. Flying B-17s and B-24s, the bomber crews conducted daylight attacks on some of the most heavily defended targets, such as Berlin and Schweinfurt. Before long-range fighter escorts became available, the bombers were subject to vicious attack by German fighters. The attrition rate was high; on any given mission a member of the bomber crew had a 4 percent chance of not making it back (i.e., a 4 percent chance of being killed or shot down and captured). At the time, a bomber crewmember was expected to fly twenty-five missions. With a 4 percent chance of not returning on each mission, what were the odds that a crewmember would make it through all twenty five missions? Here is how you figure it:

The probability of making it back on a given mission is .96. We get that by applying rule PR-2: The chance of *not* making it back is .04, so the probability of making it back, is 1 − .04 = .96. These are pretty good odds for one mission, but to last through 25 you have to make it through mission 1, and mission 2, and mission 3, . . . and mission 25, with a .96 chance of getting back on each one. How do we figure the odds of making through all 25? If the chances of making it on each mission are independent (and we assume that they are), then what is the chance of making it through two missions? Let a = making it back on mission one and b = making it back on mission two. In this case p(a & b), assuming independence, is calculated using the special conjunction rule, PR-3: p(a & b) = p(a) x p(b) = .96 X .96 = .92. Still good odds, but they are going down. To figure making it through three missions, we take making it through the first two missions as one event, and multiply its probability, .92, by the chance of making it through the third mission, .96. The chance of making it through three missions is .88. As you can see, the chance of making it through all 25 missions is .96 multiplied by itself 25 times. As you can quickly find out with your calculator, this comes out to a 36 percent chance of making it through all 25 missions, or, using PR-2 again, there is a 64 percent chance of not making through all 25 missions. Not good odds.

The sobering lesson is that actions that bear a small risk on a single occurrence can get very risky indeed if the actions are repeated a number of times. The chance of getting an STD on one occasion of having unprotected sex may be quite small, but the odds quickly get much worse if the behavior becomes habitual. Likewise, an event that has a very small chance of occurrence in a given year can become very probable over geological time. Thus, the chance of a large asteroid or comet hitting the earth in a given year is very small, but over 100 million years, the chances become very good indeed, as the dinosaurs learned to their chagrin.

EXERCISES FOR CHAPTER 7

1) Classify the following pairs of events as independent or not independent.

   (a) washing your car/rain the next day

   (b) watching the pot/the water boiling

   (c) the days get longer and warmer/flowers bloom

   (d) your boss yells at you/you yell at your spouse

   (e) politician's lips are moving/politician lies

   (f) wreck on freeway/traffic backs up

2) Classify the following events as mutually exclusive or not mutually exclusive.

   (a) IRS calls you in for an audit/mother-in-law phones to say she is visiting for three weeks

   (b) you roll "snake eyes" on a toss of a pair of dice/you roll seven on the same toss of the dice

   (c) you attend a conference in New York/you attend a conference in Beijing at the same time

   (d) your boss has a birthday party/you forget to bring a gift

   (e) a politician makes promises/the politician keeps his promises

   (f) you flunk out of school/you make the dean's list every term

3) Calculate the following probabilities.

   (a) I figure that I have a 10 percent chance of making an "A" on the test and a 30 percent chance of making a "B." What is the probability that I will make an "A" or a "B"?

   (b) What are the chances (referring to the above situation) that I will make a "C" or lower?

   (c) What are the chances that a couple with three children has all boys (assume a 50 percent chance that a live birth is a boy and regard each child as an independent "event").

(d) What are the chances that a couple will have at least one girl out of three children (assume a 50 percent chance that a live birth is a girl)?

(e) Suppose that there is a 10 percent chance that the condom will fail. If the condom fails, there is a 5 percent chance that Alice will become pregnant. What are the chances that the condom will fail and that Alice will get pregnant?

(f) If I have ten brown socks and ten blue socks all mixed up in a drawer, what is the probability that the first two socks I pull out at random are both blue (assuming I don't replace the first one)?

(g) If I have ten brown socks and ten blue socks all mixed up in a drawer, what is the probability of drawing out at least one blue sock if I pull out two socks at random without replacement?

(h) To get his football scholarship to Mega University, Moose must score at least 700 on his SATs and graduate high school with at least a 2.0 grade point average. Moose has a .3 chance of scoring at least 700 on his SATs and a .6 chance of graduating from high school with at least a 2.0 GPA. What are Moose's chances of getting the football scholarship to Mega University?

(i) Every time Joe Leadfoot takes the I-10 there is a 5 percent chance that Officer Dan will give him a speeding ticket. What are the chances that Joe could take the I-10 ten times in a row without getting a speeding ticket from Officer Dan?

(j) On a TV game show: Behind door 1 is a new car. Behind door 2 is a dream European vacation for two. Behind door 3 is a goat wearing a straw hat. You can only choose one door. What are the chances that you will get the new car or the dream vacation?

(k) The state of Texas issues license plates that have three letters followed by three numbers. Some people have objected that they got license plates with the letters F-A-T. Others objected that they got plates with the numbers 6-6-6, numbers associated with the devil. What are the chances, assuming that numerals and letters are assigned at random, that you would get the plate FAT 666?

(l) If I get a cold this winter, I'll have to miss two days of work. If I get the flu this winter, I'll have to miss a week of work. There is a .7 chance I will get a cold and a .3 chance I'll get the flu. What are my chances of missing at least two days of work this winter? Assume that getting a cold and getting the flu are independent events. .79

(m) Suppose that the chances that an unwed mother will not finish high school are 70 percent. Suppose that if an unwed mother does not finish high school there is a 70 percent chance her child will grow up in poverty. What are the chances that an unwed mother will not finish high school and that her baby will grow up in poverty?

Chapter Eight

THE THEOREM OF DR. BAYES

T he story goes that a boy's mom asks him what he learned in Sunday school. He says that the teacher told them about the evil Pharaoh and how Moses led the children of Israel out of slavery in Egypt. "Well, what did she say?" asks Mom. The boy replies: "She said that Moses led the people out of Egypt, but Pharaoh got mad so he ordered his army to attack Moses, but they couldn't get away "cause they were all backed up to the sea. So Moses gets on the radio and he calls in artillery and an air strike and wipes out Pharaoh's army." Mom's eyebrow arches: "Now, Billy, she didn't really say that, did she?" "No," says Billy, "But you wouldn't believe the story she really told us."

Billy is on to something. When is a tale so tall that you shouldn't believe it, even when it comes from a trusted authority like a teacher or a preacher? The ancient Romans had a saying: "I wouldn't believe that story even if Cato told it." Cato was a figure of such renowned rectitude that, generally speaking, anything he told you was sure to be so. But there are limits to credibility, even for Cato. Recall saintly Mother Teresa, the nun who was awarded a Nobel Peace Prize for her work with the poor in Calcutta. What if she had announced, with a straight face, that she had flown to receive her Nobel award, not in a jetliner, but simply by flapping her arms? Who would have believed her? It seems, then, that there are some claims that are so extraordinary, so intrinsically unbelievable, that they should not be believed, even when they are supported by testimony from a seemingly impeccable source.

This point was famously emphasized by the eighteenth-century Scottish philosopher David Hume (1711–1776) in his notorious essay "Of Miracles," published as section X of his *Enquiry Concerning Human Understanding*. The thing that made Hume's essay so controversial was that he said, or seemed to be saying, that reports of miracles should not be believed, even if those reports came from persons of incontestable holiness and sanctity. Since many religions, Christianity in particular, proclaim miraculous happenings as part of their teaching and doctrine, Hume's critique was bound to strike a nerve. Indeed, at least one miracle, the bodily resurrection of Jesus of Nazareth, seems essential for Christianity, for as St. Paul says in I Corinthians 15:14: "If Christ be not risen, then is our preaching vain, and your faith is also vain." So if the resurrection of Jesus is not credible, then Christianity is not believable.

Hume's actual argument does not draw quite as hard a line as some have thought. He does not say that there are no conceivable circumstances in which it would be reasonable to believe a miracle report; in fact, he concedes that there could, in principle, be such circumstances. He does say that anyone who wants to convince a skeptic that a miracle has occurred has an extraordinarily heavy burden of proof, a burden so heavy that, in actuality, it is practically impossible to bear. Hume is concerned with those who invoke miracles for *apologetic* purposes, that is, those who try to use miracle claims to provide skeptics with a rational basis for religious belief. The religious apologist tries to convince the skeptic by showing that a particular miracle, like the resurrection of Jesus, has likely occurred, and that the occurrence of this miracle certifies the Christian revelation as the true and authentic one, a revelation from God Himself.

The reason why the apologist's job is so hard, says Hume, is that a miracle, by definition, is a violation of a law of nature. To try to define the term "law of nature" would take us far afield into a jumble of philosophical complexities. Let's just say that we all recognize that some occurrences, while conceivable, are physically impossible. In chapter 1 we talked about logical impossibility, things that we cannot even coherently *suppose*, because even trying to suppose them lands us in a self-contradiction. On the other hand, there are conceivable events which we can imagine happening, but which just cannot be physically accomplished. There is a skit from the old *Monty Python* TV series about a sleazy character who exploits a pathetic, deranged individual by setting him to such impossible tasks as leaping across the English Channel, eating a cathedral, and tunneling to Java with a shovel. If you have a vivid enough imagination you can imagine a man eating a cathedral, and it is logically possible (there is no logical contradiction in supposing it), but it just physically cannot be done.

Now when somebody says that something occurred, there are two factors that should enter into our assessment of the believability of the claim: (1) the *reliability of the testimony*, that is, how likely is that person to say that something occurred *if and only if* the event really occurred, and (2) what we might call the *background credibility* of the claim itself, that is, how credible it is on the basis of our **background knowledge**, that is, everything we know *apart* from the evidence provided by the present testimony. The first factor is obvious. Everyone knows that some people are dishonest and, further, that under many circumstances even the most honest persons can misreport what they saw. But we tend to overlook the second factor, that is, when we make spontaneous assessments of the believability of claims, we often forget to figure in the intrinsic plausibility, what I call the background credibility, of the claim. As we shall see in the next chapter, this is a pervasive and often harmful foible of human rationality.

When somebody claims that a miracle has occurred, he generally is claiming that something physically impossible really occurred: Someone walked on water, or fed thousands with a few loaves and fishes, or was raised from the dead. The problem here is that we have someone saying that something has occurred when, apart from that person's testimony, we have grounds as solid as any can be for thinking that such things just don't happen. In fact, if we know anything at all about the world, then we know that certain things are physically impossible; for example, nobody, using only human muscle power, can jump the English Channel in one bound. So when we hear a report claiming that something obviously physically impossible has nonetheless happened, like someone walking on water or feeding thousands with one Happy Meal, our *initial* reaction should be one of deep skepticism. We should initially think that the probability of such a report being true is nearly zero. Why nearly zero, and not just zero? Well, philosophers today generally regard all of our beliefs as fallible so that even our best supported generalizations about the world are not *absolutely* certain. Also, maybe all of the laws of nature are, in the end, merely statistical generalizations, so that on very, very rare occasions the "impossible" spontaneously happens. So let's just say that such a miracle report has a background credibility of nearly, but not quite, zero.

Hume's argument then is that when someone offers testimony claiming to have witnessed a miracle, that person is claiming that something occurred despite the fact that its background credibility is nearly nil. That is, that person is making a claim that, based on our background knowledge, is as implausible as a claim can be. In order to make that claim believable, therefore, the testimony supporting that claim has to be so flawlessly reliable that it would be *even more* implausible that the testimony is wrong than that the event actually occurred. In other words, we should believe a miracle report only if it would be an *even bigger* miracle for the testimony to be false! Hume goes on to argue that in reality it is extremely unlikely that, in the real world, anyone will ever achieve this degree of reliability as a witness. Even if we can be absolutely sure that someone is not lying, no one is infallible, and we are familiar with many different circumstances in which even intelligent and educated people can be made to believe that they have witnessed a miracle when no such event occurred.

It is important to be very clear on just what Hume is arguing here. It may sound like he is arguing in a circle by *assuming* that miracles are impossible, and then using that assumption to dismiss reports of miracles. But this is not his argument. Hume does not assume that miracles are impossible; he merely notes that, as with any claim, the believability of a miracle report has to be assessed both with respect to the reliability of the testimony and with respect to the background credibility of the claim. With miracles, since they involve a physically impossible event, the background credibility will be extremely low, so low, he argues, that it is practically impossible for testimony to ever be so reliable as to make the report credible overall.

Hume's argument is about the believability of a claim, that is, he asks how much credence we should give to reports of miraculous events. In the last chapter we considered the probability as it applies to the frequencies of events, but probability language can also be used to express our level of *confidence* in a claim, that is, our *degree of belief* that something is so. Such a construal of probability is called **personal probability**, and on this personal interpretation, the probability calculus measures our personal level of confidence or degree of belief that something is so. Thus, when we are talking about personal probabilities, if we are absolutely certain that a particular claim, c, is so, we say $p(c) = 1$; if we are sure that it is not so, we say $p(c) = 0$. If we think that c is so, but are not sure, then we give $p(c)$ a value between .5 and 1. If we think that c is unlikely but not absolutely impossible, we say that $p(c)$ is between and .5. In general, low probabilities will indicate a low level of confidence, and high probabilities will indicate a high level of confidence. In other words, presuming a personal interpretation of probability, when we say that the probability of a claim c is x percent, that means we are personally x percent confident that c is so.

Hume argues informally, without the aid of the machinery of the probability calculus, but Hume's miracles argument can be expressed with the mathematical tools of probability. To do this, we assume a personal interpretation of probability where probability is a measure of a personal degree of belief. We also assume that the theorems of the probability calculus can be used to model *rational* belief change. That is, we assume that a rational person's personal probabilities, his or her levels of confidence or degrees of belief, will satisfy the rules of probability. For instance, if my degree of personal confidence in claim c is .4 and my degree of personal confidence in claim c^* is .2, then, assuming that the truth of claim c is independent of the truth of claim c^*, my degree of confidence that both c and c^* are true should conform to the special conjunction rule of the probability calculus: $p(c \& c^*) = p(c) \times p(c^*) = .4 \times .2 = .08$. That is, if I am rational and I have a .4 degree of confidence in c and a .2 degree of confidence in c^*, then I will only have a .08 degree of confidence that both c and c^* are true.

A contemporary of Hume's, Reverend Dr. Thomas Bayes, established a theorem of the probability calculus, and called **Bayes's theorem** in his honor, which is extremely useful for modeling how rational belief changes when we get new evidence. We will derive Bayes's theorem in a general form in a little while, but let's first give the theorem as it applies to Hume's argument on miracles. Also, here and in the rest of this chapter, let's remember that we are assuming a personal interpretation of probability, that is, probability will measure degree of belief.

$$p(m \mid t \& k) = \frac{p(t \mid m \& k) \times p(m \mid k)}{p(t \mid m \& k) \times p(m \mid k) + p(t \mid {\sim}m \& k) \times p({\sim}m \mid k)}$$

Let's take this formula apart one piece at a time: $p(m \mid t \& k)$ is the probability that miracle m has occurred given that we have a body of testimony t and background knowledge k, and $p(t \mid m \& k)$ stands for how likely it is that we would have the given testimony for a miracle given that the miracle actually occurred and given our relevant background knowledge. $p(m \mid k)$ is the probability that miracle m occurred given only our relevant background knowledge. The numerator of the formula is the product of these two expressions. The product of these two expressions is also placed in the denominator, on the left hand side of the + sign. $p(t \mid {\sim}m \& k)$ is the probability that we would have the testimony given that miracle m did *not* occur and given our relevant background knowledge. $p({\sim}m \mid k)$ is the probability that miracle m did *not* occur given only our background knowledge. The product of these last two expressions is put on the right side of the + sign in the denominator of the formula.

What the whole formula tells us is how much credence should be given to a miracle claim given that it is supported by certain testimony and given relevant background knowledge. If our calculations result in $p(m \mid t \& k) < .5$, then a rational person will not believe that the claimed miracle has taken place.

OK, to see how the formula works, let's plug in some reasonable values for each of these expressions. $p(t \mid m \& k)$, the probability that the alleged witnesses would say that they had seen a miracle if one had actually occurred, and given relevant background knowledge, is sure to be pretty high. After all, miracles are usually pretty impressive events, and if one actually happened where you could see it, you would probably say what you saw. So let's say that $p(t \mid m \& k) = .99$. On the other hand, we have seen that $p(m \mid k)$, the probability of a miracle given only background knowledge, is very low, close to zero. So let's say that $p(m \mid k) = .000001$. How high is $p(t \mid {\sim}m \& k)$, the probability that the alleged witnesses would *say* that they had seen a miracle, even if one has *not* occurred, and given our relevant background knowledge? Alas, this has to be pretty high, or at least not terribly low. People are not always honest, and even when they are, they are fallible and liable to misreport what really happened. So let's say that $p(t \mid {\sim}m \& k) = .1$, a figure that is low but not extremely low. Finally, by PR-2, $p({\sim}m \mid k) = 1 - p(m \mid k) = 1 - .000001 = .999999$. So:

I'm curious about these

$$p(m \mid t \& k) = \frac{p(t \mid m \& k) \times p(m \mid k)}{p(t \mid m \& k) \times p(m \mid k) + p(t \mid \sim m \& k) \times p(\sim m \mid k)} =$$

$$\frac{.99 \times .000001}{.99 \times .000001 + .1 \times .999999} = \frac{.00000099}{.00000099 + .0999999} = \frac{.00000099}{.10000089} = .0000099.$$

This is a very small number, far below the .5 necessary to make it as likely as not that the miracle occurred given the particular testimony. So it looks like, and Reverend Bayes probably would be unhappy with the result of this application of his theorem, that applying Bayes's theorem substantiates what Hume argues: If the background probability of a miracle is close to zero, testimony in favor of the miracle is not going to be enough to make it more likely than not that the miracle really occurred.

But, of course, the final result you get depends on what values you plug into the formula. Critics of Hume could say that Hume's argument only seems to work because he only includes in the background knowledge information about what is physically possible or impossible. However, many people, religious people, think that in addition to the physical world there is a supernatural being, God, who has the power to bring about miracles and who will occasionally do so. Therefore, critics could argue, religious people would include such religious beliefs within their background knowledge, and this will dramatically raise their estimate of the background credibility of a miracle report. For these people, since the background likelihood of miracles for them is not nearly as low as Hume thinks it is, testimony would have a much better chance of establishing a miracle. But Hume is not arguing that *nobody* should believe in miracles, that is, that it is not a rational belief for *anybody*. His argument is a defensive one; he says that people who are skeptics, who *start* with background beliefs that place a low order of credibility on miracle reports, are not at all likely to be persuaded by the arguments of religious apologists when they adduce testimony for miracle claims. For the skeptic, such claims are initially very improbable, and there are just too many ways for people, however honest and well intentioned, to be wrong when they report something seemingly miraculous. As a defensive maneuver, defending the right of skeptics to remain skeptical in the face of miracle claims, Hume's argument seems perfectly sound.

What else can Bayes's theorem do for us, besides give us a tool for evaluating miracle claims? First, though, why should we accept Bayes's theorem? How does it derive from the rules of probability already given? Recall PR-4, the general conjunction rule: $p(a \& b) = p(a) \times p(b \mid a)$.

If we divide each side of this equation by $p(a)$, we get

$$\frac{p(a \& b)}{p(a)} = p(b \mid a)$$

or

$$p(b \mid a) = \frac{p(b \& a)}{p(a)}$$

We assume that $p(a) > 0$ so we won't have to divide by zero.

Now, a is equivalent to $(a \& b) \lor (a \& {\sim}b)$, as we can easily show with a truth table:

a	b	~b	(a & b)	(a & ~b)	(a & b) v (a & ~b)
T	T	F	T	F	T
T	F	T	F	T	T
F	T	F	F	F	F
F	F	T	F	F	F

So, since a and $(a \& b) \lor (a \& {\sim}b)$ are equivalent, we can replace $p(a)$ with $p[(a \& b) \lor (a \& {\sim}b)]$ in the above formula:

$$p(b \mid a) = \frac{p(b\ \&\ a)}{p[(a\ \&\ b)\ v\ (a\ \&\sim b)]}$$

Applying the special disjunction rule to the denominator, which we can do since (a & b) and (a & ~b) are mutually exclusive, we get

$$p(b \mid a) = \frac{p(b\ \&\ a)}{p(a\ \&\ b) + p(a\ \&\sim b)}$$

Since we know by the rule of commutation that a & b is equivalent to b & a and that a & ~b is equivalent to ~b & a, we get

$$p(b \mid a) = \frac{p(b\ \&\ a)}{p(b\ \&\ a) + p(\sim b\ \&\ a)}$$

Applying the general conjunction rule to the denominator twice we get

$$p(b \mid a) = \frac{p(b\ \&\ a)}{p(b) \times p(a \mid b) + p(\sim b) \times p(a \mid \sim b)}$$

Finally, applying the general conjunction rule to the numerator we get

$$p(b \mid a) = \frac{p(b) \times p(a \mid b)}{p(b) \times p(a \mid b) + p(\sim b) \times p(a \mid \sim b)}$$

and this is Bayes's theorem (Note that in this version of Bayes's theorem, we did not include symbolization for background knowledge, usually denoted by "k." Bayes's theorem is often given with background knowledge implicit rather than explicitly denoted. I shall always specifically represent it, since it is often so important in our Bayesian calculations).

In English, Bayes's theorem tells us that the probability of b given a is equal to the probability of b by itself, apart from a—usually interpreted as the probability of b given only background knowledge—multiplied by the probability of a given b (for technical reasons that need not concern us here, statisticians would call p(a | b) a "likelihood," not a "probability," but for our purposes we can just call it a probability). The product of these two is then divided by what is called the "total probability" of a, that is, the probability of a given either b or ~b. This total probability of a is figured by multiplying the probability of a given b times the probability of b and adding this product to the probability of a given ~b times the probability of ~b.

As a theorem of the probability calculus, Bayes's theorem can be put to many uses. In general, it is used to tell us **inverse probabilities**. If we know the probability of a given b, then Bayes's theorem can tell us the probability of b given a. However, Bayes's theorem is most often used by philosophers to model rational belief change. With Bayes's theorem we can model how a rational person's beliefs will change given new evidence, that is, how a rational person learns from experience. A rational person proportions his or her belief to the evidence, so that as the evidence for a hypothesis mounts, the rational person's degree of belief in that hypothesis will also increase. Suppose we start with a hypothesis h, which we regard with a certain degree of belief on our background knowledge k. We then get some positive evidence, e, for h. Bayes's theorem allows us to calculate p(h | e & k), our new degree of belief given that new evidence and background knowledge.

Let's consider a concrete example. Why did the dinosaurs go extinct at the end of the Cretaceous after 160 million years as the dominant form of terrestrial life? This is a fascinating question that, prior to 1980, had generated much speculation but few testable hypotheses. Then, in 1980, Nobel laureate physicist Luis Alvarez, his son Walter, a prominent geologist, and two other colleagues published an article attributing the mass extinctions at the end of the Cretaceous, the so-called K-T extinction event, to the impact of a large extraterrestrial body and the consequent catastrophic effects of such an impact. The advantage of the Alvarez hypothesis over many earlier ones is that it was testable; it made definite predictions that could be checked by competent investigators.

Paleontologists and geologists were initially quite skeptical of the impact hypothesis, as it was called. The earth sciences had long accepted and practiced a methodology that looked to the earth itself for explanations of earthly changes. Furthermore, they expected that major changes, such as mass extinctions, would occur slowly, over a million years or more. That large changes in earth history could have been brought about by an extraterrestrial cause operating effectively instantaneously, seemed to earth scientists like a throwback to primitive geological theories that invented massive catastrophes to account for the large-scale changes that had affected the earth over geological time. Also, most earth scientists believed that major impacts by large extraterrestrial bodies had occurred very early in the earth's history and had not occurred since. Therefore, explanations of major earth events in terms of asteroids, comets, or other extraterrestrial influences, went against the grain and made the impact hypothesis highly controversial. Putting it in terms of Bayes's theorem we could say that, given their background knowledge, earth scientists initially rated the believability of the Alvarez hypothesis as quite low. That is, where h is the impact hypothesis and k is background knowledge, for the earth sciences community in 1980 p(h | k) was quite low.

However, the impact hypothesis was testable, as a good scientific theory should be, and evidence began to mount in its favor. One prediction of the hypothesis is that at every site around the world where the strata of sedimentary rocks contain a record of the end of the Cretaceous, the so-called K-T boundary layer, there should be a significantly higher concentration of certain elements in that rock. Certain elements such as iridium and other "iridium group" elements are normally very rare in the earth's crust but are much more abundant in asteroids, meteorites, and other extraterrestrial bodies. Therefore, if an asteroid with a 10-kilometer diameter hit the earth at the end of the Cretaceous, it would have been vaporized on impact and spread a cloud of debris worldwide. That cloud should have been much richer in the iridium-group elements than the sedimentary rock it settled on and the sedimentary rock that was later deposited on top of that layer. Therefore, the impact hypothesis predicted an iridium-group "spike" in the concentration of these elements in the thin K-T layer marking the end of the Cretaceous, wherever in the world such a layer is found. Sure enough, as such layers from around the world were tested, they consistently revealed a "spike" of the iridium-group elements, just as the Alvarezes had predicted. This accumulation of evidence enhanced the credibility of the hypothesis.

Bayes's theorem can be used to model how the accumulating evidence enhanced the credibility of the impact hypothesis. If h is the impact hypothesis, e is the accumulated evidence of an iridium "spike" at the K-T boundary worldwide, and k is background knowledge, we can calculate the effect of the evidence, e, on the credibility of the hypothesis with the following version of Bayes's theorem:

$$p(h \mid e \ \& \ k) = \frac{p(e \mid h \ \& \ k) \times p(h \mid k)}{p(e \mid h \ \& \ k) \times p(h \mid k) + p(e \mid {\sim}h \ \& \ k) \times p\,({\sim}h \mid k)}$$

In this formula, $p(e \mid h \ \& \ k)$ gives us our personal probability that we would have a certain body of evidence e given that the impact hypothesis h is true and given our background knowledge k. From what we know about the constitution of extraterrestrial bodies and the effects of large impacts, we can say that we regard it as highly likely that we would have the evidence, the iridium-group "spikes," if, in fact, a major impact occurred at the end of the Cretaceous. So let's say that $p(e \mid h \ \& \ k) = .9$. However, given background knowledge, what was known—or at least believed—by earth scientists prior to 1980, the background probability of the hypothesis was quite low, let's say that $p(h \mid k) = .0001$. The probability that we would have the worldwide iridium-group "spike" given that no impact had occurred would be very low, let's say that $p(e \mid {\sim}h \ \& \ k) = .0001$. Finally, $p({\sim}h \mid k)$, the probability that the impact did not occur given only background knowledge is $1 - p(h \mid k) = 1 - .0001 = .999$. So plugging in the numbers we get

$$p(h \mid e \ \& \ k) = \frac{.9 \times .0001}{(.9 \times .0001) + (.0001 \times .999)} = \frac{.00009}{.00009 + .0000999} = .474$$

In other words, if we add evidence e to our background knowledge, we see that the overall credibility of h has increased enormously compared to its probability solely on background knowledge. The addition of the evidence increased its credibility from very low, .0001 to .474, still on the unlikely side, but just barely below the .5 needed to be counted as likely as not.

Another interesting thing these figures show is that when we have evidence that is surprising, that is, apart from our hypothesis and considering only background knowledge it is highly unexpected, then the discovery of such evidence greatly enhances the credibility of the hypothesis. In the above formula e is unexpected given our background knowledge and given that the impact did not occur; we stipulated that $p(e \mid \sim h \ \& \ k)$ =.0001. This result, the strong confirming power of unexpected evidence, fits with our intuitions about evidence and how it supports hypotheses. If we find fingerprints on the murder weapon we normally consider this highly incriminating evidence against the accused, but *only* if the prints were very unlikely to be on the weapon unless the accused was the murderer. If the accused's fingerprints *were* likely to be on the weapon in any case (suppose the accused is the gardener and the weapon was a pair of shears he frequently used), the presence of the prints is little evidence against him. If, however, the butler is accused, and the butler never normally handled the garden shears, then the presence of his fingerprints on the shears is highly unlikely unless he was the murderer, so the presence of his prints on the weapon is strong evidence of his guilt.

Getting back to the K-T extinctions and the impact hypothesis, suppose we find even more predicted evidence. Another prediction of the impact hypothesis is that we would find granules of a particular sort of "shocked" quartz in the K-T boundary layer. Shocked quartz has crystals that have been deformed in a particular way due to sudden, massive overpressure. The only known causes of certain types of shocked quartz are large impacts and nuclear explosions. Finding these particular types of quartz granules in worldwide K-T boundary layers would therefore be further support for the impact hypothesis. Suppose we call this new quartz-granule evidence e*. What we want to know now is $p(h \mid e^* \ \& \ e \ \& \ k)$, that is, the credibility of the impact hypothesis given the new evidence, e*, added to the previously acquired evidence, e, and the background knowledge, k. Our formula will therefore be

$$p(h \mid e^* \ \& \ e \ \& \ k) = \frac{p(e^* \mid h \ \& \ e \ \& \ k) \times p(h \mid e \ \& \ k)}{p(e^* \mid h \ \& \ e \ \& \ k) \times p(h \mid e \ \& \ k) + p(e^* \mid \sim h \ \& \ e \ \& \ k) \times p(\sim h \mid e \ \& \ k)}$$

$p(e^* \mid h \ \& \ e \ \& \ k)$ is the likelihood that we would have the quartz evidence given that the impact hypothesis is true and given our other evidence and background knowledge. This has to be pretty high because if such a huge impact occurred, then, given our other evidence and background, it is quite likely that shocked quartz would have been produced. Let's say then that p(e* | h & e & k) = .9. We saw previously that p(h | e & k) came out to .474, so that is now our background probability for h. The likelihood of e* given that h is not true, that is, given that there was no impact, is quite small since the only known causes of shocked quartz of that type are massive impacts and nuclear explosions, and it is highly unlikely that the dinosaurs possessed thermonuclear weapons. So let's set p(e* | ~h & e & k) = .001. Further, p(~h | e & k) = 1 – p(h | e & k) = 1 - .474 = .526. So, plugging in the numbers, we get:

$$\frac{.9 \times .474}{(.9 \times .474) + (.001 \times .526)} = \frac{.426}{.426 + .000526} = .999$$

So, with the accumulation of enough good evidence, a hypothesis that on our background knowledge is very unlikely can be made very credible indeed: We now have a 99.9 percent degree of confidence in the hypothesis! Good evidence, especially evidence that is very unexpected or surprising given our background knowledge, can raise the credibility of a hypothesis from nearly nil to nearly certain. Of course, this is really just a highly simplified and idealized model of the complex and rough-and-tumble process whereby hypotheses are evaluated in real life. Real scientists usually don't actually figure out the strength of their beliefs using Bayes's theorem. Still, the model shows that we can and should greatly increase the credence we give to hypotheses when there is enough really good evidence supporting it, even if our initial assessment of its probability is very low. What about miracles? In fact, even if our hypothesis is a miracle claim, so its background probability is extremely low, enough good evidence could, *in principle*, convince us that it actually occurred. Hume concedes this possibility, but replies that in the real world, in the world where people are often dishonest and fallible and appearances are so often misleading, then you should be so lucky as to ever get such evidence!

EXERCISES FOR CHAPTER 8

1) Use Bayes's theorem to solve the following problems. The first one is set up for you.

(a) A hospital is having a hard time with infections by the drug-resistant MRSA bacteria. The hospital has two wards, Ward A and Ward B. In Ward A, 2 percent of patients get the MRSA infection. In Ward B, 7 percent of patients get MRSA. We know on background knowledge that 2/3 of the hospital's patients stay in Ward A. If a patient in the hospital comes down with the MRSA infection, what is the probability that he/she was in ward A?

Partial solution:

Let a = the patient was in Ward A; b = the patient was in ward b, and m = the patient was infected with MRSA. What you want to know is p(a | m & k). By Bayes's theorem:

$$p(a \mid m \ \& \ k) = \frac{p(m \mid a \ \& \ k) \times p(a \mid k)}{p(m \mid a \ \& \ k) \times p(a \mid k) + p(m \mid \sim a \ \& \ k) \times p(\sim a \mid k)}$$

p(m | a & k) = .02

p(a | k) = .67 (since Ward A has 2/3 of the patients)

p(m | ~a & k) = .07 (The patients who are not in Ward A are in Ward B, where the MRSA infection rate is .07.)

p(~a | k) = .33 (The patients who are not in Ward A are in Ward B, where there are 1 − 2/3 = 1/3 of the hospital's patients.)

Now you only have to plug in the numbers.

(b) Steven Stocks won the National League MVP award last year. Eight out of the last ten National League MVPs have used steroids. 75 percent of players who use steroids deny that they have ever used them. 100 percent of players who did not use steroids deny using them. What is the probability that Stocks used steroids, given that he denies ever using them?

Let p(s | d & k) = the probability that Stocks used steroids given that he denies using them; p(d | s & k) = the probability that Stocks denies using steroids, given that he used them; p(s | k) = the probability that Stocks used steroids given only background knowledge; p(d | ~s & k) = the probability that Stocks denies using steroids given that he did not use them; and p(~s | k) = the probability that Stocks did not use steroids given only background knowledge.

(c) If the Democratic candidate is elected president, there is a 60 percent chance we will have universal healthcare in eight years. If the Republican candidate is elected president, there is a 20 percent chance we will have universal health care in eight years. Las Vegas odds makers say that the Republican candidate, who has a slight lead in the polls, has a 55 percent chance of being elected. Assume that the Democratic and Republican candidates are the only candidates, that is, that one is elected if and only if the other is not. Judging by the Las Vegas odds, given that we have universal healthcare in eight years, what is the chance that the Republican candidate was elected?

Let r = the Republican candidate is elected and h = we have universal healthcare in eight years.

(d) Your friend Gerry likes hot and spicy food. Three days a week he eats lunch at Curry Favor, the Indian restaurant. Four days a week he eats lunch at My Thai, the Thai restaurant. The problem is that the hot and spicy food he eats at these restaurants sometimes gives him heartburn. When he eats at Curry Favor, he gets heartburn 20 percent of the time. When he eats at My Thai, he gets heartburn 30 percent of the time. Suppose Gerry ate lunch a couple of hours ago and it gave him heartburn, what is the probability that he ate lunch at Curry Favor?

(e) In the town of Armadillo Crossing, Texas, 60 percent of drivers drive Dodge pickup trucks, 30 percent of drivers drive Ford pickup trucks, and the remaining 10 percent drive GM pickup trucks. Last night, an accident was caused when a truck ran the only stoplight in Armadillo Crossing. Billy Ray was the only witness of the accident, and he claims that he saw a GM pickup truck run the light and cause the accident. Now, Billy Ray knows his pickup trucks. When a truck goes by, even at night, Billy Ray correctly identifies it as a Dodge, Ford, or GM pickup 90 percent of the time, and misidentifies it the other 10 percent of the time. Given this information, how likely is it that the truck that caused the accident was a GM truck?

2) My friend Bob claims that he has paranormal powers and can accurately predict future events. I am skeptical and ask him to prove it. He agrees and says that he will confirm his prognosticating powers by predicting that the next bird I see will be a grackle. Note that in this part of the world 80 percent of the birds are grackles. Explain, in terms of Bayes's theorem, why this prediction is a poorer test of his alleged psychic abilities than if he had predicted that the next bird I see will be a cassowary (a bird which, as far as I know, has never been seen around here except in zoos).

3) Patient A is admitted to the hospital with symptoms of delirium, fever, nausea, and muscle spasms. Standard tests show nothing, so the famous diagnostician Dr. Home is called in. Home examines the case carefully and begins to suspect that A has a rare condition known as Glaubner's syndrome (n.b., as far as I know there is no such disease as Glaubner's syndrome; I just made this up). Glaubner's is a rare condition, afflicting only one patient out of a thousand with symptoms like patient A's. There are two tests for Glaubner's syndrome. One, test t, gives immediate results and is 90 percent reliable, that is, it will give a true positive 90 percent of the time and a false positive 10 percent of the time. The other test, test t*, is 98 percent reliable, giving true positives 98 percent of the time and false positives 2 percent of the time, but it takes several days to get results. Home does the first test, test t, and it is positive. Use Bayes's theorem to

determine Home's rational degree of confidence that A has Glaubner's, on the basis of the results of test t. A few days later the results of the second test, test t*, come in, and they are also positive. Use Bayes's theorem to show how Home's rational degree of confidence that patient A has Glaubner's syndrome increases in the light of this new evidence.

Chapter Nine

PROBABILITY ILLUSIONS

Why We Are So Bad at Inductive Reasoning

We have spent the last two chapters learning about probability and how to reason about it. There are no tools of human inquiry more important than the rules of probability and the associated methods of statistics. Hardly any field of the natural, social, or human sciences can be studied without the aid of these rules and methods. Yet it is remarkable that we ever mastered these techniques adequately to make use of them because probabilistic and statistical thinking just does not come naturally to us. In fact, our spontaneous judgments about probabilities are prone to go woefully wrong. Our "gut reactions" about things often just do not match their actual probabilities.

Consider our assessments of dangerous situations. Our perceptions just do not match reality. Prior to the attacks of 9/11, one of the leading news stories of the summer of 2001 had been shark attacks along the Gulf Coast. People read with lurid relish accounts of how several swimmers had been attacked off popular beaches. As the mayor of Amity, New York, observed in the movie *Jaws*, you yell "Shark!" and people panic. Some people were not putting a toe in the water because they were afraid that it would be bitten off. Yet even in a "bad" summer for shark attacks, they are extremely rare. Your chances of being injured or killed on the road driving to the beach are much, much greater than your chances of being mauled by a shark once you get in the water.

Clearly, we are irrational about our fears. People will shrink in terror at the sight of a harmless spider, a creature that an average human outweighs by a million times. If our reactions were in line with the real level of danger something poses, we would flee at the sight of a cigarette. A double-meat bacon cheeseburger with supersized fries and triple-thick shake would send us screaming. Dangers come in degrees. True, around the world in a given year some people will be killed by sharks, crocodiles, or tigers. Vastly more people die in automobile accidents or house fires. Indeed, far more people are killed by dogs than by sharks, yet sharks are loathed and dogs are "man's best friend." In the 1990s in the United States, 18 people were killed annually by dogs and only .4 by sharks, that is, 45 people were killed by dogs for every person killed by a shark. One hundred thirty persons per year were killed in vehicular collisions with deer, so you are 325 times more likely to be killed by a deer than a shark. What we perceive as dangerous, therefore, simply does not match the real likelihoods that something will kill or injure us.

Maybe it is easy to see why our fears match so poorly with actual dangers. What scare us are the things that really were dangerous to our pre-human or early human ancestors, like predatory or poisonous animals. *Homo erectus* did not have to worry about the danger of automobile travel or cigarette smoking, but he did have to worry about lions. Deer were prey for *H. erectus*, not collision hazards. Science and technology have made us much safer from predators and pathogens, but have also rendered us susceptible to other dangers that we are not evolutionarily disposed to fear. In this, as in many other ways, evolution has not adapted us well for the high-tech world we live in.

The disturbing fact is that when it comes to probability estimates, our spontaneous judgments are often at odds with the real probabilities. Suppose that you hear about a really nasty incurable disease that brings about an unpleasant, lingering death. Fortunately it is rare, only afflicting one in ten thousand people. You decide to get tested for it anyway, even though you have no symptoms and do not belong to any high-risk subgroup that would make it more likely that you have the disease than the average person. There is a test for the disease that is highly accurate.

An ideally accurate test for a disease would be one that tells you that you have the disease if you do and that you don't have it if you don't. In the real world, almost every such test will have some rate of false positives and false negatives, that is, it will sometimes tell you that you have the disease when you don't and that you don't when you do. A good test will have low rates of both false positives and false negatives. Note that these rates need not correspond; indeed, these measures of reliability are independent. A test could, for instance, have low rates of false positives and high rates of false negatives, or vice versa. Let's suppose though that our test has a rate of false positives of 2 percent and also a rate of false negatives of 2 percent. This is a very good test. Suppose you take it, and, to your horror, it comes back positive. Is it panic time? Should you start writing your last will and testament? Actually, you shouldn't get too excited. Though the test is very accurate with very low rates of false positives and false negatives, it is, on the basis of just this one test, highly unlikely that you have the disease. How can this be?

Let's do the math. We learned about Bayes's theorem in the last chapter, so let's use it. What we want to know is $p(D \mid P)$, the probability that you have the disease, given that you tested positive. Bayes's theorem tells us that

$$p(D \mid P) = \frac{p(P \mid D) \times p(D)}{p(P \mid D) \times p(D) + p(P \mid \sim D) \times p(\sim D)}$$

How do we find $p(P \mid D)$, the probability that you test positive if you have the disease? Well, we assumed that only 2 percent of those who have the disease will test negative, and since the test has only two possible outcomes, positive or negative, then 98 percent of those with the disease will test positive. In other words, the rate of true positives, $p(P \mid D)$, is the inverse of the rate of false negatives, $p(\sim P \mid D)$, so $p(P \mid D) = 1 - p(\sim P \mid D) = .98$. We have assumed a base rate of the disease, the chance that a randomly selected individual from the population has the disease, of only one in ten thousand, so $p(D) = .0001$. We have also assumed that the rate of false positives is only 2 percent, so $p(P \mid \sim D) = .02$. The probability that a randomly selected individual does not have the disease $p(\sim D)$ is simply the inverse of the probability that one does, so $p(\sim D) = 1 - p(D) = 1 - .0001 = .9999$. Now we are ready to plug in the numbers.

$$p(D \mid P) = \frac{.98 \times .0001}{(.98 \times .0001) + (.02 \times .9999)} = \text{(approximately) } .005$$

That is, there is only about a .5 percent, chance, one half of one percent, that you have the disease.

If this still sounds fishy to you, think of it this way: Out of a randomly selected population of 10,000, on average, 9,999 people will not have the disease. The test has a rate of generating false positives of 2 percent, so of those 9,999 disease-free people, 9,999 × .02, or on average about 200 people, would get false positive results. Out of those 10,000 randomly selected persons, on average, only one person would have the disease, and that person would very likely test positive for it. So, if 10,000 randomly selected persons were tested for the disease, on average, there would be about 200 persons who test positively for the disease but do not have it for everyone that tests positively for the disease and does have it. If you tested positive for the disease, you are far more likely to be in the group of those who got a false positive simply because the number of people who do not have the disease (9,999) is so much higher than the one person who does. In other words, as we saw above, you would only have about a 1/200th or one-half of one percent chance of having the disease even if you tested positive.

This result goes strongly against our intuitions. Since the test is highly accurate, generating false positives only 2 percent of the time, we naturally feel that we are doomed if we get a positive test result. But reasoning in this way commits the **base rate fallacy**; we overlook the base rate of the disease in the population, which is only 1 in 10,000. The high accuracy of the test does not compensate for the fact that it is just so unlikely that you have the disease.

Ignoring base rates is one of the most common problems with inductive reasoning, and it crops up again and again in all sorts of contexts, from the scientific to the everyday. For instance, as I've mentioned before, I live in the Houston area, where bad driving is a way of life. The motto of the Houston driver is "My time is more precious than your life." Now it seems to me that when I'm out on the road and somebody is driving extremely rudely, like tailgating me at 70 mph, about half the time it is some guy in a big pickup truck. My natural conclusion is that a disproportionately high percentage of drivers of big pickup trucks are colossal jerks. But such a conclusion, though natural, may be guilty of the base rate fallacy. If, as could be the case in Southeast Texas, about half the drivers on the road are driving big pickup trucks, then you would expect about half the rude jerks tailgating you to be driving big pickups even if the rate of jerks among big pickup drivers is no higher than the percentage of jerks in the general population of drivers.

The foibles of human inductive reasoning have been studied extensively by two well-known psychologists, Daniel Kahneman and Amos Tversky. Their findings are both enlightening and alarming. Anybody who wants to think of humans as "rational animals" might have to significantly qualify that judgment after reading the works Kahneman and Tversky. Massimo Piatelli-Palmerini is a cognitive scientist who has written an amusing and engaging book titled *Inevitable Illusions* that identifies what he calls "mental tunnels," blinkered patterns of thinking that come naturally to us but lead us to irrational conclusions. Just as optical illusions fool the eye into seeing something that isn't so, cognitive illusions lead the mind to conclusions that are "obvious" but wrong. In either case, whether the illusion is optical or cognitive, it happens automatically and without our awareness. Even when we are made aware of them, optical illusions do not go away and we continue to see things the wrong way. With cognitive illusions, fortunately, we can learn to think about things the right way. But it is tough. These cognitive illusions can be highly resistant to the effects of education, cropping up even with people who, it seems, should know better. For instance, Kahneman and Tversky found that even most *medical students* failed to take base rates into account when presented with a scenario like the one about the rare disease and the reliable test (described previously).

One of the most remarkable ways that our reasoning goes awry has to do with what Kahneman and Tversky called **framing**. Suppose you want to go to law school and you are anxious (as you probably should be) about taking the Law School Admissions Test (LSAT). You are considering whether to take a test-preparation course. Suppose that these courses are quite expensive, about $1,000, so you check into two test-preparation agencies that charge the same for their courses. Legal Eagle's ad reads as follows:

Taking the LSAT? It is a tough exam. When unprepared students take the LSAT, 70 percent fail to get into the law school of their choice. But only 40 percent of applicants who take a Legal Eagle LSAT prep course fail to get into their school of choice. Get the Legal Eagle edge! Sign up today!

TestMaster's ad reads as follows:

> Taking the LSAT? It is a tough exam. When unprepared students take the LSAT, only 30 percent get into the law school of their choice. But 60 percent of applicants who take a TestMaster LSAT prep course get into their school of choice. Get the Test-Master edge! Sign up today!

Which ad sounds more appealing? Which one would you be more willing to drop $1,000 on? Extensive studies with similar examples indicate that most people would find TestMaster's ad more appealing than Legal Eagle's. TestMaster promises a doubled rate of success; Legal Eagle only promises a somewhat lower rate of failure. However, the obvious fact is that both are making *the same claim* (recall that the probability of p is always equal to $1 - \sim p$, so a 70 percent chance of failure is just one minus a 30 percent chance of success, and a 40 percent chance of failure is just one minus a 60 percent chance of success). Each agency is claiming the same level of success for its students as opposed to those who take no preparation classes. The only difference is that one expressed it in terms of failing to get into the school of your choice and the other expressed it in terms of succeeding. In short, people often make choices, even important ones, not on the basis of the information provided, but on how that information is framed. Politicians are keenly aware of this fact, as are advertisers (Legal Eagle should fire its ad agency). "Sell the sizzle, not the steak," is an old advertising maxim. Framing often constitutes the "sizzle" in an ad.

Another fascinating foible of our inductive reasoning can be illustrated with the following example:

> Linda is 31 years old, single, outspoken, and very bright. She majored in philosophy. As a student, she was deeply concerned with issues of discrimination and social justice, and also participated in antinuclear demonstrations.[1]

Given this information about Linda, rank the following statements in order of their likelihood of being true:

Linda is a teacher in an elementary school.
Linda works in a bookstore and takes yoga classes.
Linda is active in the feminist movement.
Linda is a psychiatric social worker.
Linda is a member of the League of Women Voters.
Linda is a bank teller.
Linda is an insurance salesperson.
Linda is a bank teller and is active in the feminist movement.[2]

People consistently say that the last statement, that Linda is a bank teller and a feminist, is more likely than the statement that Linda is a bank teller. But recall that we figure the probability of a conjunction by multiplying the probabilities of the individual conjuncts. If the probability that Linda is a feminist is .9 and the probability that she is a bank teller is .1, then, assuming independence, the probability that Linda is *both* a feminist and a bank teller is .9 X .1 = .09, which is less than .1, the probability that she is a bank teller. When you multiply quantities between zero and one, the product will be less than either of the quantities you multiplied. Anybody who knows anything about probability knows this, but even people who know better often make judgments that run against the simplest rules of probability. Why? What seems to be going on here is that we form a mental picture of Linda based on the few facts we know about her (Whatever else she is, she's *got* to be a feminist, right?). Our judgments about Linda then conform to that mental image rather than to a rational assessment of probability.

Well, so what? What if we make such a mistake, what does it matter? Who cares if Linda is a bank teller or not? The problem is that such mistakes in reasoning pop up in contexts where they can do a lot of harm. We very quickly, and unconsciously, stereotype people and file them under labels. Once we have formed a mental image of someone (e.g. "feminist," "nerd," "jock," "gay") even on the basis of very meager information, we make judgments about that person based on our mental image—and consequently our prejudices—not according to the rules of probability. Racism, bigotry, and bias of all sorts can easily exploit such propensities to base our judgments on a mental picture rather than logic.

Why are people often so bad at science? Why do even people with a natural talent for science have to spend many years learning how to do it? Maybe one reason is that some of the basic kinds of reasoning used in science don't seem to come naturally to us. For instance, testing hypotheses is one of the main jobs of scientific reasoning. Suppose four cards are spread out on a table, and each card is blank except for a single numeral or letter printed on it. The four cards have these numerals or letters printed on the faces that we can see:

7   4   A   H

Now you are asked: "Supposing that you can turn over only two cards, which two cards do you turn over to test the hypothesis 'If a card has an odd number on one side, then it has a vowel on the other side?'" The right answer is you turn over the 7 and the H. Research into such "selection tasks" by British psychologist Peter Wason shows that the vast majority of people would select the 7 and the A cards to be turned over.

But think about it. The point of a test is to see if a hypothesis is true or false. The hypothesis is "If a card has an odd number on one side, then it has a vowel on the other." This hypothesis is expressed in the form of a conditional. Recall (from chapter 2) that a conditional sentence is false when the antecedent is true and the consequent false and is true otherwise. This is what the truth table for the conditional sentence form showed:

p	q	$p \rightarrow q$
T	T	T
T	F	F
F	T	T
F	F	T

So the only way our hypothesis—"If a card has an odd number on one side, then it has a vowel on the other"—can be false is for the 7 to have a consonant on its other side or the H to have an odd number on its other side. These are the only circumstances with these four cards in which the antecedent of the hypothesis would be true and the consequent false, so these are the two cards that need to be checked. You don't need to check the 4 because the antecedent is false in this case, and you don't need to check the A because the consequent is true in this case. The problem is that most people, even logic students who know about the truth table for conditional sentences, just don't see its applicability to a problem of this sort.

Fascinatingly, if we take a problem like the Wason selection task and put it in a social context that people find more familiar, they reason much more successfully. Suppose, for instance, suppose you are a bouncer at a bar and you suspect that some underage drinkers are consuming alcohol. Four young people are sitting at a table. Each has a drink and each has his or her ID card on the table. With two of the drinkers, you can see what they are drinking, but they have covered their ID cards. One has a beer, and the other has an iced tea. With the other two, you can see their ID cards, but they have their hands over their drinks so you cannot tell what they are drinking. One's ID card says she is 22, and the other's ID card says he is 19. How do you check to see if anyone is violating the rule "If someone is consuming alcohol, then he or she must be 21 or older?" Obviously, you ask the beer drinker to show you his ID and you ask the 19 year old to show you what he is drinking. You won't bother to check the iced tea drinker or the one whose ID says she is 22. In contexts like this—though the problem is really the same as with the numbered and lettered cards—people find it much easier to reason correctly.

Psychologists debate the significance of findings like these. Such results seem to show that people have problems with abstract, uncontextualized reasoning, but do much better when the problem is placed in the context of a social interaction. Again, perhaps, an evolutionary explanation beckons. Perhaps we are evolutionarily adapted to deal with complex social situations that often involve things like monitoring rules of behavior, but we are not adapted to reason about such rules when they are stripped of that context and put in an abstract situation. Unfortunately, doing science often requires that we think abstractly and in unfamiliar contexts.

As a final instance of the foibles of our inductive reasoning, we look at one that fooled even some professional mathematicians and statisticians, the notorious Monty Hall problem, named after famous (or infamous) game show host Monty Hall. You are a contestant on the show and Monty directs your attention to three lowered curtains. He tells you that behind one curtain there is a terrific prize but that there is nothing behind the other two. If you pick the curtain with the prize, you win it;

if you pick one of the other curtains, you get nothing. So you pick a curtain at random. Monty, who of course knows where the prize is, then devilishly raises one of the curtains you did not choose to show that there is nothing behind that curtain. Now he gives you the chance to switch your choice and pick the other lowered curtain. Do you switch or stick with your first choice?

When the Monty Hall problem was first introduced by a popular newspaper columnist a few years ago, it precipitated a storm of controversy that became quite heated, and even led to PhD mathematicians and statisticians taking opposite sides of the question of whether or not to switch. Most people seem to reason like this: Once Monty raises the curtain and they see that there is no prize behind it, they then know that the prize is definitely behind one of the two remaining curtains. Therefore, they conclude, there is a 50 percent chance that it is behind one curtain or the other, so it would be pointless to switch their choice. Once they know that the prize has to be behind one curtain or the other, they tend to have an overwhelming intuition that there is a 50/50 chance of it being behind either one of the two curtains.

The correct answer, though, is that you should always switch to the other curtain. The reason is that there is only a 1/3 chance that the prize is behind the curtain you chose, but a 2/3 chance that it is behind the one you did not choose. How can this be, when the prize definitely has to be behind one of the two curtains? The third one has been eliminated, leaving only two, so how can it be twice as likely that the prize is behind the curtain you did not choose? Surely—so our gut instincts tell us—the choice here has to be 50/50. But think of it like this: If you could play Monty's game an indefinite number of times, about what percentage of the times would you choose the right curtain? About 1/3 of the time. What percentage of the times would you choose a wrong curtain? About 2/3 of the time. This means that if you switched every time you would lose about 1/3 of the time and would win about 2/3 of the time. On the other hand, if you stuck with your original choice each time you would lose about 2/3 of the time and win about 1/3 of the time. Therefore, it is good strategy to switch every time. The fact that Monty raises the curtain has no bearing on this. You already know that at least one of the curtains you did not choose has nothing behind it, and, of course, Monty will always raise the curtain with nothing behind it. The logic behind the decision to always switch is unassailable, but the gut feeling behind the wrong answer is almost impossible to resist.

So what do we make of these demonstrable foibles of human reasoning? Don't be misled by the fanciful nature of some of the examples given in this chapter. Incorrect reasoning about probabilities costs us enormously in wasted time, money, effort . . . and lives. The only way to avoid this wastage is to resolutely follow our best calculations and not our gut instincts. This is hard to do. People who have taken pilot training have told me that one of the hardest lessons is that when you are "flying blind"—in a heavy fog, for instance—you must learn to trust your instruments and not your feelings. Pilots who learn to trust their instruments land safely; those who go by feeling commit what air traffic controllers call "a controlled flight into terrain." There are times to go with gut feelings. If you get an e-mail from someone you've never heard of and who claims to be a wealthy Nigerian who must get out of the country and will give you millions of dollars to help if you will only give your bank account number, then go with your gut feelings and delete it. As the saying goes, an offer that sounds too good to be true usually is. But when you have to figure a probability, don't go with your gut. Calculate.

EXERCISES FOR CHAPTER 9

1) Rate the following pairs of dangers by what *feels* more dangerous, and then look up some statistics from a reliable source to see which really *is* more dangerous (assume that all cases apply to the United States):

   (a) (1) being murdered by a stranger
       (2) being murdered by a family member

   (b) (1) being killed in a terrorist attack.
       (2) choking to death in a restaurant

   (c) (1) drowning in a backyard pool.
       (2) being killed in an airliner crash

(d) (1) being attacked by a grizzly bear while hiking in a national park
   (2) being injured by a forklift while working in a warehouse

(e) (1) dying of carbon monoxide poisoning in your home
   (2) being killed by a drunk driver

(f) (1) being killed by lightning
   (2) being killed by a tornado

(g) (1) dying of complications from a legal abortion
   (2) dying of complications from childbirth

(h) (1) being killed by a poisonous snake
   (2) being killed by a fraternity initiation

2) Consider the following description of Sam:

> Sam is 27 years old, largely self-educated, and works as a firefighter in a suburb of Atlanta. He is white and married. He drives a pickup truck, is an evangelical Christian, and he attends church weekly. Sam's father and both grandfathers were pastors of evangelical churches. Sam is deeply concerned about church/state issues.

Explain how most people (presumably not you, since you have had the benefit of reading this chapter) would rank the following assertions about Sam from most to least likely, and what factors would influence people to make such a ranking.

> Sam voted Republican in the last presidential election.
> Sam reads the Bible regularly.
> Sam opposes gay rights legislation.
> Sam is a fan of the University of Georgia Bulldogs.
> Sam listens to Rush Limbaugh on the radio.
> Sam supports the death penalty.
> Sam voted Republican in the last election, opposes gay rights legislation, supports the death penalty, and listens to Rush Limbaugh on the radio.

3) Check TV, newspaper, or magazine ads to find three possible instances of "framing." That is, find three ads that present information in such a way that makes the information sound remarkable or exciting. For instance, if a beer brand claims that it is the most popular, this might mean that it has a market share of 11 percent of all beer sales and its nearest competitor has 10 percent.

4) Mr. Smith's hobby is bird watching. He is fairly new at the hobby, and his identification skills are already good, but he still has some problems identifying certain species. For instance, when he sees a lesser bittern he identifies it correctly 80 percent of the time, but 20 percent of the time he says it is a least bittern. Also, 80 percent of the time when he sees a least bittern he identifies it correctly, but 20 percent of the time he says it is a lesser bittern. Suppose you are birding with Mr. Smith and he says that he just spotted a least bittern. You happen to know that only 10 percent of the bitterns in that area are least bitterns and that the other 90 percent are lesser bitterns. What is the probability that Mr. Smith saw a least bittern?

NOTES

1. Massimo Piatelli-Palmarini, *Inevitable Illusions: How Mistakes of Reason Rule Our Minds* (New York: John Wiley & Sons, 1994), p. 65.

2. Ibid.

SUGGESTIONS FOR FURTHER READING

The book to read here is the one cited above, *Inevitable Illusions* by Piatelli-Palmarini. It is both amusing and alarming to find out how spontaneously irrational we really are. Piatelli-Palmarini argues that there are cognitive illusions just as there are optical illusions. He says that we all too easily get trapped in "mental tunnels" and it requires considerable effort to extricate ourselves. He is particularly good at explaining the findings of Daniel Kahneman and Amos Tversky, which detail how badly we tend to reason about probabilities. It makes you wonder how we survived the Paleolithic if we couldn't figure probabilities better than that! Anyway, our ineptitude is particularly alarming now that we depend on statistical information and probability estimates more than ever.

Chapter Ten

"STUDIES HAVE SHOWN"
... OR HAVE THEY?

Suppose that you like eggs for breakfast. Scrambled, boiled, poached, or fried, you like them, and every week you eat about a half dozen. One day, though, as you are watching the evening news, a grim-face commentator announces a new study by a major medical school that shows that eggs are a leading contributor to clogged arteries and heart disease and that doctors now recommend consumption of no more than two eggs per week. Dutifully, you switch from eggs to yogurt on most mornings because, even though you don't care much for yogurt, you are careful about your health. After two years of mostly egg-free breakfasts, you are relieved to see a newspaper headline reading: "Major Study Puts Eggs Back on the Menu." You read that a new study by another prominent institution shows that consumption of up to a half dozen large eggs a week shows no correlation with increased rates of heart disease or artery blockage. Happily (you were getting pretty sick of yogurt), you resume your egg breakfasts until two years later when—you guessed it—another somber commentator reports another study published in a leading medical journal that, of course, tells you to get off eggs again.

What the hell is going on? Why do studies, supposedly conducted by reputable institutions and leading scientists, seem to contradict each other so often? What is the average person supposed to do? Why not live your life however you like, smoking and drinking and eating as you please, confident that there will eventually be a study saying that your lifestyle is fine?

That would probably be a bad idea. We do know some things—like that cigarettes are bad for you. Even the big tobacco companies now admit this. If you are drinking a six-pack of beer each night, you don't need to wait for a study to tell you that this isn't good for you. There are plenty of facts that everybody agrees on. Another problem is that a lot of the time studies don't contradict, but appear to when reported in the mass media. The results of scientific studies are carefully qualified, with lots of "ifs," "ands," and "buts." When reported in the popular media, these careful qualifications are usually stripped off, leaving the impression that the study makes a much stronger and more certain claim than it does. When properly qualified, a new study may be seen only to modify or restrict earlier results rather than contradict them.

What is a "study"? What is it supposed to do? What is it a study of? Let's answer the last question first: A study is usually about us, at least indirectly. Even if a study is about the effects of an experimental medicine on lab rats, what we really want to know is how it will affect us. Studies are especially widely used in the social, behavioral, and biomedical sciences, the sciences that have the most direct bearing on our health, well-being, and self-understanding. The focus of these sciences on us makes such fields important, but it also makes them problematic. It is relatively easy to be objective about active galactic nuclei, or neutrinos, or crustal plates. Such topics pique our curiosity, but we have little personal stake in how some galactic cores generate large amounts of energy. Whether one mechanism or another is the cause is pretty much irrelevant to how everybody except astrophysicists live their lives. But consider a recent study which concluded that men talk as much as women. A long-lived stereotype is the image of gabby women and strong, silent men. Men are the doers, and women are the talkers, right? Actually, one researcher had men and women carry around tape recorders all day so that all their conversations were recorded for a number of days. Other people, probably exploited, low-paid grad students, then counted the actual number of words spoken in a day by the test subjects. The announced result of the study was that there is no significant difference in the number of words spoken daily by men and women.

Now which report would catch your eye if they were side by side in the science section of the newspaper: "New Theory of Black Holes," or

"Men as Gabby as Women, Study Finds"? It is a no-brainer that the latter would get ten times as many readers as the former. But when the topic is us, this creates special problems for objectivity. How can we be sure that bias does not creep into the design of the study, the way that it is carried out, or the interpretation of the results? How do we assure ourselves that what our studies determine corresponds with reality and is not simply a projection of our own wishes, biases, or predilections? Maintaining objectivity is a problem in every science, but it is fair to say that in the human sciences, where we are the subject matter, it is the most difficult of all.

The problem with objectivity in the medical, social, and human sciences is not merely a matter of avoiding bias but is an intrinsic problem of the methodology. A study is really a kind of experiment, but it is hardly ever possible to do a study on human beings that is like experiments on, say, a protein or a proton. Clearly, there are ethical limitations on how we can study human beings that do not apply to experiments on inanimate molecules or particles. What would be the best way to see if cigarette smoking causes lung cancer? Well, you could take 100,000 randomly selected sixth graders and divide them up randomly into two groups of 50,000. One group you would addict to cigarettes, getting them to smoke three packs a day. The other group you would prohibit from somoking at all. At the end of thirty years, you compare the incidence of lung cancer in the two groups. I hope it is obvious to every reader that this experiment has never and should never be done. It would be monstrous, like the insane "medical" experiments at Auschwitz or the Tuskegee study of the 1930s in which African American men were left untreated for syphilis so that the course of the disease could be studied.

What, then, is a study? Basically, a study aims to provide a rigorous test of a hypothesis. What kind of hypothesis? A hypothesis evaluated by a study is generally one of two types. There are **statistical hypotheses** and **causal hypotheses**. A statistical hypothesis is one that claims that a particular numerical relationship exists between the values of certain variables. A **variable** is simply a general property possessed by members of some population such that the property can take a range of possible values. A variable may have only two possible values, such as the sex of newborns (ignoring hermaphrodites); or it may have a range of many possible values, such as height in humans. Further, the values that a variable may take can be continuous, able to take any value within a given range, or discrete, only able to take certain values within the given range. Human height continuously varies between the heights of the shortest and tallest persons. You can be 5'9" or 5'9.25" or 5'9.257" or 5'9.2571384" and so on. IQ, on the other hand, has to take whole-number values. Nobody has an IQ of 130 1/2.

Statistical hypotheses frequently claim that a **positive correlation** or a **negative correlation** exists between the values of two variables. A positive correlation between two variables means that the values of each variable tend to go up or down together. As the value of one variable increases, so the value of the other tends to increase; as the one decreases, so the other tends to decrease. A negative correlation is just the opposite. If two variables are negatively correlated, an increase in the value of one tends to go with a decrease in the value of the other, and vice versa. Height and weight are positively correlated. Taller people also tend to be heavier people and vice versa. It is not a perfect correlation. Some short people weigh more than most tall people, and some tall people, like those cadaverous runway models, weigh very little, but there is nonetheless a positive correlation between weight and height. In other words, in the majority of cases (and it might be a slight majority), if person A is taller than person B, person A will also be heavier than person B; also, in the majority of cases, if one person is heavier than another, he or she will also be taller. An example of negative correlation is the relationship between formal education and religious belief. The more formal education one has, the less likely one is to accept religious doctrines. The correlation is far from perfect, of course. There are many very highly educated and very religious people (like, for instance, the pope), and many unbelieving ignoramuses. Still, there is some degree of negative correlation: people with bachelor's degrees are more likely to be skeptical of religious claims than people with no college education, and people with PhDs tend to be more skeptical still.

As the above paragraph implies, not only can we say that some variables are positively or negatively correlated, we can speak of the **strength of a correlation**. A perfect correlation, one that is maximally strong, means that the values of two variables change in lockstep. Any change in one always means a change in the other. Air temperature, for instance, is perfectly positively correlated with the height of the mercury column in an old-fashioned thermometer. Any increase in the one means an increase in the other; any drop in one means a drop in the other—that's why thermometers are so handy. On the other hand, there is a perfect negative correlation between the perceived brightness of a luminous object and your distance from it. The farther away you are from a 100-watt bulb, the dimmer it will appear. A correlation of zero strength means that there is no correlation at all. It would, for instance, be very surprising to find any correlation at all between fluctuations in the price of tea in China and major league batting averages (though weirder correlations have been found).

Most of the correlations studied in the medical, social, or human sciences are less than perfect. For instance, in the United States there is some positive correlation between being male and being a smoker (there is a slight negative correlation in some other countries). A perfect positive correlation would mean that all men smoked and no women did, and clearly this is not so. In fact, though, the percentage of American men who smoke is slightly higher than the percentage of American women who smoke. So in the United States there is a positive correlation, a weak one, between being male and being a smoker. Further, the strength of correlations can change over time. Eighty years ago, the correlation between smoking and being male was much stronger than now because at that time a considerably higher percentage of men smoked than now and a much lower percentage of women did. (Smoking wasn't considered ladylike in those days. Now that the percentages are nearly equal, women's lung cancer rates are closing in on men's. As the cigarette ad for women used to say, "You've come a long way, baby!")

Causal hypotheses claim more than a statistical relationship between things; they claim a cause and effect relationship, which is something *very* different. The remainder of this chapter will focus on causal hypotheses and how studies attempt to confirm such hypotheses. The exact nature of causation has long been a topic of philosophical dispute, and we do not have room to enter into those disputes here. However, I think it is clear that when we say that one thing A causes (or is *a* cause of) some effect B, we are, at bottom, postulating the existence of a **causal mechanism,** a physical process involving A that makes the occurrence of B either certain or more likely (i.e., more likely than it would have been had that process not occurred). For instance, when I say that cigarette smoking has a causal relation to lung cancer, I am not merely making a statistical claim about smoking habits and lung cancer rates in human populations. I am saying that a physical process occurs, a biochemical one, whereby the inhalation of cigarette smoke in human beings, in conjunction with other relevant physical conditions, makes the growth of cancerous tumors in human lung tissue either certain or more likely. Sometimes science permits us to isolate particular causal mechanisms. For instance, we know the mechanisms, the changes in the hemoglobin and the red blood cells, which bring about the devastating condition known as sickle-cell anemia.

Often, however, we cannot isolate the causal mechanism, but we still can identify **causal factors** at work within populations. By employing a well-designed study (usually multiple studies), we can sometimes identify A as a causal factor in bringing about B even if we cannot identify the precise causal mechanism connecting A to B. To say that A is a causal factor for B means this: Imagine two *hypothetical* populations, P_1 and P_2. To say that these populations are hypothetical means that they do not really exist; we only imagine them. Imagine then that these two populations, P_1 and P_2, are just alike. Now suppose A is applied to every individual in P_1 and to no individuals in P_2, and that otherwise these two populations are treated exactly alike. If, after an appropriate period of time, we observe a higher incidence of B in P_1 than in P_2, we would conclude that A is a causal factor for B. If, for instance, there were two hypothetical populations that were exactly alike except that one smoked three packs a day for thiry years and the other did not smoke at all, and if we found a higher incidence of lung cancer in the former, we would say that smoking is a causal factor for the occurrence of lung cancer. In short, we say that smoking is a causal factor for lung cancer if there would be more cases of lung cancer if everybody smoked than if nobody did. Of course, we cannot actually perform tests on hypothetical populations, but only on real populations, so people who design studies to detect causal factors have devised ways to make real populations effectively correspond to the hypothetical populations we imagined.

By the way, to say that A is a causal factor for B is not to say that A is the *only* cause of B. In the real world, most complex phenomena have complex causes. For instance, criminal behavior no doubt has many causes, perhaps involving genetic predispositions (which themselves are very complex) toward criminality, family background (a history of having been abused seems particularly significant), peer pressure, drug use, social status, economic disadvantage, educational opportunity, and so forth. If crime had a single, simple cause, it probably would be much easier to eliminate. Further, each particular causal factor will be limited in its effect. Beware of those, like politicians or ideologues, who propose simplistic solutions to complex issues like crime ("Lock 'em up and throw away the key!"). Crime has no simple cause and can have no simple cure. Nevertheless, complex problems like crime are not completely intractable because we can identify some of the contributing causal factors, and this may allow us to mitigate its occurrence, even though it seems highly unlikely that we will ever, so long as we have human beings, be completely crime free.

Here we also must note, most emphatically, that cause and correlation are *not* the same things. To say that two things are correlated, as we note above, is merely to say that they tend to vary together, either directly or inversely. To say that one thing, A, causes another, B, is to say that A, wholly or in part, *brings about* B or *makes* B occur, or, at least, makes B *more probable*. In other words, when we say that A causes B we are, explicitly or tacitly, postulating a causal mechanism connecting A to B. Confusion often arises because causally related things are correlated. Lightning and thunder are correlated; the occurrence of one is always accompanied by the occurrence of the other, and the reason is that lightning causes thunder. The problem is that the converse relationship does not always hold; things can be correlated, even perfectly positively correlated, without there being a causal relationship between them. For instance, being made of copper and having "In God We Trust" stamped on it are two perfectly correlated properties of US pennies (ignoring some noncopper pennies minted in World War II). Yet, clearly, there is no causal relationship between being composed of copper and having "In God We Trust" stamped on.

So, though all causes involve correlations, the converse does not hold: not all correlations between two things involve a causal relationship between those things. Unfortunately, human beings have a strong psychological propensity to attribute causality whenever striking correlations are observed, and this has often led to error and mischief. Let me illustrate with a historical episode: When I was a kid, the comic books all carried a stamp saying "approved by the Comics Code Authority." The Comics Code Authority (CCA) was created in 1954 in response to concerns of the public and public officials about allegedly excessive sexuality and violence in comic books. In that year psychiatrist Dr. Frederick Wertham had created a stir with his book *Seduction of the Innocent*, which claimed that comics were corrupting America's youth and contributing to juvenile delinquency. Out of fear of government censorship, the comics industry created the CCA to monitor itself, and comic book distributors refused to sell comics that did not have the CCA stamp of approval. The result was that I had to settle for some pretty bland comics, until I discovered *Mad* magazine (whose publisher, William Gaines, had refused to submit to the CCA).

Supporters of Dr. Wertham could certainly point to evidence that juvenile delinquents, <u>insofar as</u> they read anything at all, preferred horror comics, which often included gruesome scenes of decayed corpses rising from the grave to exact a horrible revenge. Being an avid reader of horror comics and being a delinquent seemed to be correlated. So comics caused juvenile delinquency, right? Not necessarily. There might indeed be a fairly strong positive correlation between delinquency and reading horror comics, but that, by itself, is no indication of a causal connection. Comic book reading and delinquent behavior might be correlated for any number of reasons other than because the comics caused the behavior. Another consideration was that delinquent behavior and comic book reading were *both* correlated with being a high school dropout. Isn't it possible that what was actually going on was that low academic achievement was a causal factor contributing both to delinquent behavior and to the preference for comics? After all, a high school dropout is probably not going to be running around with a copy of James Joyce's *Ulysses* tucked under his arm; more likely it will be *Weird Tales of the Crypt*. The upshot is that correlation is not cause, and if you mistakenly think that it is, you could wind up with something a lot worse than bland comics. So one aim of a good study designed to test a causal hypothesis is that it will provide effective checks to make sure that we do not mistake a mere correlation for a cause.

So how do we test for causal factors? When we find that A is associated with B, how do we tell whether A is causally connected with B or whether they are merely correlated? Recall that we defined "causal factor" in terms of *hypothetical* populations—the imaginary population in which the suspected causal factor is present in every case and the population in which it is absent in every case. But obviously real-world tests can only be performed with real populations. Imagining hypothetical populations allow us to construct a **causal model**, an imaginary representation of a possible causal relationship.

Scientific thinking very often involves the creation of **theoretical models**. A causal model is a kind of theoretical model. A theoretical model is an imaginary representation of possible states of affairs, thought to approximate aspects of physical reality, and intended to be a part of a theoretical account of some body of natural phenomena. For instance, Nicholas Copernicus famously created a heliocentric model of the cosmos, a representation of the cosmos with the sun at (or, rather, very close to) the center of the universe. A model is not an exact representation of physical reality, but a stripped down, simplified, idealized picture that, in actuality, exists only in scientists' minds. Though theoretical models are imaginary, they can fit reality in the sense that models depict an imagined world that can be similar to the real world in important respects. Likewise, a road map cannot possibly represent every bump, pothole, curve, or dip in a real road, but it can show you, for example, that if you make a right turn on Smith Street and go four blocks to Capitol Avenue, a left turn will take you to the freeway. When scientists test a theory, this amounts to seeing if, indeed, the theoretical model is a good map of the physical reality. It turned out that Copernicus's map was good, better than the old, geocentric (earth-centered) one, anyway.

So suppose we want to test a causal claim, say, the claim that reading horror comics contributes to juvenile delinquency. We first imagine a causal model. Let's say we imagine the entire population of 11- to 15-year-old males in the city of New York. Now let's imagine one hypothetical population in which all of the 11- to 15-year-old males in New York read two particularly lurid horror comics a week. Let's call this hypothetical population the "X" group. Now let's imagine another hypothetical population of that same group of 11- to 15-year-old New Yorkers where everything is exactly the same as in the previous hypothetical population except that nobody reads horror comics. Let's call this hypothetical population the "K" group. We would expect, if horror comics contribute to juvenile delinquency, that the rate of delinquency would be higher in the hypothetical X group than in the K group. As we say, though, you cannot do an actual test on a hypothetical population, but only on a real population. The trick of testing for causal factors is to come up with real populations that approximate, as closely as possible, the idealized hypothetical populations of our causal models. The best way to do this is with a **randomized experimental design**.

A randomized experimental design begins by making a *random* selection from a real population—say, the population of 11- to 15-year-old males in New York City. To say that a member of a population was selected randomly means that every individual in the population had the same chance of being selected. Suppose, then, we could randomly select 1,000 boys between the ages of 11 and 15 from the entire population of 11- to 15-year-old boys in New York. We then divide this population again and assign five hundred to one group, which we call the **control group**, and the other 500 to another group we call the **experimental group**. It is essential that the assignment of individuals from the group of 1,000 to either the control or the experimental group is also random— that is, each member of our group of 1,000 must have a 1/2 chance of being put into the experimental group and a 1/2 chance of being put into the control group. The control group is our real-world group that is supposed to approximate the ideal K group in our causal model. The experimental group is the real-world population that approximates the ideal X group in our model. In our experiment we get members of the control group to read two nonhorror comics a week (say, Archie comics—ugh!) and get members of the experimental group to read two particularly hideous horror comics per week. We then wait and see what happens (I hope it is obvious, by the way, that this is another one of those experiments that should not be done in real life).

The *two* random selections are both crucially important. What random selection does for you is that it tends to wash out all of the differences between your test subjects that might skew your results. For instance, if our initial selection of 1,000 from the general population of 11- to 15-year-old boys in New York were nonrandom, if it were biased, say, toward boys from households with incomes considerably greater than the median income of New York households with 11- to 15-year-old boys, then the selected group would hardly be representative of the general population. This would mean that whatever results we got from our test would be compromised since our goal is to find out something about the whole population and not just the selected group. A random selection from the whole population of 11- to 15-year-old male New Yorkers makes it unlikely that the 1,000 you select will come from households with a significantly higher median income. Likewise, when we divide our initial group of 1,000 into two groups of 500, another random selection will help prevent the intrusion of all sorts of factors that could bias our results. If we select, say, all of those 11 to 15 year olds in our group of 1,000 who already have records as juvenile delinquents and put all of these in one of our groups of 500, clearly, this will bias our findings.

In any study, the use of a control group is essential. The members of the control group and the experimental group should be as alike as possible except that every member of the experimental group is exposed to the suspected causal factor and no member of the control group is. If we try to do a study without a control group, our results will not be reliable. For instance, suppose we just took our first group of 1,000 11- to 15-year-olds and had all of them read horror comics. Let's suppose that after a year we found that, say, 115 of the boys had been involved in some sort of delinquent behavior. Would this show that reading horror comics contributed to delinquency? Of course not, since we have no idea, because we have no control group for comparison, what the rate of delinquency would have been had the group not read the horror comics. It could have been the same or possibly even higher. Conceivably, reading horror comics *prevents* juvenile delinquency! We just have no way of knowing if we don't use a control group.

OK. Suppose then that after a couple of years we find that the boys in the experimental group have a slightly higher rate of delinquency than the boys in the control group—that is, we find that delinquency is somewhat positively correlated with reading horror comics. Suppose that the delinquency rate in the experimental group is 11.5 percent and in the control group it is 10.5 percent. Do we therefore conclude that reading horror comics is a causal factor for juvenile delinquency? No. We have only discovered a slight correlation, and, as we say, a correlation is not the same thing as a cause. However, correlations can be used to *test* causal models if we follow the right procedures. If we have selected the members of our experimental and control groups by our two random selections, then we can be pretty sure that we have washed out most of the significant differences between the two groups that might skew our results. But we cannot be completely sure. No matter how carefully we design the experiment and no matter how scrupulously we randomize our selection procedures, we cannot rule out chance factors that can bias the results. For instance, our random selection of 500 boys for the experimental group might, purely by chance, include more "at risk" boys than the control group. If this were so, our results would likely show a somewhat greater incidence of delinquency in the experimental group even if horror comics are not a causal factor.

In the language of statistics, we have to ask whether our results are **statistically significant**. In effect, we are asking whether the difference between the rates of delinquency in the experimental and control groups is likely due to "statistical noise," the chance factors that enter into any statistical measurement, or due to the influence of an actual causal factor. To say that results are statistically significant means that we have a certain level of confidence that our result reflects a real difference between the two groups and is not simply due to chance. What level of confidence? Usually a result is deemed statistically significant if we are 95 percent confident that the result indicates a real difference and is not due to chance fluctuations. As statisticians like to put it, we want results that are significant at the .05 level (i.e., there is only a .05, or 5 percent, probability that the results were due to chance).

To check for statistical significance we have to understand the concept of the **margin of error** of a statistical measurement. Any statistical measure will—or should—come with a margin of error. Consider when we take a sample from a real population and measure the value of some variable in the sample group. We cannot be confident, no matter how careful we are, that the measurement we get for the value of that variable in our sample *exactly* matches the value of the variable in the real population from which the sample was taken. If we poll a random sample of 500 boys aged 11 to 15 in New York and find that 27 percent read two or more horror comics weekly, we cannot say that exactly 27 percent of *all* 11- to 15-year-old New York boys read two or more horror comics weekly. We can only say that the percentage of New York boys in that age group who read horror comics *probably* (usually, we mean with a 95 percent probability) falls within a certain range, say, 23 percent to 31 percent, so we say that we have a margin of error of plus or minus 4 percent. Everyone is familiar with such margins of error from the polls that abound at election time.

Likewise, when we are performing a test of a causal hypothesis, and our measured results in our control and experimental groups are supposed to support projections for values in our hypothetical X and K populations, we also use margins of error. If 11.5 percent of the experimental group in our test of the horror comic hypothesis became delinquent, we could not project that *exactly* 11.5 percent of the hypothetical X group of all 11- to 15-year-old New York boys (the hypothetical group where they all read the horror comics) would become delinquent. Our projection would have to also include a margin of error. We would say that our test results indicate that if all New York boys in the selected age group were to read two horror comics weekly, we would expect (supposing we have a margin of error of 4 percent) somewhere between 7.5 percent and 15.5 percent to become delinquents (11.5 percent plus or minus 4 percent). Similarly, using the same margin of error, we would say that our results with the control group (a 10.5 percent rate of delinquency) indicate that the members of our hypothetical K group, none of which read horror comics, would likely have a delinquency rate of between 6.5 percent and 14.5 percent (10.5 percent plus or minus 4 percent).

Are the results of our study statistically significant, reflecting a real causal factor, or likely due to chance? Note that there is very considerable overlap in the intervals determined by the margins of error in our projected values for delinquency in the X and the K groups. The minimum projected delinquency percentage for the X group is 7.5 percent and the maximum projected delinquency percentage for the K group is 14.5 percent. Such a large overlap in the intervals means that the results of our study are not statistically significant at the .05 confidence level (see a statistics text for the details). The small 1 percent difference in the delinquency rates (11.5 percent to 10.5 percent) is more likely due to chance factors than the alleged corrupting influence of horror comics. Our causal model is not confirmed. So our imaginary study (sorry, Dr. Wertham!) fails to confirm that horror comics contribute to juvenile delinquency.

Suppose that the two intervals had not overlapped. Suppose that in the experimental group the delinquency rate had been 23 percent and only 9.5 percent in the control group. In this case, keeping the margin of error at 4 percent, we would say that the X group would have a projected delinquency rate of between 19 percent and 27 percent, and the K group would have a projected delinquency rate of 5.5 percent to 13.5 percent. So the intervals would not overlap. This would mean that the results are statistically significant and that it is very unlikely that the measured difference in delinquency rates between our experimental group and control group is due to chance. Rather, it likely has a cause, and since we have made the two groups as alike as possible except for the comics they read, it would look like the horror comics are the culprit.

What if the two intervals had overlapped, but by not as much as in our imaginary example? If the overlap is relatively small, and the number of individuals in our sample is relatively large, then the results might still be deemed statistically significant (again, see a statistics text for the details). In fact, in actual hypothesis testing, getting no overlap at all in our margins of error would be rather rare. So with most tests of a causal hypothesis about the best we can say is that if the overlap in the projected values of our X and K groups is not too great, and if the sample size is large enough, then the results are probably statistically significant. We see then, that even when we use the best sort of study design, the randomized design, our results will often not be terribly robust. Worse, as we said, a randomized experimental design of hypotheses like Dr. Wertham's could not be carried out and should not even if it could. It would be unethical. If Dr. Wertham was right, and reading horror comics contributes to delinquency, we would be contributing to the delinquency of minors by having some of them read comic books in our study! So an actual test of the comic book hypothesis would have to employ another experimental design.

When it is impractical or unethical to do a randomized experimental design in a given circumstance, we have to use other designs. The randomized design is the gold standard, the optimal design for achieving reliable results in our study. Everything else is second-best, but this is often the best we can do. Often, the best we can do is to use a **prospective experimental design**. What often makes a randomized design unethical is that it would be wrong to intentionally expose the people in the experimental groups to something that might harm them. If smoking or reading horror comics is really harmful, and we do not know until we check, it would be wrong to get people to smoke or read horror comics. But what if people make these choices themselves? Some people choose to smoke or to read horror comics without being prompted by experimenters. In other words, we sometimes find a "natural experiment" in which some people voluntarily expose themselves to possible causal factors and others refrain from doing so. The essence of the prospective design is that you regard those who do choose to smoke, or read horror comics, or whatever, as the members of the experimental group. The ones who choose not to do or engage in those things are put in the control group. You make sure that nobody in either group already shows the effect that you think the suspected causal factor might cause. For instance, if you are doing the horror comics study, you make sure that none of the boys chosen for the study have already exhibited delinquent behavior. Basically, then, you wait and see what happens. If, after an appropriate period of time, the self-selected experimental group shows significantly more of the suspected effect than the self-selected control group, then you might be able to conclude that a causal factor is at work.

You have to be really careful, though. The biggest problem with the prospective design is that you have to be as sure as possible that the subjects you put in the experimental group and those you put in the control group are as alike as possible except for that one crucial suspected factor. For instance, we would try to make the group of horror comic readers as much like the nonreaders as possible except, of course, for their horror comic reading behavior. If we do not effectively do this, our results could easily be biased. Remember that the kinds of effects we are interested in when we do studies in the medical, human, or social sciences are usually complexly caused, with many causal factors at work and interacting in intricate ways. If, for instance, you let a considerably higher proportion of boys from single-parent homes go into the experimental group, this might be the factor that increases the delinquency rates, not reading the comics. Cigarette manufacturers for years claimed that the correlation between cancer and smoking was not necessarily due to the smoking but possibly to other causal factors that the studies had not ruled out. They suggested, for instance, that smoking was correlated with living in urban areas, and that other features of the urban environment might cause the higher cancer rates.

For ethical or practical reasons, therefore, a prospective experimental design is often the best that we can do. It is not as reliable as the randomized design studies, and this is why no one such study, however carefully conducted, is hardly ever definitive or final. Usually, a number of studies are needed to confirm an important result, and unsurprisingly, some studies will probably contradict others because of the inherent and unavoidable uncertainties involved in the examination of complex phenomena. Results obtained from studies in the medical, human, or social sciences are usually not as "clean" as the results of experiments in particle physics—that is, our findings in the medical, human, and social sciences are usually less clear cut and require more analysis and interpretation. Eventually, though, consensus can emerge, but it takes time, and the path to agreement is often convoluted and strewn with discredited studies. Further, there is no question that some studies that were incompetently designed or carried out still make it into print in the professional journals.

Of course, every science progresses only by stepping over the bodies of dead hypotheses, and even particle physics has its failed, incompetently-designed experiments. Why, then, does it seem that studies in the medical, human, and social sciences contradict each other so much more often than in the physical sciences? Again, it is largely a matter of publicity. Occasionally spurious results derived from incompetent experiments in the physical sciences make the front page, as with the cold fusion debacle of the late 1980s. Generally, though, a bad study in the medical, human, or social sciences will get much more attention than, say, a flawed experiment to detect gravity waves. As we say, few people really care about things like gravity waves, but studies about cancer or gender relationships or self-image interest many people. A gravity wave experiment gets a few articles in the physics journals; a study of eating habits and obesity will make the front page of the *New York Times* and the *CBS Evening News*. The failures of some fields are much more public than those of others.

Some people have scorned the whole practice of conducting studies of human behavior and have regarded the fields of psychology and sociology, for which such studies are methodological bread and butter, as no more than pseudosciences. For instance, classical scholar Bruce S. Thornton comments:

> The difficulty, of course, is that both fields [i.e., psychology and sociology], despite wrapping themselves in the procedures and jargon of real science, have about as much legitimacy as mes-

merism and phrenology . . . [classical pseudosciences of the nine-teenth century].[1]

As Thornton sees it, all that studies do is lend a spurious appearance of scientific validity to conclusions that are either trivial truths or vast over-simplifications:

Anytime a sentence is prefaced by the phrase "studies have shown," you can be sure to hear either some truism ponderously restated, or some half-baked oversimplification the authors of the study already believed to be true before they ever began. And when the "study" purports to prove some truth about the intri-cate, complex, quirky, unpredictable, unique creature that is a human being, then you can be equally sure that its conclusions add one more disease to the syndrome of false knowledge.[2]

As an instance of how a flawed study can produce misinformation, Thornton cites the well-known "self-esteem" study commissioned by the American Association of University Women in 1991. Thornton comments:

Starting from the assumption that girls are shortchanged in school, and hence wounded in their self-esteem, because of the subtle gender biases of teachers, the study went ahead and, *mirabile dictu*, discovered that little girls, between the exact ages of eleven and seventeen, *are* short-changed in school by the gender biases of their teachers, and so suffer from wounded self-esteem, which in turn prevents them from excelling in traditional male pursuits. The study ultimately provided the intellectual support for the $360 million Gender Equity in Education Act.[3]

Thornton points out that these sweeping conclusions were reached by asking preteens to self-report on their attitudes and feelings, which does not seem to be a reliable means of getting accurate or useful information. Further, the study assumed that there is a definite and distinct property called "self-esteem" that can be meaningfully measured and expressed quantitatively. Finally, the study assumed a simplistic cause-and-effect relationship between what it calls "self-esteem" and achievement. The problem with this, and all such studies, says Thornton, is that human behavior is so complex in its character and causes that it is unfathomable and impervious to scientific investigation.[4]

There is no question that there has often been an ideological agenda behind the "findings" of studies. This is inexcusable whether the ideology is fundamentalism, feminism, or whatever. Yet Thornton's total skepticism about studies in the human and social sciences does not seem warranted. There is no question that human beings are enormously complex, and this is a daunting challenge for any would-be student of human individual or social behavior. Yet in the natural sciences we have seen in recent years that the "complexity horizon" has receded, that is, powerful techniques have been developed, such as computer modeling, that permit precise, repeatable, and firm results to be obtained even in the "sciences of complexity" such as climatology, neuroscience, artificial intelligence, and cellular biology. Perhaps in the human sciences also complexity is a difficult but increasingly tractable problem. Even John H. Fennick, whose book *Studies Show* is the definitive guide to studies and how they can go wrong, concludes with a chapter titled "They're Not All Bad."[5] It seems that we can use the methods outlined in this chapter to learn *some* things about human beings and their individual or collective behavior. Nevertheless, when you hear that a study has reached some sweeping conclusion about a "hot-button," emotionally charged issue, take it with a grain—no—a tablespoon of salt.

EXERCISE FOR CHAPTER 10

Check some science magazines like *New Scientist, Science News, Scientific American, Discover,* or *American Scientist,* or good online science news sites and find two studies of causal models in the medical, social, or human sciences (if you are not sure whether a site is a good science news source or not, check with a reference librarian). Make sure the studies employ either a randomized experimental design or a prospective experimental design, and identify the design used for each study. With each study, identify the X group and the K group (the experimental group and the control group). Identify the variables being measured in each study.

Give the sample sizes of the experimental and control groups. State the causal model or hypothesis being tested and say whether the study confirmed the hypothesis or not. State whether the results were reported as statistically significant at a given confidence level. Compare and contrast the two studies and state your overall evaluation of the reliability of the studies. Does one seem more reliable than the other? Why or why not? Are there any reasons for particular skepticism about the reported results?

NOTES

1. Bruce S. Thornton, *Plagues of the Mind: The New Epidemic of False Knowledge* (Wilmington, DE: ISI Books, 1999), p. 11.
2. Ibid.
3. Ibid., p. 12.
4. Ibid., p. 13.
5. John H. Fennick, *Studies Show: A Popular Guide to Understanding Scientific Studies* (Amherst, NY: Prometheus Books, 1997), p. 211.

SUGGESTIONS FOR FURTHER READING

The book I relied upon the most in writing this chapter is Ronald Giere's classic *Understanding Scientific Reasoning*, 3rd ed. (New York: Harcourt, Brace, Jovanovich, 1991). This is a terrific book, very clearly written, though with perhaps a bit too much detail for some readers. I attempted to teach from this book once, and my students found it a bit overwhelming. A considerably more succinct but reliable guide to the same territory is Stephen S. Carey's *A Beginner's Guide to Scientific Method*, 3rd ed. (Belmont, CA: Wadsworth, 2004). The definitive guide to the critical evaluation of scientific studies is the book *Studies Show*, by John H. Fennick, cited in the notes. It is readable, authoritative, and eye opening. This book is a wonderful antidote to the knee-jerk deference we tend to show to studies presented as "scientific." While I cannot go along with Bruce S. Thornton's attitude of total skepticism toward the social and the human sciences, his book *Plagues of the Mind* (cited in the notes), makes many good points. He is very good at puncturing the balloons of ideologues who try to wrap themselves in the mantle of scientific respectability.

Chapter Eleven
INFERENCE TO THE BEST EXPLANATION

Years ago in elementary and high school, my science textbooks used to talk about something called "The Scientific Method." The idea was that there was some simple set of procedures such that, if you followed them carefully, you would be doing "science" and you could depend upon those methods to guide you to scientific discovery. The problem is that there really is no such thing as "science," but only a quite complex and diverse set of sciences that can be divided up or categorized in different ways. There are physical sciences and earth sciences and life sciences and social sciences. Each of these broad divisions is comprised of smaller subdivisions, and there is no reason to expect that all of these diverse kinds of inquiry will share more than the most general sorts of methodological principles and standards. True, in all sciences you are expected to postulate hypotheses and test those hypotheses rigorously by experiment, measurement, or observation. But saying this doesn't tell us much more about the actual practice of scientists than the advice to buy low and sell high tells you how to be a successful stockbroker. Different sciences go about their business very differently. You cannot do particle physics with the same sorts of methods you use in archaeology. So, really, it is hard to offer any one-size-fits-all characterization of scientific method, one, that is, that is not so generalized as to be virtually devoid of content or so detailed that it applies to only a small subset of sciences.

However, we can make *some* useful generalizations about the kinds of reasoning that enter into all, or at least most, of the natural sciences. One kind of reasoning of central importance to most sciences is **inference to the best explanation** (IBE), the form of reasoning where we say that the hypothesis most likely to be true is the one that best explains the facts.

Perhaps the most famous example of the use of IBE comes from Daniel Defoe's novel *Robinson Crusoe*. According to the story, castaway Crusoe has been alone on his island for many years and has not seen another human being during all that time. One day, however, when he is walking on the beach, he sees an unmistakable human footprint. He instantly realizes that he is no longer alone on his island. Now the inference from a human footprint to the earlier presence of a human foot happens so rapidly that we are unconscious of it. It is an inference nonetheless. It is possible that something looking just like a human footprint could be caused by an accident of wind and tide, but this seems very unlikely. By far the *best* explanation of a footprint is that it was left by a human being because that is what *best* explains the marks in the sand. Every other possible explanation is much more implausible.

We use IBE in everyday life; in fact, probably not a day goes by that we do not use inference to the best explanation in some basic way. Here's a hypothetical example: Suppose that I keep a box of breakfast biscuits in the freezer of the suite refrigerator to heat in the microwave and have at my desk with morning coffee. I thought I had counted two biscuits left after I got one yesterday, but when I looked today, I only found one. How do I explain the discrepancy between my expectations and what I found? Possible explanations are (1) I was mistaken in thinking that I had two biscuits left, when, in fact, I only had one, (2) A colleague was feeling peckish and decided to help himself or herself to one of my biscuits, or (3) Some person on the nighttime cleaning staff had it for a midnight snack. These seem to be the most feasible possible explanations. Which is likely to be true? Well, I am pretty absentminded, but I usually can accurately distinguish between one item and two, so (1) is probably not the explanation. (3) is probably not the explanation because the cleaning staff is carefully supervised and has to pass a strict background check before hiring. Sadly, I have to conclude that the best explanation of the missing biscuit is that a hungry colleague grabbed it.

The sciences make copious use of IBE. One thing we expect from the natural sciences is that they provide insightful, informative, and well-grounded explanations of the occurrences in the world around us. Why are tornadoes common in the Midwest in spring? Because in springtime moist, warm air from the Gulf of Mexico flows north over midwestern states where it interacts with cold, dense air moving south out of Canada and dry air flowing down the slopes of the Rocky Mountains. This clash of air masses produces an extremely unstable atmosphere, which results in super-cell thunderstorms that sometimes spin off destructive tornadoes. Why are some galactic nuclei extremely active, producing prodigious quantities of energy that can sometimes be seen across the visible universe? Most likely because accretion disks form around monster black holes in the centers of these galaxies and, as the matter from these disks spirals into the black hole's maw, compression and friction generate tremendous energies that are emitted in inconceivably powerful jets. Why did Neanderthals disappear from Europe about 30,000 years ago after flourishing there for nearly 300,000 years? Perhaps they vanished in part because of competition with modern humans, *Homo sapiens*, who had recently arrived in Europe after following a circuitous route from Africa. In sciences as different as meteorology, astrophysics, and paleoanthropology we seek to infer the scientific explanations that will best account for puzzling facts.

What is a scientific explanation? Philosophers have proposed various models of scientific explanation, but I think it is fair to say that no one of these models has proven to be wholly satisfactory; each one fails to accommodate some instances of legitimate scientific explanation. Here it will be more fruitful to describe what a scientific explanation is supposed to *do*, the *pragmatics* of scientific explanation as philosophers call it.

In science, as in daily life, we often ask "Why?" When we ask why, we are focusing on a particular "topic of concern," as, for instance, when we are concerned to know why the Neanderthals disappeared 30,000 years ago. When we ask a why question about a particular topic of concern, we tacitly assume that the event we want to explain is part of a "contrast class" of possibilities, only one of which—the one we are trying to explain—was actually realized. For instance, when the topic of concern is the disappearance of the Neanderthals 30,000 years ago, the contrast class could be alternative, unrealized possibilities such as these:

(1) the Neanderthals continue into historical times (as depicted in the movie *The 13th Warrior*), or
(2) they disappear even longer ago than 30,000 years.

In effect, when we ask why the Neanderthals disappeared 30,000 years ago, we are asking why *that* possibility was realized as compared to others. Why did they go extinct *just then*, and not at some other time or not at all? We also expect answers to why questions to meet a "relevance condition," that is, we expect them to answer the question in the respect in which it was asked. For instance, in asking for a scientific account of Neanderthal extinction, we would not be happy with a theological answer, say, "The Neanderthals were sinful and the Lord smote them." We are instead asking for the *physical cause* of their extinction. For instance, did their contact with *Homo sapiens* expose them to diseases to which they had no immunity? Finally, we are looking for a "telling answer" to our why question, that is, one that tells us why the actual outcome was to be expected over the other possibilities in the contrast class. What factors, for instance, brought the disappearance of the Neanderthals at just that time? Also, the "telling answer" will have to meet the relevance condition and answer the question in the respect in which it was asked. So a good scientific explanation should provide an answer that tells us (1) why one particular possibility of the contrast class (the one that really happened) was to be expected over the other possibilities, and (2) meets the relevance condition by answering our question in the respect that we asked it.

Good scientific explanations will have other virtues as well, and the best one will be the one that in our judgment is the most virtuous. Good explanations will have four virtues. First, they will be *deep*, that is, they will connect the occurrence to be explained with more basic or fundamental features of physical reality. For instance, when astronomers learned to explain the apparently erratic and unpredictable behavior of comets in terms of Newton's laws of motion and gravitation, they achieved a deep explanation because those laws are among the most basic and general for explaining the physical world. Second, the best explanations should be *simple*, elegantly explaining the observed phenomena in terms of a few simple relations and a small number of terms. Newton's law of universal gravitation is a good example here, also. It says that the force of gravity between two massive objects is directly proportional to the product of their masses and inversely proportional to the square of the distance between them. This very simple and beautiful relationship has proven enormously successful in explaining many things in our cosmos. Third, ideal explanations should also have a great deal of *unifying power*. That is, they should not only explain one small set of phenomena but include that small set with many other kinds of occurrences and show that they all fit into a common framework for explanation. Darwinian evolution has proven to be one of the most successful explanatory theories in this regard. Darwin himself noted that his theory encompassed many apparently diverse phenomena, from embryology, to paleontology, to comparative anatomy, to ecology, and many other fields. Each of these seemingly disparate sets of facts, like the common structure of animals' forelimbs, or the close resemblance of their embryological forms, or their geographic distribution, or their distribution in the fossil record, could be brought under the common explanatory framework of descent with modification, that is, evolution. Fourth, finally, good explanations should *fit our background knowledge*. We will not judge an explanation as good unless it is consistent with the other things that we know. How do we explain the fact that the year 1816 was so cold that it was called "the year without a summer?" We know that large volcanic eruptions can eject vast quantities of particulate matter into the upper atmosphere and that this matter can reflect sunlight back into space, reducing the amount of solar energy that reaches the ground. So the best explanation of the "year without a summer" seems to be the massive eruption of the Indonesian volcano Tambora in 1815.

Now that we have an idea of what a good scientific explanation should do and what virtues it should possess, let's look at an actual example of scientific inference to the best explanation. We shall then look at the objections that some skeptics have raised about IBE as a reliable form of reasoning, meaning one that leads to conclusions that we should confidently regard as true or probable. Finally, we shall assess the skeptics' case against IBE and see how important their objections are.

In the early decades of the twentieth century, a German meteorologist named Alfred Wegener proposed a startling new geological theory called "continental drift." Geological orthodoxy of the day held that when the earth formed it was a molten mass that gradually cooled. As it cooled, the earth's crust solidified. As the crust continued to cool, it contracted and this contraction caused some parts to rise and others to sink. The result was the formation of ocean basins and continents, and such features as mountain ranges and the ocean's abyssal trenches. According to this this view, after the continents formed, they remained in the same relative positions. After all, what possible force could move a continent?

Local changes took place, mountains rose and were eroded, and the sea level changed, but the continents themselves remained in place. Wegener proposed that, on the contrary, the continents had drifted over geological times and at one time had, in fact, come together to form a massive supercontinent he called "Pangaea" ("All-Earth").

What prompted Wegener to propose such an unorthodox and bold theory? Wegener noticed a number of very unusual facts about the earth's surface. For one thing, the continents sometimes look as though they belong together. Schoolchildren often notice that the eastern coast of South America looks as though it would fit snugly into the western coast of Africa. Other facts were even more suggestive. Mountains are not all alike. Geologists note that different mountain ranges have different and highly distinctive features, such as their particular mineral composition. Wegener noticed that there are mountain ranges and geological provinces (areas with distinct types of rock) in the Old World continents, Europe and Africa, that match up perfectly with counterparts across the Atlantic Ocean in North and South America. If the continents could be pushed together, those mountain ranges and geological provinces would constitute continuous formations, instead of just breaking off at the shore of the Atlantic and apparently continuing across the ocean. Wegener also noticed that the distribution of many fossil animals and plants was very puzzling unless, at one time, we imagine the continents together. Part of the fossil range of a land-dwelling creature might be in South America and part in Africa. How could there be two populations of the same creature, which certainly could not have swum the Atlantic Ocean, unless those now separate ranges were contiguous during the animal's lifetime? For Wegener, the only reasonable conclusion given these odd facts was to infer the explanation that the continents had at one time been joined together.

The geologists of Wegener's day were practically unanimous in condemning his idea. One derided the notion of continental drift as "geopoetry." The main objection of traditional geologists was that continental drift seemed physically impossible. The floors of ocean basins consist of dense basaltic rock. The continents, on the other hand, are composed mostly of lighter siliceous rock. How could the less dense continents plow through the dense oceanic floor? Any force adequate to do so would simply shatter the continents. So Wegener's proposal looked impossible. Yet, in the 1960s, over thirty years after Wegener's death, geologists began to discover strong confirmation of continental drift. One of the most convincing lines of evidence was that the seafloor had spread over time, which, if true, could explain how the continents move without having to plow through the dense basaltic rock in the seabed. Instead of having to plow through ocean crust, the continents could just move with the seafloor as it spreads.

When minerals containing iron solidify from a molten state, they become magnetized, taking on the north/south polarity of the earth's magnetic field. However, the earth's magnetic field sometimes reverses its polarity, and it has done so many times over the earth's history. That is, at certain times in the earth's history, the earth's magnetic field will have a normal north/south polarity, but at others the polarity will switch and the north magnetic pole will move to the south and the south to the north. Naturally, any iron-containing minerals that solidify during a period of reversed polarity will themselves take on that reversed polarity. When geologists examined the rock on either side parallel to the mid-ocean ridges, they discovered a very distinctive pattern in the orientation of the magnetic fields in those rocks. Mid-ocean ridges, by the way, like the mid-Atlantic ridge, are enormous structures in the middle of oceans that run north to south for vast distances. When geologists examined the magnetic orientation of seafloor rock on either side of the ridges, they found a remarkable pattern. Successive bands of normal and reverse-polarity rocks to the east of the ridges were exactly matched by a mirror-image pattern in the seafloor to the west of the ridges. That is, the pattern of polarity in rock to the east of the ridge—say, normal, reverse, normal, reverse, normal—is exactly matched by the polarity pattern in the rock to the west of the ridge—normal, reverse, normal, reverse, normal. Further, the relative widths of the bands were virtually the same. Wide bands of normal polarity on one side were matched with wide bands of normal polarity on the other; narrow bands of reversed polarity were matched with narrow bands of reversed polarity in the same relative position on the other side of the ridges. What could possibly explain these very odd and striking findings? When we find an unexpected pattern in nature, we know there has to be a reason for it.

Geologists ultimately concluded that the explanation of the matching bands of magnetized rock on either side of the mid-ocean ridges had to be this: Molten seafloor matter wells up in the mid-ocean ridges and flows to the east and west. As it does so, the older seafloor pushes further away from the mid-ocean ridges. When the new seafloor solidifies, it naturally takes on the polarization of the earth's magnetic field, either normal or reversed, as the case may be at that given time. So the matching bands of rock to the east and to the west of the mid-ocean ridges are really a record of the spreading of the seafloor over geological time. If the seafloor spreads, and the continents move with it, then Wegener could have been right, and the continents could have moved across the earth's surface. Further work developed the theory of plate tectonics, which holds that the rock underlying the earth's crust, the lithosphere, comprises rigid crustal plates that ride atop a deeper, denser, semi-plastic layer in the upper mantle called the asthenosphere. The earth's heat moves the asthenosphere by convection, causing it to well up under the mid-ocean ridges and so push the seafloor apart, making room for new molten seafloor to flow to the surface and solidify. Research also discovered subduction zones, areas where old seafloor is pushed below continental crust. So geologists now had a workable model of how the continents could move, and Wegener's theory was finally vindicated.

How did geologists reach these conclusions about crustal plates, the asthenosphere, mantle convection, and other features and occurrences deep within the earth? Has anyone actually seen deep down inside the earth? No, and almost certainly nobody ever will. The deepest mines only go down a few miles, barely scratching the earth's crust. Geophysicists have techniques and tools for examining the interior of the earth indirectly, but nobody has ever been more than a few miles below the earth's surface. Yet geologists are very confident of these theories; in fact, plate tectonics brought about a true revolution in the earth sciences and is now the central theoretical foundation of geology. How can geologists be so confident that they have inferred the correct explanation when nobody ever has or ever will penetrate into the earth's mantle? The short answer is that the plate tectonics explanation is the best. It is deep (it connects crustal movements to fundamental forces within the earth), it is simple (the model itself is simple although the way things actually work on the earth's surface is complex), it has enormous unifying power (it explains many different sets of facts), and it is the only one that fits everything we know about the earth. In fact, there just is no other viable alternative. Some matching patterns in the magnetization of seafloor rock could be due just to chance, and require no special explanation. But a consistent pattern, occurring repeatedly over time just cannot be a chance occurrence. There has to be some underlying cause, and seafloor spreading from mid-ocean ridges seems to be the only feasible one. Further, *if* the continents move, and there is now little doubt that they do, then plate tectonics seems to be the only reasonable way to provide a physically possible mechanism. As the geologists of Wegener's day noted, lighter continents cannot just plow through dense seafloor basalt. The only feasible answer is that the continents and the seafloor move together since both float on the mobile asthenosphere beneath. IBE is often inference to the *only* explanation that makes sense given everything else that we know.

As I say above, IBE is a common pattern of reasoning in the sciences, so common that it is hard to see how most sciences could function without using it. Yet there are some philosophers who question whether such inferences are reliable in many circumstances. One who has raised skeptical doubts about IBE is Bas van Fraassen, a well-known specialist in the philosophy of science. Van Fraassen does not doubt that IBE is a form of reasoning used in science and in everyday life. He also does not question that in many contexts it does, in fact, provide us with explanations that are not only plausible, but probable. For instance, if we hear suspicious scratching and pattering in the walls, we use IBE to conclude that we have mice and we go buy some traps. In such everyday contexts, Van Fraassen does not doubt that IBE gives us explanations that are highly likely to be true. After all, we can see mice and observe their habits and propensities. Indeed, our experience of mice and other animals (we know, for instance, that elephants or crocodiles are not likely to be hiding in the walls) puts us in a position to say that mice are the *only* likely cause of the suspicious noises. True, it is conceivable that your neighbor has trained his pet mongoose to climb behind your walls and scurry about just to irritate you. But unless we have reason to think that our neighbor has a trained pet mongoose and would want to irritate us in this strange way, the mouse explanation is far more reasonable, and, surely, is the right one. Van Fraassen has no problem with scientific use of IBE so long as scientists are inferring the sorts of explanations that postulate things we *could* have seen had we been at the right time and place. For instance, when paleontologists infer things about dinosaur behavior from looking at their footprints, Van Fraassen has no objection. *Had* we been there in the late Jurassic, we could have witnessed those behaviors directly.

What Van Fraassen objects to is the use of IBE when it involves hypotheses about things that are, in principle, unobservable. Subatomic particles, for instance, are in principle unobservable. Even if, like the hero of the 1950s science fiction classic *The Incredible Shrinking Man*, we could be shrunk to molecular size, we still could not see protons because they are too tiny to be seen in visible light. Van Fraassen objects that when our explanations start talking about putative entities that cannot, in principle, be observed, we cannot have any confidence that the explanatory hypotheses we have *thought* of are the only ones likely to be true. So in using IBE to select from the explanatory hypotheses that have occurred to us, we might only be choosing the best of a bad lot. Again, when we are talking about things we can or could have seen, we might have confidence that the set of available hypotheses constitutes a good lot, that is, that the correct explanation is probably one of these. When, for instance, we see a set of footprints that have been made by two different dinosaurs, we can infer that the dinosaurs were interacting in some way, and our background knowledge of animals and their interspecific behaviors limits the number of ways they could have been interacting. If we find parallel tracks from a sauropod (plant eater) and a theropod (meat eater), we can say with some confidence that one was likely pursuing the other with the intention of predation. But when we are hypothesizing things that we never can see, things we cannot have experienced, what confidence can we have that the *true* explanation is among the ones we just *happen* to have thought of? How do we have confidence that *all* of our candidate explanations are not just figments of our imagination? If we cannot have such confidence, then we can only use IBE to select the best from among the explanatory hypotheses that happen to have occurred to us, and we could have no confidence that the one we select is probably true.

Therefore, Van Fraassen thinks that IBE is not a reliable guide to probable truth when our explanations postulate unobservables. So do electrons exist? Van Fraassen does not question that explanations postulating electrons have been enormously successful, and that such explanations have, in the history of physics, fairly won out over all rivals. But the success of electron theory, Van Fraassen says, is evidence that explanations in terms of electrons are empirically adequate, not that they are true. By saying that a theory is "empirically adequate," Van Fraassen means that the theory's predictions, what it implies about the real world, are consistent with known data, and that will continue to be so in the future. But a false theory can make true predictions, and could, conceivably, continue to do so forever. Van Fraassen therefore holds that all of the things (like the picture on a TV screen) explained in terms of electrons and their properties could, in reality, be due to something else we never will think of. Since we cannot see electrons, or have any experience of them other than through their alleged effects, he thinks that we cannot be confident that electron theory, however successfully it explains electrical phenomena, is the *true* story. He argues that the only way we could have such confidence is if we could know that the human mind has some sort of privileged access, that is, that the mind is so constructed that when it conceives of a set of possible explanations these imagined explanations probably encompass the *true* explanation. But how could we possibly argue that? Can we say that something or someone, evolution, maybe, or God, designed the human mind so that it is likely to light on true explanatory hypotheses?

Philosophers of science who oppose Van Fraassen are called "realists." They believe that electrons and other subatomic particles really exist, and that IBE is a reliable form of reasoning, even when it comes to unobservable things, like electrons. How should they respond to Van Fraassen's challenge? Probably it would be best not to take the bait and attempt to show that the human mind has some sort of privileged access, some sort of prior inkling about true explanations. In fact, it seems very unlikely that our minds do possess such an aptitude. However, might there not be *scientific* reasons for thinking that the truth probably lies within a certain range of candidate explanations, even explanations postulating unobservables? Consider the reason that astrophysicists give for explaining some puzzling phenomena in terms of something truly bizarre—black holes. A black hole is, by definition, unobservable. It cannot be seen because its gravitational field is so intense that not even light can escape its fatal clasp. We cannot see nor in any way detect the black hole itself; indeed, the "event horizon" surrounding a black hole represents the limit beyond which no information can be extracted. Why, then, do astrophysicists place so much confidence in explanations postulating black holes, the ultimate unobservables? Let's look at their reasons.

Cygnus, the Swan, is a magnificent constellation that is due overhead in early evenings in late summer. From a point within this constellation astronomers noticed a prodigious outpouring of x-ray energy, 10,000 times that of the total energy output of the sun. They called the site Cygnus X-1 (scientific creativity does not extend to inventing fancy names). Telescopic observations revealed a supergiant star in a binary system (two objects in orbit about a shared center of mass) with an invisible companion. Using tested and reliable techniques, astronomers concluded that the unseen companion had to have a mass of at least 3.4 times the mass of the sun. What could it be?

When stars die, they have only three possible fates, say astrophysicists, and the fate of a star is determined by its mass. Medium to low mass stars, like our sun, will first pass through a red giant stage, and then shed their outer layers into interstellar space. The star's remnant will then shrink to form a white dwarf, an ultradense, ultrahot body that squeezes vast amounts of matter into a sphere about the size of the earth. Larger mass stars suffer an even more bizarre fate. First they go supernova; they die in a cataclysmic explosion so powerful that observers can detect them even when they occur in very distant galaxies. The supernova explosion leaves behind a stellar remnant, and if this remnant is between about 1.4 and 3 solar masses, it will collapse into an extremely bizarre object called a neutron star. A neutron star has an inconceivable density of a hundred million metric tons per cubic centimeter. A neutron star spins very rapidly, up to hundreds of times a second, and this rotation generates a magnetic field a trillion of times stronger than the earth's. These ultrastrong magnetic fields generate intense beams of microwaves that rotate with the star. When one of these beams sweeps past an earthly observer, it is seen as a very brief microwave pulse, and so rapidly spinning neutron stars are known as "pulsars." Stars that go supernova and leave a remnant of greater than 3 solar masses experience the strangest fate of all. Such stellar remnants undergo infinite collapse. They shrink to an infinitesimal point of literally infinite density and where the structure of spacetime itself is infinitely distorted. When physical values become infinite, the laws of physics no longer apply, and physicists call such a situation a "singularity." The "event horizon" we mentioned earlier surrounds the singularity and marks an absolute boundary around it. Nothing, not even light, can escape once it passes the event horizon; it is captive forever, and hence we say that it has fallen into a black hole.

How do we know all this? How can we say that such bizarre events actually take place when we are not, and never will be, in a position to observe them? The short answer is that this is what *has* to happen. We know that these things happen, not because we have privileged access, but because what we know about matter and the forces of nature tells us that this is what has to happen. We know enough about matter and its properties to say what will happen when it is subjected to extreme gravitational compression. Some of our most basic and best-established theories, like the theory of general relativity, tell us what will happen to matter in extreme gravitational fields. So when astrophysicists infer that the invisible companion of the visible star in Cygnus X-1 is a black hole, they say this because, so far as they can tell, it just cannot be anything else. It cannot be a white dwarf or a neutron star. Our best theories tell us that matter cannot take these forms if the gravitational field is too intense, and that infinite collapse is the only alternative. Of course, we could be wrong. Even our best theories could be wrong; this is a truism that everybody admits. Science cannot give us absolute certainties. Van Fraassen and other skeptics of IBE have to be saying more than merely repeating such a truism. They have to deny that we can ever have legitimate scientific grounds for inferring the probable truth of explanations that postulate unobservable things or events. But the black hole case appears to indicate that we sometimes can.

The upshot is that IBE seems to be a reliable form of reasoning, one that leads us to explanations that are probably true, even sometimes when those explanations postulate things that we cannot observe. IBE has other opponents. Some followers of the Bayesian approach to the confirmation of hypotheses, the approach we studied in chapter 8, say that Bayes's theorem provides the correct model of the reasoning we use to confirm explanatory hypotheses, not IBE. Recall that in the Bayesian model we begin with hypotheses that are quite improbable according to our background knowledge. We then discover evidence that is highly likely given that hypothesis, but highly unlikely given any other hypothesis. If we get enough such evidence we can revise our subjective probability assessments to the point that hypotheses that initially looked very implausible now can appear highly probable. Defenders of IBE claim that it is a more realistic model of the way that we reason about explanatory hypotheses in science and in everyday life. They argue that scientists do not actually make assessments of subjective probability in the light of new evidence but do frequently weigh alternative explanatory hypotheses in the light of their criteria for good explanations. These debates are far too technical and detailed to enter into here. It seems to me that humans at different times spontaneously use Bayesian-style reasoning, perhaps even unconsciously, and at other times employ IBE. My suspicion is that it is a matter of "both/and" rather than "either/or" when it comes to our thinking about explanatory hypotheses.

SUGGESTIONS FOR FURTHER READING

The book on inference to the best explanation is Peter Lipton's *Inference to the Best Explanation* (London: Routledge, 1991). Some call it a classic of the philosophy of science. It is very good, but may be too technical for beginners. Certainly too technical for novices are the works of Bas van Fraassen, one of the leading philosophers of science in the world today. He develops his pragmatist view of explanations in his *The Scientific Image* (Oxford: Clarendon Press, 1980). A very clear and useful exposition of Van Fraassen's pragmatist position, as well as the various theories of explanation, is found in Karel Lambert and Gordon G. Brittan Jr.'s *An Introduction to the Philosophy of Science*, 4th ed. (Atascadero, CA: Ridgeview, 1992). Van Fraassen's critique of inference to the best explanation is in his *Laws and Symmetry* (Oxford: Clarendon Press, 1989). For an elementary exposition of Van Fraassen's critique and a defense of IBE against those criticisms, see my book *Copernican Questions: A Concise Invitation to the Philosophy of Science* (Boston: McGraw-Hill, 2006), which goes into somewhat more detail than does this chapter. An authoritative account of the revolution in geology leading to plate tectonics is A. Hallam's *A Revolution in the Earth Sciences: From Continental Drift to Plate Tectonics* (Oxford: Clarendon Press, 1973).

Chapter Twelve

RHETORIC: THE ART OF PERSUASION

I mentioned Aristotle (384–322 BCE) at the beginning of chapter 5 as the founder of formal logic. Being the universal genius that he was, and having the good luck to have lived near the beginning of the Western intellectual tradition, he founded a number of other fields of study also. Aristotle was a pioneer in the study of **rhetoric**. In fact, his book *Rhetoric* was the first systematic study of the subject. What is rhetoric? In Aristotle's day, rhetoric was chiefly the art of orators, public speakers who sought to present the most persuasive case before a given audience. We may define "rhetoric" more broadly as the art of persuading or motivating people through the effective use of spoken or written communication. Of course, we have many ways of communicating other than by the explicit use of language. We can glare, scowl, wink, sigh, roll our eyes, or "give someone the finger." These nonverbal forms of communication are very important and no doubt often effective persuaders or motivators—they might even have their own "rhetoric"—but in order to maintain a manageable focus we shall restrict attention to explicitly written or spoken communication.

These days the term "rhetoric" often carries a bad odor and is spoken of disparagingly in the sense of "mere rhetoric," that is, deceptive or misleading language that uses various tricks to fool people into accepting dubious claims. As we shall see in the fourteenth chapter, when rhetorical techniques are used to deceive or manipulate people, we now call these tricks "spin." Aristotle did not see all rhetoric as deceptive and manipulative spin, and neither do I. Of course, there are many dishonest ways of persuading people, and we shall examine some of these in subsequent chapters. But rhetoric need not have such negative connotations.

Two arguments can be equally honest and equally worthy from a logical point of view, but when presented to the same audience one is a hit and the other bombs. Why? Because one was presented with rhetorical skill and the other was not. If you are interested not only in proving your point but in actually persuading people, then you have to be interested not just in *what* you say but in *how* you say it.

For Aristotle, rhetoric is an essential part of the art of governing. It is easy to see why he says this, since all good politicians need to be proficient at rhetoric, and the greatest statesmen have been masters of rhetorical skill. Think of Winston Churchill's magnificent oratory during the Battle of Britain, when Britain stood alone against the Axis, or Lincoln's "Gettysburg Address" delivered at the height of the Civil War. When a country is facing a life-or-death struggle, great words can have transcendent value. Unfortunately, politicians far more often use rhetoric for less noble or inspiring purposes. Politicians frequently have to defend themselves before the public, and they can't afford to look too obviously stupid, callous, or deceitful on *Meet the Press*, no matter how stupid, callous, and deceitful their policies actually are. Politicians who fail to master rhetorical skills, and who come across as inarticulate, dimwitted, or duplicitous, will find themselves the butt of ridicule on the late-night talk shows and their approval ratings will drop to the nether regions.

But politicians are not the only ones who need rhetoric. We humans are social creatures. We are also incredibly fractious, opinionated, obstinate, and contentious creatures. Anybody who has to work with (or against) other humans to get things done will need skill in persuasion. For instance, reformers and activists have got to be good at rebutting hostile critics, inspiring followers, encouraging the wavering, and motivating the apathetic. Why was Martin Luther King Jr. seen as the preeminent leader of the civil rights movement in the 1950s and 1960s? Much of the reason for his prominence, then and now, has to be due to his great rhetorical skill, both as a speaker and as a writer. If you listen to his "I have a dream" speech delivered at the Washington Monument in August 1963 or his "I have seen the Promised Land" speech given in Memphis in 1968 on the night before his assassination, you can still feel the thrill of inspiration. King's "Letter from the Birmingham Jail" eloquently answers critics who challenged his tactics of civil disobedience.

Who else needs rhetoric? Trial lawyers, obviously, and preachers, too (the rhetoric of delivering effective sermons is called "homiletics" in seminary), and it certainly does not hurt for educators to be rhetorically adept. A teacher who has the unenviable burden of explaining, say, tariffs, or covalent bonds, or the subjunctive mood, is also trying to convince an audience, in this case to convince largely unmotivated and distracted students to give a damn. Any administrator, planner, boss, or bureaucrat needs rhetoric. No matter how much authority you have, saying "Do it because I said so" has limited motivational traction. Persuading people to *want* to do what you want them to is much more effective—and they won't hate you while doing it. Scientists, social scientists, doctors, and engineers need rhetoric too because just having good evidence often is not enough. Many good ideas, and even major discoveries, have languished because they were not effectively presented.

Every human being who is not a hermit will often have to convince at least one other person to believe or do something. So just about everyone really could use some skill at persuading and motivating people. But isn't there, after all, something a little bit sleazy about persuading people with anything other than cold facts and clear reasoning? Doesn't rhetoric have at least a mildly foul odor? Couldn't you just stick to provable points, presented in a detached and dispassionate way, and thereby avoid tainting your logic with irrelevant emotion and personal feeling? Shouldn't this be the ideal we strive for, to present evidence and argument in a disinterested and objective manner that avoids any rhetorical posturing or grandstanding? The articles in a professional scientific journal, for instance, are composed in accordance with rigorous stylistic standards that are designed to exclude feeling and put the evidence foremost. Take a look at any article in the leading science journal *Nature*, for instance, and you will find only data, analysis, and interpretation, presented in a stark, clipped, unadorned style devoid of expressions of personal preference or feeling. But this does not mean that there is no rhetoric of scientific writing. On the contrary, there is just as much an art of effective scientific writing as there is of any sort of writing. The rhetorical minimalism of scientific writing *is* the accepted rhetorical style of scientific communications, and part of learning to be a working scientist is learning to write in that style.

The stark style of professional scientific journals is entirely appropriate for that medium. Scientists dismiss "hand wavers" who try to sway colleagues by dramatics rather than the straightforward presentation of evidence and argument. Why not adopt this scientific style in all of our communication? Why not always do as 1960s TV detective Joe Friday used to admonish—stick to "just the facts, ma'am"? The problem is that with just about any issue there are two entirely distinct questions we can ask: (1) "What is the truth about that issue?" and (2) "Why should I care?" Put another way, it is one thing to show that something is so and another to get people to *listen* to why it is so or *care* whether it is or not. Often the impetus of facts is insufficient to overcome the sheer inertia of settled opinion. People are rational, but, as the subtitle of this book hints, only intermittently so. Rhetoric, in its best form, is the art of motivating people to be reasonable.

How do we apply this additional motive force without resorting to grandstanding, hand waving, manipulation, or deception? The art of rhetoric does not consist in learning tricks that *substitute for* evidence and reasoning but in employing the most effective *means* of presenting the rational argument and supporting evidence to a given audience. How do we discover those means? You will need to know four things: You must (1) know yourself, (2) know your subject, (3) know your opponent, and (4) know your audience.

KNOW YOURSELF

"Know Thyself" was the advice of the Oracle of Delphi 2,500 years ago, and it still holds good today. Knowing yourself is the hardest of the four things you have to know to be good at rhetoric. Are you angry and bitter? Are you given to self-pity or self-righteousness? Are you condescending or arrogant? When speaking or writing you are, among other things, projecting your inner self, your personality, and you are projecting it on a big screen for people to see. Your charm, wit, learning, and intelligence will be on display, but so also will be your fears, hatreds, and prejudices. You can easily lose an audience if you come across as hostile, smug, or pompous. On the other hand, if you try too hard to ingratiate yourself to an audience by adopting an overly friendly and familiar tone, they will regard you as patronizing and glib.

Suppose, then, that you are brutally candid with yourself and admit, let's say, that you are bitter and angry or smug and self-righteous. What should you do about it? Well, it depends. Eloquently expressed bitterness and anger can be a big hit with people who are similarly bitter and angry. Many of the most popular radio pundits are mad as hell, and their legions of listeners love them for it. The listeners share the pundits' bitter resentment against "bleeding heart" liberals, "ivory tower" academics, "tree hugging" environmentalists, "activist" judges, "liberal news media," "big government," "illegal aliens," and so on. Self-righteousness also has an audience of millions. Look at how many people tune in to the radio personality who has made a career out of humiliating callers and telling people how good she is and how sinful they are. Even sheer paranoia has great appeal to an audience of paranoiacs. Listen to some of the late-night radio shows and you will hear that the world is run by a cabal of Freemasons, Jewish bankers, Illuminati, and members of the Tri-Lateral Commission. So you can turn your personal foibles into rhetorical strengths by making sure that you always preach to the choir.

However, most of us do not have the luxury of always addressing people who share our worldviews, attitudes, biases, or obsessions. It's a diverse world, and we often have to communicate with people, on our jobs or in our communities, who do not share our perspectives or predilections. What should you do if you are pretty sure that your personality and opinions will clash with a given audience? Face it: barring mental illness, or severe head injury, and especially if you are over forty, your basic personality and outlook are unlikely to change radically. What can you do if you find yourself in a situation where you know that you and your audience are likely to clash?

One of the most important and least appreciated rhetorical skills is to know when to shut up. There are plenty of situations in which just about anything you say will make things worse, and the best course is to say nothing. In general, if you feel too strongly about a subject to be calm and reasonable about it, it is usually best to refrain from comment. Over the years I have occasionally gotten essays from students written on topics that they felt so strongly about that they were unable to articulate a coherent and logical argument. This puts me in a no-win situation. When I give these rants the bad grades they deserve, I just make these students madder and convince them that I am prejudiced against their views. That is why in classes like ethics where you have to deal with controversial subjects I caution students not to write about hot-button topics—abortion, homosexuality, or creationism, for instance—if they are too passionate about that topic to compose a reasonable argument.

Another option, if silence is not feasible, is to use tact, an option hardly ever employed these days. Suppose you are at a meeting on your job where you have to negotiate something with the head of another department, someone you think is an idiot. You don't have to actually say or intimate that you think that he or she is an idiot. *Dilbert* is funny because people in that comic actually say to co-workers and bosses the contemptuous, insulting, and brutally frank things that everyone thinks but, in reality, should be left unspoken. The most effective way of dealing with the stupidest idea you ever heard is probably not to announce that it is the stupidest idea you ever heard. Much better would be something like this: "I see your point, Bob, but don't you think that by shutting down our service department we would drive away some of our best and most loyal customers?" Hypocritical? Maybe, but the form of hypocrisy we call "diplomacy" is a necessary tool for cooperation and, indeed, for survival. Henry Kissinger once commented that campus disputes are so vicious because so little is at stake. When it is a matter of life and death, people learn to disagree politely.

Be honest and realistic about your intentions when you speak or write. Are you honestly trying to persuade someone or nudge them toward cooperation . . . or are you just venting? On the other hand, venting sometimes has its uses. There are good and bad ways to express indignation, however. I recently read of an elderly woman whose cable TV company promised on three separate occasions to come by her home to connect the equipment, but each time she waited all day and they never showed up. She gathered up the cable equipment and took it down to the local office of her cable provider and asked to see the manager. She was shown to a bench and told to wait. After sitting three hours, she was informed that the manager had gone home for the day. She went home, returned with a hammer, and proceeded to smash up the cable company's office until the police led her away in handcuffs. Bully for her! However, though her anger was entirely appropriate, perhaps it was not expressed in the most effective way. In *Ethics*, Aristotle says that the virtuous person expresses anger on the appropriate occasion, for the right reason, in a reasonable degree, and toward the right person. Anger expressed calmly and rationally, as Aristotle recommends, is usually much more effective as a tool of persuasion than when expressed with a hammer.

In summary, then, you have to be diplomatic in dealing with others, but you need to be brutally honest with yourself. Should you speak or shut up in a given situation? Honestly ask yourself whether you can say anything that will not just make things worse. On many occasions, if you cannot bring yourself to be diplomatic and tactful, a discreet silence may be best. When you do choose to speak, ask yourself frankly what kind of effect you want to achieve and how likely you are to achieve it. Be honest with yourself about what your goals are. Don't pretend that you are trying to get someone's cooperation, agreement, or goodwill when you insult or belittle them (even if they deserve insulting or belittling). If you are too passionately committed to an opinion to defend it calmly and rationally, then you probably should stay quiet. If you are angry, ask yourself whether you can express your anger in a way that will get people to help or only make things harder for you.

KNOW YOUR SUBJECT

You could read this and a dozen other logic books and still not be an effective persuader. Logic only tells you *how* to present a reasonable case; it does not guarantee that you know what you are talking about. Unless you are preaching only to the very gullible or the willfully deceived, you had better know your stuff. Of course, everyone hears about fast-talking con men who can make you think that they are experts on something, and even fool a lot of people for a while, before their cover is inevitably blown. Some slick talkers have passed themselves off as doctors, lawyers, secret agents, or billionaires. However, as Lincoln observed, you cannot fool everybody all the time, and someone will eventually blow your cover. The basic point, then, is that if you want to make your case, you need to do your homework.

Genuine expertise in any field is hard to come by. Many of the issues of greatest interest turn on technical points that few people really understand, and those who do understand them have often spent many years in the effort. Don't despair! You do not have to know as much biology as E. O. Wilson or as much physics as Stephen Weinberg or as much history as Norman Davies to have intelligent and well-informed opinions. But there is no substitute for doing the hard work of informing yourself. If you are not an expert, learn what the experts are saying, not just the ones who agree with you, but the ones on the other side. There is a saying, attributed to George Bernard Shaw, that goes "Those who are down on something usually are not up on it." That is exactly right. People are quick to condemn things that they do not understand. There is all the difference in the world between an ignorant rant and an informed critique. Unfortunately, knowing next to nothing about a subject seldom prevents people from aggressively grinding their axes. They assume that other people are just as poorly informed as they are, and will lack the knowledge to rebut their confidently asserted claptrap. All too often that assumption is correct. If you know your subject, though, you can deal with people like that.

One of life's more satisfying experiences is to see an arrogant, ignorant blowhard deflated by somebody who really knows what he or she is talking about. I am an avid reader of the "letters to the editor" section of the local paper. These letters are often far more stimulating than the essays of the syndicated columnists. Often a person will write a letter expressing a strong opinion on a complex issue that he or she knows little about. For instance, I recently read one, clearly written to cast doubt on scientific findings about human-caused global warming, stating that the global temperature of Mars is steadily rising and that its polar ice caps are disappearing. Gosh. I didn't know that, and I bet most other readers didn't either. Well, if Mars is getting warmer without human intervention, then the warming of earth's climate might not be due to human causes either! The letter writer's claims might have stood unchallenged had not another letter appeared in the next day's paper written by a professional planetary scientist who specializes in Martian climatology. The scientist pointed out that Mars's global warming has not been observed for long enough to extrapolate long-range trends. Also, the short-term warming is related to unique conditions of the Martian environment, such as the intensity of hemispheric dust storms. So the claimed analogy between Mars's global warming and Earth's simply collapses when examined from a standpoint of knowledge rather than ignorance.

Unfortunately, the current intellectual environment is polluted with slick nonsense packaged to look legitimate. Why? Because there are many powerful economic and ideological motivations to obscure the truth and to stymie the spread of accurate information. Recall the tobacco company executives who stood before Congress a few years back and, to a man, testified that they did not regard cigarettes as addictive (the video is probably on YouTube). The tobacco industry fought a long, bitter rearguard action against the findings of medical researchers about the carcinogenic and other harmful effects of cigarettes. For years they conducted their own in-house research trying, unsuccessfully, to rebut the claims of the scientific community. What do you do when you are making profits beyond the dreams of avarice by selling a noxious and addictive product that, science shows, kills many thousands of people each year? You deny the science.

Ideologues, those who zealously defend rigid doctrinal systems, are also highly effective obscurantists. It doesn't matter whether the ideologues are, for instance, fundamentalists or feminists; they excel at promoting self-serving falsehoods. For years I would occasionally hear or read the story that NASA scientists supposedly were performing a calculation of planetary orbits and discovered that an entire day was missing from the time that should have elapsed over the last several thousand years. It turned out, so the story goes, that the missing time could be explained by the Lord commanding the sun to stand still in the book of Joshua so that Joshua and the Israelites could have enough daylight to kill more enemies. What a marvelous scientific demonstration of the truth of scripture! The only problem is that NASA never discovered any such "missing day." Careful investigation showed the whole "missing day" story to be a baseless fiction mindlessly repeated in fundamentalist tracts. Then there was the story spread by a number of feminist activists, and widely repeated in the media, that on Super Bowl Sunday the incidence of domestic violence rises alarmingly. According to the story, football-loving macho guys, primed with beer and testosterone, get so pumped by the glorified violence of the Super Bowl game that they take it out on their wives and girlfriends. Men! Again, however, careful research failed to turn up any basis for this canard, but the fact that the story was baseless did not prevent it from being eagerly repeated by those who wanted it to be true.

The moral of the story is that there is a vast amount of misinformation masquerading as the truth. Some of it arises spontaneously in the form of "urban legends" and other rumors and misconceptions that seemingly arise from nowhere. Some of it is intentionally disseminated by those with a vested financial or ideological interest. Logic alone is not enough to combat widespread, entrenched ignorance. Knowledge is the only effective antidote. Only diligent research *and* clear thinking can dispel the fog of obfuscation and obscurantism, but cutting through the haze is often difficult. Politicians and CEOs surround themselves with a retinue of spin doctors, PR men, press secretaries, lobbyists, and lawyers whose job is to make the people who pay their (handsome) salaries look good, or, failing that, to blow so much smoke that it is hard to pin anything bad on them. "Speak truth to power" says the slogan, but the powerful are very good at obscuring the truth. Take a look at the old movie *All the President's Men* about the two *Washington Post* reporters who broke so many of the stories about the Watergate scandal. As the movie shows, ferreting the truth out of all the lies, stonewalling, and deception coming from the Nixon White House took hundreds of hours of determined, diligent, relentless digging. Once disclosed, though, the truth brought down the most powerful man in the world.

KNOW YOUR OPPONENT

It is fun to watch a politician trying to make a speech without saying anything that might offend potential voters. He supports our men and women in uniform. He is for strong families. He loves his wife, kids, and dog. He is for lowering taxes and raising benefits (sometimes in the same breath). He likes baseball, apple pie, motherhood, and the flag. He doesn't like terrorists, crime, or drugs. The reason why the politico's efforts are amusing is that in striving to say something without stepping on anyone's toes he only succeeds in adding some greenhouse gases to the atmosphere. To say anything worth hearing, you have to say something controversial. The simple fact is that, except for the "motherhood" issues beloved by the politicians, if you are for something, then somebody is going to be against it. If you think it is important that people believe X or do Y, there will be somebody just as convinced that X is false or that Y shouldn't be done. The consequence is that when you take a stand for or against something, you are going to have to make your case in the face of opposition—sometimes powerful, well-financed, organized, smart, articulate, and knowledgeable opposition. Not all situations in which you need rhetoric are adversarial; sometimes you are merely speaking to an audience that may be neutral or friendly toward you. But if you take a stand on a hot issue, expect controversy.

There is nothing wrong with controversy. On the contrary, it is the lifeblood of free societies and free inquiry. Free and open societies are always contentious; closed societies silence dissent with guns and gulags. Also, every intellectual inquiry is rife with controversy. Scientists argue all the time and a scientific meeting often is an intellectual brawl. Most new ideas are bad, even the ones that sound plausible and are supported by the big names in a field. Argument is the crucible in which ideas get tested, so only by arguing things out can we see which ideas are really worthwhile, that is, which ones survive the most determined attempts to prove them wrong. The few ideas that survive this rigorous culling are the ones we finally dignify with the name "knowledge." So to make a contribution in any field, you have to be able to confront opponents who are going to do their best to prove you wrong and could not care less about how you feel about it.

One good thing about debates in scientific or academic communities is that, though the debates sometimes get heated, the disputants usually fight fairly. That is, opposing sides are straightforward in the presentation of their data and evidence and usually do not intentionally resort to fallacy or fraud. Scientists and academics disagree, sometimes vehemently, but outright cheating is rare, if only because scientific and academic communities punish such behavior severely. When debating in a scientific or academic context, you might encounter an opponent who is egotistical, obnoxious, belligerent, and rude, but generally not one who is simply dishonest.

Unfortunately, this generalization does not hold in many other cases. Sometimes when two people debate an issue, one takes the high road—scrupulously sticking to established facts, good science, and sound argument—while the other party takes the low road—slinging mud, presenting bad science as good (see chapter 15), and arguing fallaciously (see the next chapter) if not outright lying. When a high-roader debates a low-roader, which one wins? You guessed it. The low-roader can dump so much mud and blow so much smoke that the high-roader has no chance. What's the answer? Should you forget logic and evidence and fight just as dirty as your opponent? No, what you do is to refuse to play the low-roader's game. Don't play into the low-roader's hands by going on the defensive and trying to dig your way out of the mud or blow away the smoke. He can dump more mud and blow more smoke than you can clear away. Call your opponent's bluff. Make his dirty tricks the focus of your argument. Expose his dishonest tactics for all to see. For instance, suppose you are arguing that we should not support a president who misled the country into an unnecessary, preemptive war. Your opponent responds by charging that you are "unpatriotic" and "not supporting the troops." Don't get defensive. Point out precisely what your opponent is doing—trying to stifle legitimate disagreement by hitting you with a bogus accusation rather than by addressing your substantial points.

The point is that you need to know your opponent. You need to know if you face a fair fight or an attempted mugging. If your opponent has a reputation for using dirty tricks, be ready for them. If your opponent has a track record of previous public debates or publications, you need to research these so you will have a very good idea what your opponent is going to say. Know your opponent's talking points ahead of time and have incisive responses prepared. In any such encounter, the old saw holds: forewarned is forearmed.

Another big mistake to avoid is underestimating your opponent. I have followed the debates between evolutionists and creationists for many years, and even participated in a couple of them. Early on, before evolutionist debaters wised up, they nearly always lost. One reason why was that they consistently underestimated the creationists. They apparently assumed that anyone who defends creationism must be a barefoot, Bible-thumping, banjo-strumming yahoo. They were unpleasantly surprised by an opponent who was urbane, smart, articulate, poised, and prepared. I have seen big-name philosophers, scientists, and scholars come off badly in debates because they had not bothered to see what they were up against by familiarizing themselves with their opponents and their opponents' arguments.

KNOW YOUR AUDIENCE

An audience is fickle. They might come to tar and feather you and wind up cheering. Or vice versa. Whether you are participating in a formal debate before a live or broadcast audience, speaking at a meeting of colleagues or coworkers, writing a letter to the local paper, or making comments at your district's school board or town council, you have got to remember that you have an audience, and you have to think carefully about how you will come across to them. You have to form as accurate an idea as you can of the kind of audience you will have and tailor your presentation accordingly. Also, remember—and this is crucial—an audience is not just a collection of individuals. People in a group often behave differently, sometimes better and sometimes much worse, than they would if they were on their own. "Group dynamics" or, in the vernacular, "mob psychology" is a fascinating study. Groups really do have their own personalities, which is more than the sum of the personalities of the individual members. Stand-up comics know that the same routine can have one audience in stitches but leave another one petulantly unamused. Nothing is *guaranteed* to work with a given audience. Even flattery and humor can fail—catastrophically.

Audiences are more than the sum of their individual members, as we say, but, clearly, different kinds of people will form different kinds of audiences. Nobody would give the same kind of talk to fourth graders that they would give to their local AARP group. Obviously, you have to consider an audience's age, education, cultural background, interests, outlook, mood, and so on. Academics tend to be especially bad at tailoring their talks to their audiences. Most scientists, philosophers, and scholars are used to speaking to audiences of their peers, but many are terrible at addressing laypersons. A talk that wows the professional association of philosophers or geophysicists will fall flat before the local Kiwanis or Rotary Club. It is a serious problem when scientists, educators, and scholars can only communicate with their peers and not the broader public. Is it any wonder that people are misinformed about issues like evolution vs. "intelligent design" or global warming or "abstinence only" sex education, when scientists cannot communicate with the public but the self-servers and ideologues can?

I have taught in institutions of higher education for about twenty-five years. A class is an audience. Sometimes while lecturing, the connection will be perfect and communication seems effortless. At other times the students are distracted, uncomprehending, fidgety, or sleepy, and nothing I say seems to work. There are many ways to lose an audience and no magic formula for reaching them. The main thing you have to remember about an audience is that they are *people* like you, and the best rule for dealing with an audience is the same as the best rule for dealing with individuals: Treat people the way that you would want to be treated. I remember professors who were condescending and arrogant and who answered honest questions with contempt. Others were self-indulgent and indifferent and clearly did not care about students. I once had a professor (in a logic course!) who would occasionally ask for questions. When I would ask, he would go through a routine: he would give me a dirty look, look down at the floor, give me another dirty look, and then rephrase my intelligent question as a stupid question and answer the stupid question. I didn't like being treated like that, and I try not to treat my students that way.

Sometimes, through no fault of your own, you will get a hostile audience. I have experienced hostile audiences. I once took the "No" position in a debate on the question "Is Christianity True?" My opponent was a leading Christian philosopher and apologist, and the debate was held at a Dallas-area mega-church. Of the 4,500 people in attendance, about 4,450 supported my opponent's position. Rather than patronize the audience, I began by telling them candidly that I would argue vigorously for views they would likely find disagreeable and reminding them that by attending such an event they have signaled their willingness to have their beliefs challenged. While I was scrupulous not to call names or engage in mockery, I did not pull any punches. In interacting with members of the audience after the debate, a few were still confrontational, hinting that I had a future in a region warmer even than Dallas, but most seemed at least willing to regard my arguments as honest and reasonable. I considered that a victory. It is unlikely that you will win over all members of a hostile audience, but by expressing your views politely but forthrightly, and thereby showing respect for your audience's intelligence and judgment, most will return the favor to you.

IN CONCLUSION

Of course, there are many other aspects of rhetoric than I have mentioned in this chapter. I cannot teach eloquence, and I am not sure it can be taught; it seems to be a natural gift. Also some people are just better at "thinking on their feet" than others. Like playing tennis or the piano, persuasive communication is a skill some people have more talent for than others. But the basic guidelines I have given here are essential to developing that skill. Remember, your basic aim in rhetoric is to motivate people to be reasonable, and to do that effectively you have to know who you are, what you are talking about, who your opponents are, and who your audience is.

SUGGESTIONS FOR FURTHER READING:

If you are interested in rhetoric, you should at least read the material from Aristotle's *Rhetoric* in a good book of selections, such as *Aristotle: Selections*, translated with introduction, notes, and glossary by Terence Irwin and Gail Fine (Indianapolis: Hackett, 1995). An excellent study of Aristotle's rhetoric is *Aristotle on Political Reasoning* by Larry Arnhart (DeKalb: Northern Illinois University Press, 1981). A classic textbook on rhetoric and informal reasoning is *Logic and Contemporary Rhetoric: The Use of Reason in Everyday Life* (Belmont, CA: Wadsworth, 2006) by the late Howard Kahane and Nancy M. Cavender. This is an update of a book first published by Kahane in 1971. Kahane was a superb expositor of both informal and formal logic. This book is engaging and highly informative.

Chapter Thirteen

WON'T GET FOOLED AGAIN

(Fallacies and Other Foibles)

Why is it so hard to think rationally? We can all do so occasionally, and even be rational pretty consistently in some types of situations. Consider auto mechanics. Suppose your car is exhibiting strange symptoms: There is an unidentifiable knocking sound coming from your engine, or it is overheating, or maybe the "check engine" icon is lighting up. When you take your car in for servicing, your mechanic performs a diagnostic on the car not unlike the diagnostic procedures followed by medical doctors. Tests are run, results are evaluated, competing hypotheses are compared in the light of the available data, and finally a diagnosis is made and treatment is prescribed. A good mechanic follows impeccable scientific procedure, procedure no different in principle than that followed around the world in leading laboratories. The same thing goes for a good plumber or computer technician. When finding the source of a leak or the cause of a computer glitch, a competent worker follows eminently rational procedures to identify the problem, assess likely causes, weigh hypotheses, test predictions, and finally arrive at the solution indicated by the evidence.

Now here is an interesting problem: Why is it that someone can think with impeccable scientific logic about auto engines but, when it comes to other issues, that same person can gullibly swallow the most outrageous pseudoscience rather than face the scientific evidence? For instance, numerous polls show that many Americans—including, no doubt, many top-notch auto mechanics—are staunch supporters of fundamentalist "young earth" creationism that rejects geology and evolutionary science while accepting as literal, scientific truth the biblical creation story. The reason is obvious: Nobody, not even your auto mechanic, is likely to have any deep, personal feelings at stake in diagnosing your car troubles. It is easy to be dispassionate and objective about alternators and fuel injectors. Not so with topics like evolution vs. creationism, which ride on deep and powerful emotions. When issues evoke strong emotions, rationality is in danger. This is why it is so hard to think rationally about politics or religion.

Now, emotion is not always the enemy of reason. On the contrary, all great thinkers have been passionate about their theories. An emotionless Mr. Spock would be a third-rate scientist at best. Creativity—and great scientists are as creative as any artist or composer—requires deep inspiration and passionate commitment. Much of what we now accept as scientific knowledge began as a hunch a or gut feeling. Sometimes scientific insights come with an overwhelming sense of epiphany. Now hunches, gut feelings, and epiphanies are far more often wrong than right, but the point is that the ones that turned out right started off as feeling, not fact. So if you get rid of feeling, you get rid of creativity and insight.

The problem is that sometimes our emotions get the better of us, and we feel so strongly about something that it derails our thinking process. Consider the following propositions (which I offer as examples of inflammatory utterance, not because I necessarily personally endorse any of them):

(1) Liberalism is a mental disease.
(2) Rush Limbaugh is a big, fat idiot, and the people who listen to him are even bigger dopes.
(3) We should invade Islamic countries, kill their leaders, and convert the people to Christianity.
(4) "Pro-life" people think that life begins at conception—and ends at birth.
(5) Environmentalists are just a bunch of wacko tree-huggers.
(6) Evangelical Christians are ignorant, sexist, homophobic hypocrites.
(7) Feminists want women to leave their husbands and children and become lesbians and witches.

Now most people will be aroused by one or more of these propositions, and anyone voicing such an opinion in a mixed group of people would almost certainly soon have a heated argument going. In fact, anyone who makes an assertion like any of those listed above is probably trying to provoke a fight. Once our emotions, especially anger, get the better of us, rational thinking is impossible.

All you have to do is turn on the television to see the extent to which violent emotion has replaced rational thinking in the public arena. If you watch any of the programs on television where current issues are supposed to be debated, you will find very little rational debate. There will be lots of shrill assertion, character assassination, and mudslinging, combined with plenty of catchphrases and emotionally laden "code" words (see below). There is very little in the way of thoughtful give-and-take, with cogent, careful argument and reasoned rebuttals. On most "public affairs" programs, you don't need logic, just a loud voice and some slick talking points. This is not only a disgraceful situation, but a dangerous one. When people can no longer reason with each other, the only alternative way to settle differences is to fight it out, first with weapons of propaganda, and then with guns. Prior to the Civil War, feelings between the North and the South ran so high that people were no longer able to reason about the issues that divided them.

The problem with trying to think clearly today is not just that our emotions sometimes get the better of us, but that we live in an age where rational thought is under assault as it never has been before. Of course, sophistry, double talk, propaganda, false advertising, and demagoguery have been around since human society began, but now these things have gone high-tech and are broadcast to us by satellite 24/7 on cable TV. We live in a "mediascape," a world of proliferating, vivid, and all but unavoidable electronic images that continually assault our senses and infect our minds. They call it the "Information Age," but that is not right. Really, it should be called the "Age of the High-Tech Hard Sell." The fact of the matter is that there are powerful vested interests that have a great deal at stake in getting you to think a certain way and believe certain things. Advertisers, most obviously, have your thoughts in their target, but so do politicians, pundits, and preachers. Anybody with a product or ideology for sale considers your mind to be prime hunting grounds. They want *you*! But not like Uncle Sam in the famous recruiting poster—they don't want you to serve your country. They want you to buy, buy, buy. And they will resort to just about any tactic to get you to do so.

What we need, then, is some means of self-defense, some way to fight back at those who want to dupe us into buying their beer, political candidate, or religion. Fortunately, unlike getting a black belt in karate, or training to be a Navy SEAL, it is relatively easy to master the self-defense techniques to use against media hype. The thing that makes most of the hard-sell techniques so effective is that they are sneaky. We don't realize what is being done to us while we are being manipulated. Often, all we really need to do is to realize what the shills are trying to do to us, that is, to recognize their tricks and dodges.

One of the oldest and still most effective kinds of trick is the counterfeit argument, the argument that looks like the real article, that is, it impersonates a legitimate argument, but actually it lacks any logical or evidential force. Logicians call these counterfeit arguments "fallacies," and they have made long lists of these. I am not going to offer you anything like an exhaustive list of fallacious arguments (probably an impossible task anyway, since there seem to be endless ways that arguments could go bad), but merely alert you to some of the ones that are the most common and that do the most damage. Also, some logicians have tried to organize all the types of fallacies into categories. I am not going to offer any comprehensive taxonomy of fallacies, since, again, my aim here is just to acquaint you with some of the dirtiest tricks, not get you to memorize lists of fallacies and schemes of categorization. All I shall do by way of classifying fallacies is note that several different kinds of fallacies might turn on the same sort of stratagem. For instance, the first kinds of fallacies we'll look at are what we might call **fallacies of relevance**, because they operate by tricking the listener to focus on considerations that are irrelevant to the conclusion being promoted.

One of the most common fallacies of relevance is the ***ad populum***, or what we might call the "appeal to popular feeling." Humans are social creatures. That just seems to be our nature. Being social creatures, we are strongly motivated to want to belong and not to be left out or ostracized. Everybody can remember junior high school when nothing was more important than to be cool and to be accepted by the other cool kids. The worst fate was to be totally uncool, one of the rabble or "dorks," "dweebs," "geeks," "nerds," and other assorted pariahs, who would be snubbed by the cheerleaders and football players and given wedgies by the bullies. Fortunately, we grow out of junior high, but we never, or hardly ever, reach the point where we are truly indifferent about what other people think of us, or how we stand with our peers. In short, nobody likes to be the weirdo. There is, then, enormous pressure to act like other people act and think the way other people think. Manipulators well understand this aspect of human nature and use it against us. They give us arguments that, either subtly or not so subtly, try to get us to accept or reject some belief, opinion, or idea because, well, you don't want to be a weirdo, do you?

Consider the following argument:

> The most recent and reliable polls show that only about 1.4 percent of the population lists its religious preference as "atheist." Consistently, in excess of 95 percent of Americans indicate that they believe in God. Further, when asked whether they would prefer that a child marry an atheist or a Muslim or a member of another race, far more parents indicated that they would prefer that a child marry a Muslim or a member of another race than an atheist. Atheists therefore constitute a small, despised, and extremist fringe element.

If someone offers this as an argument against atheism, then he or she has committed the *ad populum* fallacy. The popularity or unpopularity of atheism, or any doctrine, is simply irrelevant to the question of whether it is true or whether there are good reasons for accepting it. Even if 100 percent of the population rejected it, atheism could still be true. Whether or not there is a God does not depend upon majority opinion. Further, whether atheism is a reasonable, rational, or well-grounded belief depends on the arguments or evidence that can be offered on its behalf, not the number of its supporters or on people's attitudes toward it. Someone who makes such an argument against atheism is not trying to rationally persuade us, but merely to trick us into rejecting it because lots of people don't like it.

Another common fallacy of relevance is the **ad verecundiam**, the illicit appeal to authority. We all are dependent upon authorities for most of what we know. As individuals, what each of us knows on his or her own authority is vanishingly small. We do not have the time or resources to personally track down and authenticate more than a tiny fraction of what we hold to be true. We would be almost total ignoramuses if we refused to believe anything we heard, but only accepted what we could check out for ourselves. If, for instance, you want to learn something about what current physics believes about the universe, you are going to have to consult some experts. You will need to read a good book by one of the leading writers of popular books on physics, someone like Brian Greene, or Michio Kaku, or Lawrence M. Krauss. These are people with PhDs in physics who have a gift for explaining their abstruse disciplines to laypeople. When you want to know about physics or anything else you don't know much about, you will need to consult with an authority.

When, then, is it wrong to trust an authority? When the "authority" isn't an authority, but merely someone presented as an authority by someone who wants you to believe him or her and buy what he or she is endorsing, whether it is a product or an idea. Consider sports figures hired to endorse underwear. Why should Michael Jordan know any more about underwear than you do? Suppose you are a loyal Fruit of the Loom wearer. Why should you switch brands because Michael Jordan says his brand is the best? Why do people want to be like Mike, right down to the underwear?

Much more serious is the fact that there are many organizations that present themselves as bodies of experts who are serving the public interest by offering objective, impartial, scientific information that bears on important issues. They often have impressively scientific or authoritative sounding names like "National Center for Global Climate Research."[1] It sounds very impressive if someone, a politician or editorial writer, for instance, says something like "Dr. Rufus T. Higginbotham of the National Center for Global Climate Research says that the estimates of the extent of the retreat of the polar ice cap have been greatly exaggerated, thus discrediting a major claim of the global warming alarmists." Sounds like those "global warming alarmists" are a bunch of Chicken Littles, right? But then you check out the National Center for Global Climate Research and find that it is not a scientific body at all— they do no research—but a pressure group that presents skewed statistics, cooked data, discredited theories, and plain disinformation to promote the agenda of narrow special interests (generally big corporations who want to avoid costly and profit-shrinking pollution controls). Dr. Higginbotham, by the way, turns out to be a "Dr." because he is a dentist, and not a PhD climatologist. Here we have a particularly despicable (but all too common) instance of an organization pretending to have scientific authority in order to pursue aims that are the opposite of the goal of science—they seek to obscure truth rather than to discover it.

Actually, it is distressingly easy to produce authoritative-sounding disinformation. All it takes is a wad of cash and a lack of scruples. I have on my office door a *Dilbert* cartoon in which one character is consulting with an organization called "Rent a Weasel." He says that he needs three bitter and unsuccessful scientists and a hundred lazy journalists. He gets them and soon newspaper headlines read: "Scientists say Toddlers Thrive on Pollution."

Another all-too-common fallacy of relevance is the ***ad hominem***, or "to the person" fallacy. This trick works by diverting your attention away from the argument someone is making to the person making the argument. This trick has been around since ancient times. One Roman orator put it this way: "If you cannot defeat a speaker's argument, abuse the speaker." If you watch one of the excruciating "current events" programs on TV, you will see *ad hominem* in action all the time. Don't like what someone is saying? Are they distressingly articulate and logical with the facts at their fingertips? Here's what you do: Say that they are "extremists," "radicals," "wackos," "morons," or "feminazis." Call them old-fashioned, or bigoted, out of touch, crazy, traitors, cowards, infidels, perverts, fat, or unattractive. Besmirch them with guilt-by-association tactics. For instance, if they are defending animal rights, show clips of female activists pulling off their tops in public to protest animal experimentation. Is the opposing candidate a war hero? "Swift boat" him. Is your opponent a noted academic? Imply that college professors are all a bunch of left-wing eggheads with radical ideas who use their classrooms to harangue students with their anti-American and anti-Christian agendas. Is a respected professional woman testifying that your favored Supreme Court nominee sexually harassed her? Call her a slut. And crazy. The possibilities for vilification are limited only by your imagination!

One of the most common forms of *ad hominem* argument is the *tu quoque*. *Tu quoque* is Latin for "you too," or maybe "same to you," or a looser translation would be "So's your old man." When someone accuses you of something, one of the most satisfying kinds of retorts is the *tu quoque*, you reply by accusing them of something just as bad or worse. Now *tu quoque* does have its legitimate uses. It is an excellent way to point out hypocrisy and double standards. For instance, a number of religious writers have taken great umbrage at the rhetoric of some of the recent "angry atheists," such as Richard Dawkins, Christopher Hitchens, and Sam Harris, for making disparaging remarks and adopting a dismissive tone when discussing religion and religious belief. Yet a quick look at the writings of many religious authors shows that they often treat unbelievers with ugly, sometime scurrilous, contempt. As Jesus put it, you should take the beam out of your own eye before you tell your neighbor to take the speck out of his. Now, I wouldn't want to be so puritanical as to deny someone the right to use a really juicy *tu quoque* when the opportunity arises. Still, you have to remember that making an accusation back does not take away the charge made against you. Calling someone else a rascal does not mean that you are not a rascal. Maybe you are both rascals. So it is fallacious to distract people away from a charge against you by making a counter accusation.

Another form of *ad hominem* is the circumstantial *ad hominem*. You commit this fallacy if you try to discredit someone's argument by pointing out that they have a vested interest in the outcome. Now, admittedly, if you find that a group, like the one mentioned a few paragraphs earlier that purports to give scientific information about global warming, in fact is funded by a big oil consortium, this should make you suspicious and prompt you to examine their claims *very* carefully. However, the fact *per se* that someone stands to gain or lose by the outcome of their argument does not make their argument invalid. If it did, there would hardly be any valid arguments, since, to be honest, we have to admit that we have some sort of investment, monetary or emotional, in just about anything we would care enough about to debate. The only people who could make valid arguments would be the ones who did not care whether the debate was settled pro or con, and surely this is silly. So, yes, be an extra vigilant fact and fallacy checker when, for instance, you see someone on TV speaking out for the deregulation of the pharmaceutical industry, and you note that he is a highly paid lobbyist for big pharma, but do not think that on this basis alone you can dismiss what he says. You have to address his arguments and evidence.

Wait a second. Does the ban on *ad hominem* mean that I can't call someone an idiot, even if he really is? Aren't some people really hacks, cheats, hypocrites, liars, fools, bigots, phonies, schemers, con men, or stuffed shirts, and can't we say so when they are? Remember that *ad hominem* is a fallacy when you use it as a *substitute* for rational argument or to distract from someone else's rational argument. If you call somebody an idiot *and* you present a logical argument justifying the use of the epithet, that is, by showing that what the person did or said really was idiotic, then you might justify yourself by saying that you have not only talked the talk, but walked the walk. Really, though, the most effective way to deal with an idiot generally is not to call him one, but to *show*, by logical argument, that he is one, and let the audience figure it out.

A particularly despicable fallacy of relevance is the **ad misericordiam**, the appeal to pity. The thing that makes this fallacy especially unsavory is that it works by manipulating one of the best things about human beings, our ability to feel empathy and compassion for our fellow creatures. Empathy is the pain you feel when you see some fellow creature suffering. The helpless suffering of an injured animal, for instance, is almost unbearable to watch. Unfortunately, there are plenty of parties unscrupulous enough to want to manipulate us with our feelings of pity, empathy, and compassion. Now, there are plenty of horrible things going on in the world, and you do *not* commit the fallacy of *ad misericordiam* if you merely point out that horrible things are happening, such as the genocide in Darfur, and that we should do something about it. Motivating people by pointing out suffering is perfectly legitimate. It is illegitimate when you try to derail someone's rational thought by overwhelming them with pathos. For instance, I've seen commercials on TV that basically imply that you are starving poor children if you do not immediately drop whatever you are doing and call *right now* to pledge support for the Something-or-Other Children's Relief Fund. Nonsense. You should check out any charity before you send a contribution. Lots of so-called charities channel most of the money to the people running the organization and only give negligible amounts to the people they are supposed to be helping. Also, each of us has to decide, and it is a very personal matter that nobody can decide for you, how much and to what causes we can contribute. Even charitable giving requires clear, critical thinking.

Another class of fallacies we might call **fallacies of meaning** because they work by playing upon the ambiguity, vagueness, or connotations of terms. To say that a term is ambiguous is to say that it has two or more meanings. An expression is vague when it has no clear meaning at all. The **connotation** of a term should be distinguished from its **denotation**. The denotation is the "dictionary" definition, the "literal" meaning of the term. The connotation is what we might call the "emotional meaning" of a term because use of that term evokes a certain emotional response. The clearest example of a term's denotative and connotative meanings is illustrated by ethnic or racial slurs. During World War II, Americans generally referred to Japanese as "Japs." "Jap" meant, literally, "person of Japanese ancestry," but the connotation of "Jap" for war-weary Americans was something like "sneaky, little, treacherous bastard." The Japanese had similarly offensive names for Americans, by the way. Less obviously, there are all sorts of **loaded terms** that can be used to illicitly sway the listener to an argument. Consider the following template for an attack ad in an election:

> Senator Smith has pursued a radical agenda while in office. She has opposed every measure to stem the floodtide of illegals pouring into our state; she has worked with extremist groups such as Planned Parenthood to oppose the teaching of abstinence in our schools; she promotes the efforts of far-out environmentalist organizations that want to choke our vital petrochemical industry with excessive regulation; she supports anti-Christian organizations, such as Americans United for Separation of Church and State, who deny our children the right to pray in school. Senator Smith is out of touch with Texas values and Texas voters. Smith: Wrong for Texas.

When you throw around terms like "radical" and "extremist" you will create a negative impression, whether or not the people you call by those names are really radicals or extremists. Of course, there really are radicals and extremists, like the people who want to turn the United States into a fundamentalist Christian theocracy, but consulting with Planned Parenthood doesn't make you an extremist. Talk about a "floodtide of illegals" conjures the image of hordes of *banditos* swarming across the Rio Grande to rob banks and sell drugs. Calling people "far out" and saying that they want to "choke" our industries, and calling organizations "anti-Christian" when they are not (Americans United for Separation of Church and State is headed by a Baptist minister), are clearly ploys to sway people by name-calling and alarmism.

Another underhanded tactic, beloved of advertisers, is the use of **weasel words**. Weasel words are words or phrases that vaguely seem to promise something, but really do not. We have all heard ads like this:

> Save! Save! Save! Come on down to Crazy Larry's and save! Hundreds of items marked down by as much as 70 percent! Do we finance? Yes we do! We will finance at rates as low as 0 percent with zero dollars down! Remember, up to 70 percent off on selected items throughout the store. Prices start at only $200 for a deluxe set! That's right, I'm Larry, and I'm Craaaaazy! Come on down! Crazy Larry's! Just off Highway 59 at the Beltway!

Larry is crazy—like a fox. Saying that items are marked down by "as much as" 70 percent or are "up to" 70 percent off makes it sound like you are in for some great savings at Crazy Larry's. But, of course, "as much as" and "up to" are weaselly expressions, designed to create precisely the impression of immense savings, yet cleverly promising nothing at all. Don't be the least surprised if you get to Crazy Larry's and find nothing at all at 70 percent off. Suppose you find that nothing is marked down more than 10 percent. Was Larry lying when he said that items were marked "up to" 70 percent off and you do not see anything marked down by more than 10 percent? Technically, no; Larry was not lying. Ten percent is on the way "up to" 70 percent. If you insist that Larry must have something that is 70 percent off or he is lying, all he has to do is have one item marked 70 percent off and the rest at only 10 percent off. Also, prices might start at only $200, but you should be so lucky as to find anything in the store at anywhere near that price. The $200 one was sold just before you walked in. Even if Larry is not lying, it is sneaky and deceptive to use phrases that seem to imply big savings, but do not really. As for the financing at rates "as low as" 0 percent, if you try to get the 0 percent financing, you will find that "terms and conditions" apply and you can't get it. You can't complain, though. Larry only said that financing rates are "as low as" 0 percent, not that they *are* 0 percent.

Politicians and pundits, of course, use weasel words too. One of the most common is "possible." How often have we heard things like this?

> If conditions in Iraq continue to stabilize, it is possible that we can bring 20,000 troops home by Christmas.

Well, it's possible, but is it probable? Is it plausible? Is there a finite chance of its occurrence? Lots of things are possible by some stretch of the imagination. It is possible that Godzilla will eat Tokyo tomorrow. It is possible that a sixty-year-old professor of philosophy will win the men's decathlon in the next Summer Olympics. It is possible that your cable TV company will lower its rates and improve its service. All these things are possible, but I wouldn't wait around for them to happen. In fact, saying that something is "possible" commits you to almost nothing at all.

The ways that politicians use vagueness to obscure, mislead, and befuddle have never been better stated than in George Orwell's classic essay "Politics and the English Language." Orwell noted that one way to becloud your meaning, especially when you want to make something sound not nearly as bad as it is, is to use lots of fancy Latin and Greek-derived words and a bombastic style so that you can say horrible things that do not sound horrible. He is worth quoting at length:

> In our time, political speech and writing are largely the defense of the indefensible. Things like the continuance of British rule in India, the Russian purges and deportations [take careful note, Orwell was writing in 1946, when Britain still ruled India and Stalin was the dictator of the Soviet Union.], the dropping of the atom bombs on Japan, can indeed be defended, but only by arguments which are too brutal for most people to face, and which do not square with the professed aims of political parties. Thus, political language has to consist largely of euphemism, question-begging and sheer cloudy vagueness. Defenseless villages are bombarded from the air, the inhabitants are driven out into the countryside, the cattle are machine-gunned, the huts set on fire with incendiary bullets: this is called *pacification*. Millions of peasants are robbed of their farms and sent trudging along roads with

no more than they can carry: this is called *transfer of population* or *rectification of frontiers*. People are imprisoned for years without trial, or shot in the back of the neck, or sent to die of scurvy in Arctic lumber camps: this is called *elimination of undesirable elements*. Such phraseology is needed if one wants to name things without calling up mental images of them. . . . The inflated style is itself a kind of euphemism. A mass of Latin words falls upon the facts like soft snow, blurring the outlines and covering up all the details.[2]

The most horrible things in the world—torture, genocide, oppression—can be made to sound harmless, or even benign, if you know how to talk about them. Though Orwell was writing over sixty years ago, his point is just as valid today. Waterboarding is not torture; it is an "enhanced interrogation technique."

The **fallacy of equivocation** works by switching between ambiguous meanings. Here is an obvious example:

Doctors say you should start the day with a good breakfast, so every morning I have a very good breakfast of waffles, syrup, butter, sausage, and fried eggs.

As Aristotle observed long ago, "Good is predicated in many different ways," meaning that "good" has many different senses. When doctors say that you should have a good breakfast, they mean a healthful breakfast. A high-fat, high-calorie breakfast of waffles, butter, sausage, and eggs may be very good in the sense that you really like it, but it is not good in the sense of being healthful. If you eat breakfast like this every morning then, unless you work as a lumberjack, you probably are hurting your health.

In real-life arguments, equivocations are often much more subtle and harder to spot. You have to be really on your toes to notice them. Because the equivocation is subtle, the argument will sound plausible to people, especially those who want to believe its conclusion. Over the years, I have seen many letters to the editors of local papers that make an argument like this:

The embryo, even in its earliest stage of development, is clearly human. This is a scientific fact. Its cells contain all twenty-three pairs of human chromosomes. The embryo comes from human parents. If allowed to develop normally inside the womb, the embryo grows into a human baby, not a baby giraffe or baby gorilla. The embryo is therefore clearly human, and as human, it enjoys human rights, including the right to life and the right not simply to be used or exploited.

Now, of course, such an embryo *is*, in certain senses, a human embryo. As the argument states, given a normal process of *in utero* development, the embryo will grow into a human baby, not the baby of any other species. Further, its cells contain only human chromosomes. The problem is that the meaning of "human" subtly shifts between the premises and the conclusion. One salient issue in the contentious debates over stem cell research, abortion, and related issues is whether a human embryo is a human being. Human beings, and only human beings, enjoy human rights. To say that an embryo is human is to make a statement about its status as a biological entity; it is to say that some of its biological traits identify it as an embryo of the species *Homo sapiens*. Yet to say that an embryo is a human embryo is not to say that it is a human being, that is, a human person. *Personhood* is a legal, philosophical, and, perhaps, theological concept; there is no biological criterion for determining when an entity achieves personhood. The above argument equivocates between the biological meaning of "human" in the premises and the legal/philosophical/theological meaning in the conclusion.

There are also what we might call the **fallacies of unjustified assumptions**. What these fallacies have in common is that, as the name implies, they turn crucially on an assumption that the arguer had no right to make. The most common example of a fallacy of this sort is **begging the question**. Unfortunately, many ignoramuses on TV have recently been misusing the phrase "beg the question." They use it to indicate that some point being discussed prompts us to raise a question—as when someone says that the budget has to be balanced, and then adds that this "begs the question" of how best to do it. Here is what "begging the question" really means: To beg the question is to assume what you should be proving. You beg the question when you take your conclusion, or something that your opponent will accept only if he *already* accepts your conclusion, and stick it in as one of your premises. The dirty trick here is that by begging the question you sneak a claim you need to prove into the premises, and premises, of course, are supposed to be what everybody already accepts, not what we are supposed to be proving. Here is an obvious example:

Abortion is wrong because the intentional termination of an innocent human life is murder, and murder is wrong, and abortion is the intentional termination of an innocent human life.

Clearly, anybody who disagrees with the conclusion, that abortion is wrong, will disagree with one or more of the premises, either that the intentional termination of innocent human life is always murder or that abortion is in fact the termination of a human life.

Here is a subtler and sneakier instance of begging the question:

Contrary to the bureaucratic mind-set, government regulation of commerce and industry is inevitably detrimental to social justice because free markets, left to themselves, will, in the long run, and despite transient anomalies, always assure that a maximally equitable distribution of goods and services will eventuate.

Huh? Having read the paragraph by Orwell, the contorted, inflated style of this passage should make you suspect that *something* stinks here. Usually, when prose is that tortuous and pretentious, something underhanded is going on. But if you have the patience to figure out what the conclusion is (that government regulation of commerce and industry leads to social injustice), you can see what is wrong. What stinks here is that someone who rejects that conclusion almost surely will also not accept the premise—that free markets will always assure a maximally just distribution of goods and services. After all, whether unregulated markets will deliver an equitable distribution of goods and services, which is what we mean by "social justice," is precisely the question at issue. So the premise given for the conclusion, far from supporting the conclusion, needs to be established just as much as the conclusion. Begging the question is a lazy, sneaky way of trying to fool your opponent into accepting a conclusion that it is your job to prove.

Another way of trying to sneak in an unwarranted assumption is by asking a **loaded question**. A loaded question is a question that is phrased so that however you answer it you will be forced to tacitly accept an unjustified assumption. The classic instance of the loaded question is, "Do you still beat your wife?" Clearly, either a yes or no answer would tacitly concede that the person answering either continues to beat his wife or did so at one time. Another example of a loaded question would be, "Senator, how long do you plan to continue misleading the American people about your voting record?" This question assumes that the senator has been misleading the American people about his voting record, an assumption that the senator is sure to reject. Other instances of loaded questions might be more subtle, as in the following passage:

> Atheist authors wax eloquent in describing the "holy horrors" of persecutions, pogroms, crusades, inquisitions, and witch hunts perpetrated in the name of religion. They are notably reticent, however, when it comes to considering the good that religion has done, or the terrible harm that has been committed by atheist ideologies such as communism. In fact, atheism has yet to supply us with any account of where moral value originates. When will atheists explain to us how, in the absence of any transcendent reality, there can be genuine ethical value? When will they tell us how there can be morally better or worse in a universe consisting solely of physical entities and their properties and relations?

The two questions that end this passage are loaded because they assume that atheists have not addressed these issues. But many atheist authors have, in detail and with considerable sophistication. The author of a passage such as the one above might not think that atheists have adequately answered the question of the source of moral value in a godless universe, but that has to be argued out. The author cannot avoid that task by just assuming that it has not been answered, and an atheist should reply to these questions by pointing this out. The way to deal with a loaded question is to refuse to answer it and to point out that it is loaded.

Finally, much subterfuge employs **code words**, expressions that have a straightforward but often vague meaning for most people, but for insiders, for the ones to whom the words are really addressed, there is an understood and precise meaning. The reason why the real meaning has to be encoded is that saying it openly would be unacceptable. One of the most common code terms is "family values." Lots of politicians and activists label themselves as supporters of "family values." Gosh. Who wouldn't support family values? Who doesn't want strong families? Really, though, "family values" is code for some things that are not so nice. For one thing, saying that you support "family values" proclaims that you don't like gay people. Now you could come right out and say that you don't like gay people, but that sounds ugly and will bring charges of homophobia. People who know the code, however, know exactly where a politician stands when the referendum on gay marriage is coming up and he identifies himself—wink, wink, nudge, nudge—as a supporter of "family values." There is a bumper sticker that sees through the code. It says, "Hate is not a family value."

As I've said, there are many more fallacies, and the ones given here are just a sample of some of the worst. In the next chapter we will look at political spin, and its techniques of deception. In the following chapter, we look at various pseudosciences and the various fallacies, tricks, and dodges they employ.

NOTES

1. I just made this name up. If there actually is somewhere a National Center for Global Climate Research, or something similar in name, then the similarity or identity of names with my made-up example is purely coincidental.

2. George Orwell, "Politics and the English Language," *The Orwell Reader* (New York: Harcourt, Brace, & World, 1956), p. 363.

SUGGESTIONS FOR FURTHER READING

There are many good books on the nature of fallacies and how to detect them. A helpful little handbook is *The Thinker's Guide to Fallacies: The Art of Mental Trickery and Manipulation* by Richard Paul and Linda Elder (Dillon Beach, CA: Foundation for Critical Thinking, 2006). A good textbook is *Attacking Faulty Reasoning: A Practical Guide to Fallacy-Free Arguments* by T. Edward Damer (Belmont, CA: Wadsworth, 2001). A book that is loads of good, mean fun—if you don't like Rush Limbaugh—is *Logic and Mr. Limbaugh: A Dittohead's Guide to Fallacious Reasoning* by Ray Perkins Jr. (Chicago: Open Court, 1995), which gathers the rich harvest of bad reasoning from the famous radio pundit and uses it to introduce informal fallacies.

Chapter Fourteen

SPIN, SPIN, SPIN

(Or How Not to Be a Sucker)

SPIN: RHETORIC GONE BAD

The 1960s rock group The Byrds had a hit song called "Turn, Turn, Turn" with lyrics based on verses from the biblical book of Ecclesiastes. The song had the line "there is a season—turn, turn, turn." But if the season is a political season (and it is now *always* political season) the line should end "spin, spin, spin." Spin goes back to ancient times. Top politicians of ancient Greece, like Pericles and Themistocles, were already very accomplished spin artists. What is spin? Spin is not exactly lying, but it is not exactly being honest either. Spinners are not above outright lying, but lying is clumsy and it is often hard to make a blatant lie sound really convincing. It is far more effective to say something that is technically true, or at least half true, but to present it in such a way that it is more deceptive than a lie. In general, spin is the fine art of packaging information so that it makes precisely the impression you want it to make with your targeted audience. Put another way, spin is the dark side of rhetoric. As we saw in chapter 12, rhetoric, the study of the effective presentation of information and argument, is neutral; it can be used to elevate a discussion or to muddy the waters. When rhetoric goes bad, it becomes spin, the use of rhetorical techniques to manipulate and deceive.

Spinners have a big bag of tricks, in fact, a bottomless one. One thing they know is that how you phrase things makes all the difference in people's reactions. As the Orwell quote in the last chapter noted, bombing a defenseless village doesn't sound so bad when it is called "pacification." Spin also requires expertise in the creation of vivid visual images and the packaging of visual information. The notorious TV ad used by Lyndon Johnson when he was running for president against Barry Goldwater in 1964 is a case in point. A beautiful little girl is picking daisies until her picture freezes and disappears into a thermonuclear fireball. Message: Goldwater is an unstable nut who will get your children killed in a nuclear war.

Here's a recent example of political spin, more subtle than the one LBJ had used thirty-six years earlier: When he was running for the presidency in 2000, George W. Bush touted his tax cut plan by saying that it would chiefly benefit middle-income and lower-income workers. He repeatedly gave the example of a hypothetical waitress who makes $22,000 a year and is a single mom with two children. Under his plan, said Mr. Bush, this waitress would pay no income tax at all. Technically, this claim was true. Such a waitress would pay no income tax under the Bush plan. What was not mentioned, however, and what few people would realize, was that the hypothetical waitress probably *already* had no income tax liability and would not get a large refund under the Bush plan.[1] When Bush got into office and was promoting his tax plan, he again used the example of the single mom waitress, but he gave her a raise to $25,000 a year. President Bush said that his plan would wipe out her income tax. Again, technically this was true. However, Bush's revised claim made a number of highly unrealistic assumptions. When her tax was calculated on the basis of more realistic assumptions, taking consideration of the actual circumstances facing low-wage single mothers, the Bush plan would have given her a negligible tax cut or none at all.[2] The waitress scenario, though technically correct, was presented in a way that created the misleading impression that low-income workers would get a big tax cut under the Bush plan (in fact, the wealthy benefitted far more under the Bush tax plan than middle- and lower-income workers).

Spin is amoral. It regards the human being simply as a complex of pliable wants, beliefs, and attitudes that are to be bent and molded into the desired shape. In other words, spinners view the world the way nineteenth-century huckster and circus promoter P. T. Barnum did. "There's a sucker born every minute," Barnum supposedly said. But today's spinners have far more sophisticated tools and techniques than Barnum had. Spinners can draw on all the research that has been done on public relations (PR) since Barnum's day. PR is big business, and PR mavens are nobody's fools. PR experts have done extensive research into the psychology of persuasion and the engineering of attitudes. Image control is their specialty. Suppose you are a big oil company and one of your tankers hits a reef, which causes a big oil spill and a major ecological disaster. You hire a PR firm to portray you as ecologically sensitive and deeply concerned about the environment. Suppose your candidate for high office is inarticulate and given to verbal gaffes. A PR expert will show you how to manage the candidate and stage his speaking appearances so that he will follow a script and only have to answer softball questions in front of friendly audiences.

Spin is sly. Anybody can lie, but it takes real cleverness to tell the truth in such a way that it is more misleading than a lie. A really good spin doctor has to be someone who is skilled enough to balance on a tightrope of ambiguity while juggling highly selected facts, figures, and images. Spin operates in the space between what is said and what is heard. What someone says and what you hear are two *very* different things. What you hear is determined not just by what someone says but by a host of assumptions and inferences that *you* make, usually automatically and unreflectively. Expert spinners know this. They know that if they say x you will assume y, and by assuming y you hear what they want you to hear and think what they want you to think. Recall Bush's hypothetical waitress. When you hear that the Bush tax plan would eliminate her income taxes, you immediately and unreflectively assume that this will spell some real relief for her. *No* income taxes! Wow! But $200 ($16.67 a month)—a realistic estimate of what she will actually get—isn't terribly much relief even for someone making only $25,000 a year, so your assumption is wrong. The people who came up with the waitress story know that you will unthinkingly make that wrong assumption when you hear it and they know that by making that assumption you will get the misleading impression they want you to get—that the Bush tax plan will be a big boon to people like the waitress. Sneaky, huh? The really diabolical thing about spin is that by manipulating your automatic assumptions and inferences, you get co-opted into contributing to your own deception.

Jokes often work by playing on the assumptions that we automatically make. There is a scene in one of Peter Sellars's Pink Panther movies where Sellars, as Inspector Clouseau, sees a dog sitting next to a man. He asks the man "Does your dog bite?" and the man says "No." Naturally, when Clouseau reaches to pet the dog, it mauls his hand. "You said that your dog does not bite!" Clouseau remonstrates. "That is not my dog," says the man. This joke is funny (well, at least it was in the film) because Clouseau, and the movie audience, naturally assume that the dog sitting next to the man is his and that the man would have said so if it were not. Crucially omitted information (that the dog did not belong to the man) sets up the joke. Expert spinners also know that what you do *not* say is often just as—or even more—important than what you do say, and when they intentionally leave out information, it is no joke. By judiciously omitting important information and context, spinners get you to draw the conclusions they want you to draw. You see a big advertisement for low electrical rates and you foolishly sign a contract without reading all of the fine print. You then get a whopping electrical bill and you can't drop the electrical company without a big termination fee. Technically, the ad did not lie. The rate per kilowatt hour that it listed was correct. What was carefully omitted from the ad, or hidden in tiny print and gobbledygook language at the bottom of the page, was that the amount you will actually *pay* will include taxes, regulatory fees, service charges, and so on. When you complain to the electrical company, its reply is that you should have read the fine print. In other words, gotcha.

Presumably, you do not want to be a sucker, so you need to know how spin works. Spin employs various techniques, but all of the tricks work in pretty much the same way: They fool you into making an assumption, forming an impression, or drawing a conclusion so that you get the message the spinners want you to get. Some of the tricks they use include (1) managing images, (2) managing information, (3) use of vague catchphrases and buzzwords, (4) use of misleading figures and statistics, (5) use of misleading examples, (6) creating a misleading impression of uncertainty, and (7) smearing, misquoting, and misrepresenting critics. We shall consider examples of each of these tricks. These examples will be largely drawn from the book *All the President's Spin* by Ben Fritz, Brian Keefer, and Brendan Nyhan, a searing critique of the spin tactics of the George W. Bush administration. Why am I picking on the much-maligned George W. Bush? Liberal bias? No. Fritz, Keefer, and Nyhan are the founders of the (now sadly defunct) Spinsanity (www.spinsanity .com), a scrupulously nonpartisan Web site devoted to countering the dirty tricks and deceptions of politicians of all sorts, liberal and conservative, Republican and Democrat. All politicians use spin. However, as Fritz, Keefer, and Nyhan note, the Bush administration raised the techniques of spin to an unprecedented level of effectiveness and employed spin far more pervasively and relentlessly than previous administrations. This book was written in the closing months of the Bush administration, and that administration deposited such a rich vein of spin over the last eight years that it would be foolish not to mine it for this chapter.

MANAGING IMAGES

"A picture is worth a thousand words," the saying goes, and spinners are well aware of the impact of powerful images. On May 1, 2003, Americans were presented with the televised image of President Bush landing in a military jet on the deck of the aircraft carrier USS *Abraham Lincoln*. Striding like a war hero in his flight suit, the commander in chief accepted the cheers of the assembled sailors and marines. He then spoke in praise of the United States military's personnel, congratulating them on their performance in combat operations in Iraq. Behind his head was an enormous banner reading "Mission Accomplished." This elaborately planned and staged event was designed to create an impression of heroic and decisive leadership—just what Americans love. Technically, because an image is nonverbal, it cannot state a lie, but, of course, it can create a powerfully misleading impression. When you present the image of a triumphant commander congratulating his troops after a hard-fought victory, you make people want to jump up and salute. Of course, subsequent events in Iraq soon showed that the mission was anything but accomplished, but mere facts are often helpless before a powerful image.

Images *are* powerful. Sometimes a single picture can change history. A thousand speeches and protests against the Vietnam War did not have the impact of a single photograph, taken by Associated Press photographer Nick Ut, of a naked and terrified Vietnamese girl screaming as she ran from her napalmed village. Spinners have been creating images with staged events at least since ancient Greece. The story goes that one of the early tyrants of Athens found a tall and beautiful young woman whom he dressed up as the goddess Athena and paraded through town in a chariot, proclaiming that the goddess herself had come to name him ruler of Athens. Today's PR has the enormous advantage of the use of electronic media. Even the most magnificent triumphal procession in ancient Greece or Rome would have an audience of only a couple of hundred thousand at most. Electronic media can reach many millions with messages that are broadcast 24/7, so the market can be saturated with carefully crafted images. Humans, like all primates, are strongly motivated by visual information, and spinners are as adept as Stephen Spielberg at creating images that will delight, amuse, and inspire or horrify, disgust, and sicken.

All totalitarian governments have recognized that you can control people by controlling images. Hitler's filmmaker Leni Riefenstahl directed the propaganda classic *Triumpf des Willens (Triumph of the Will)* that recorded one of Hitler's spectacular Nazi Party rallies at Nuremberg. These rallies used dramatic lighting, music, and staging to create an impression of grandeur that made even Hitler's goons look good. Spinners and other propagandists know that with human beings appearance is often far more important than reality. They also know that humans have a deep, visceral response to symbols like flags or crosses, so they make abundant use of such symbols. Spinners also are good at manipulating the human herd instinct. For instance, when political conventions show their candidate being adored by a crowd of many thousands, the viewer is tempted to join in the adulation. In short, spinners know the power of images and how to use them to get people to think and do what they want.

MANAGING INFORMATION

Information can be managed in order to increase, decrease, or alter its impact. Where, when, and how information is released affects its impact at least as much as the actual content of the message. When you know that your information is going to be received with criticism or hostility, it helps to release it when nobody is paying attention. This is why the White House so often releases controversial information late on Friday afternoons when reporters and commentators have already started their weekends. The Bush administration has also been extremely efficient at message control.[3] That is, they practice a tight discipline in delivering a set of scripted talking points, with the same stock phrases repeated over and over. When interviewed by reporters, cabinet members and other officials were instructed, whatever they were asked, to respond by simply repeating the official line with its scripted phrasing.[4] By repeating the same message in the same language over and over again, reporters were given very little to report. Another way of managing information is to stage apparently open "forums" or "town hall meetings," where there is supposedly free and candid discussion of administration policies. In fact, the people who attended these meetings were carefully vetted to make sure that they were friendly and would make supportive comments and ask easy questions.[5]

The effect of managing information through scripted responses to questions and fake forums is to undermine the process of open, frank, and critical debate that is central to the practice of democracy. In a democratic society, all proposals affecting the public welfare are supposed to be subject to free and open debate so that their strengths and weaknesses can be made plain and a rational decision reached. Information management can make a mockery of this process, preserving the appearance of open discussion while in fact stifling it.

USE OF VAGUE CATCHPHRASES AND BUZZWORDS

A catchphrase is a phrase that has a snappy sound—that's how it catches you—but not much content. "Compassionate conservative" is such a catchphrase. Conservatives have an image problem. Many people think of them as coldhearted and mean. Conservatives have a hard time shaking the stereotype that at heart they are like Dickens's Ebenezer Scrooge, who, when told of the plight of the poor at Christmastime, rasps, "Are there no prisons? Are there no workhouses?" But a *compas-*

sionate conservative sounds much better. George Bush campaigned in 2000 as a "compassionate conservative." But what exactly do you mean when you claim to be a "compassionate conservative?" What does it commit you to? Does it commit you to actually *doing* anything to help people in dire need, like, say, the millions of children in the United States who have no health insurance? In reality, the phrase "compassionate conservative" is so vague that it really doesn't put many restrictions or conditions on one's behavior.

Catchphrases are very good at creating an impression without filling in the details; this is why they are so useful as weapons. One of the most damaging things a candidate can do to an opponent is to tag him or her with a derogatory catchphrase. For instance, Fritz, Keefer, and Nyhan report that when Bush was running against Al Gore in 2000, he dismissed Gore's attacks on his tax plans as "fuzzy math" and based on "phony numbers."[6] Bush never spelled out exactly how Gore's math was fuzzy or how his numbers didn't add up, but that did not matter because he got the phrases to stick. Bush could be sure that not many people would bother to check out the numbers because most people are highly mathphobic and numbers make their heads spin.

A buzzword is a word that people like to use because it creates an appealing "buzz" in people's heads when they hear it without really saying anything definite. Politicians love to use buzzwords. They say that they are "uniters," not dividers, and "optimists" rather than doom-and-gloom types. When they are running against incumbents, politicians like to talk about how they are for "change" and "hope." These words have a good sound, but they really tell you little to nothing about their policies or themselves.

USE OF MISLEADING FIGURES AND STATISTICS

In 1954 Darrell Huff published his classic *How to Lie with Statistics*, and this wonderful little book has been in print ever since. As we say, most people are uncomfortable with figures and will even go to great lengths to avoid "doing the math." One paradoxical effect of this mathphobia is that people are far too respectful of numbers and statistics, a respect that seems to be based on intimidation. People think that if they argue with a number, the number will win. Knowing that numbers impress and intimidate people, spinners make copious use of statistics, and they know that if their statistics are shady, not many people will be willing or able to call them out. Fritz, Keefer, and Nyhan report that misleading statistics were used to deflect charges that the Bush tax plan mostly benefitted the wealthy.[7] The Treasury Department released statistics indicating that only 25.4 percent of individual income tax cuts went to those making over $200,000 a year under the Bush plan. However, this statistic was misleading because it considered only part of the tax plan and ignored the provision of greatest impact on the wealthy, the elimination of estate taxes. When the elimination of the estate tax was considered along with income tax cuts, you got a much more revealing figure: 45 percent of the overall tax cut went to just those making over $373,000 a year, that is, those with incomes in the top 1 percent.

There are many ways to lie with statistics. One of the perennially popular tricks is to confuse mean and median. The mean is the arithmetic average. If you add up the incomes of every adult in a community and you divide by the number of adults, you will get the mean income for adults in that community. If a politician wants to brag about the local economy, he or she may note that the average (meaning the mean) income has gone up significantly over the last few years. However, the mean income may have gone up simply because a small number of people have done very well, while most people's salaries continue to languish. If you live in a small town and Bill Gates moves in down the street, then the mean income of people in your town will increase significantly, though you and your friends are not making any more than before.

A more revealing measure of income is often the median rather than the mean. The median income is the one that is in the middle of the range of income distribution, and this is often quite different from the mean income. For instance, if you make $50,000 a year, five of your neighbors each make $30,000 per year and five each make $100,000 a year, your income of $50,000 will be the median of this group since it is in the middle (five incomes above and five below). To figure the mean income you add everyone's income:

$$5 \times \$30,000 = \$150,000$$

$$5 \times \$100,00 = \$500,000$$
$$\$150,000 + \$500,00 + 50,000 = \$700,000$$

Then divide by the total number of income earners, 11, so you get $700,000/11 = $63,636, quite a bit higher than the median income of $50,000. So the average income of you and your neighbors depends crucially upon whether by "average" you mean the arithmetic mean or the median of your incomes. For the many other fascinating ways to equivocate with statistics, see Huff's book.

USE OF MISLEADING EXAMPLES

People generally feel much more at ease with concrete examples than they do with abstractions like numbers. So if you want to get a point across, it always helps to illustrate your point with good examples. Unfortunately, examples can be used to mislead. First of all, you have to make sure that someone's example is not fictitious. For years Ronald Reagan would relate the story of the "Chicago Welfare Queen." As Reagan told it, this woman had dozens of aliases and addresses and multiple Social Security cards. He claimed that she cheated the government out of $150,000. Honest, hardworking Americans were outraged. Dirty welfare chiselers, living like queens on our tax dollars! One small problem: No such "welfare queen" existed. Reagan's anecdote was loosely based upon the case of a welfare cheat who used two aliases to collect $8,000. Bad enough, but nothing like Reagan's tall tale.

Examples can be real but can mislead when they are unrepresentative. Fritz, Keefer, and Nyhan again refer to the Bush tax plan to show how it was supported with spun examples.[8] The administration claimed that under its tax plan the "typical family of four" would be able to keep at least $1,600 more of its money under that plan. However, this hypothetical "typical" family was not at all representative of the benefits most taxpayers would receive:

> The majority of the ["typical"] family's tax cut, $1,000, came from a $500 increase in the tax credit it received for each child. Families without enough income tax liability to qualify for the

credit [impoverished families, in other words] or without multiple children under seventeen would have received a much smaller tax reduction. An analysis by Citizens for Tax Justice using the Institute on Taxation and Economic Policy model found that 89.6 percent would have received a smaller tax cut than $1,600. In reality, the tax cut received by Bush's "typical" family was quite unusual.[9]

Only in the world of spin can a family representing 10.4 percent of the population be considered "typical."

CREATING A MISLEADING IMPRESSION OF UNCERTAINTY

One of the most damaging and despicable tactics of spinners is to exploit the uncertainties inherent in scientific methodology in order to undercut scientific information and to create the misleading impression that there is much less evidence for a given claim than there actually is. As we noted in the last chapter, for decades the tobacco companies fought a diehard rearguard action against mounting evidence that cigarettes cause lung cancer. Their defiance was possible because, as we saw in the chapter on empirical studies, a degree of uncertainty is built into any such study and the conclusions of legitimate studies are always carefully hedged and qualified. Further, results of individual studies will differ and sometimes contradict each other. When we are dealing with a complex relationship that can only be measured using statistical techniques, such as the relationship between the incidence of cancer and its various causes, our conclusions will be based on cumulative evidence arising over time from multiple independent studies. This means that the evidence for something like the smoking/cancer connection builds over time and becomes increasingly difficult to deny.

Up to a point it will be reasonable to question studies, to note their inconclusiveness or contradictoriness and highlight the limitations of their conclusions. But at some point the evidence will accumulate until skepticism is no longer warranted. When spinners don't like a scientific conclusion because it undercuts their financial or ideological interests, they continue to pose as "skeptics" long after the evidence has convinced reasonable critics. Even the rhetoric of calling themselves "skeptics" is part of the spin. Every field of inquiry needs its skeptics, those who set the evidence bar high and will not accept a claim until the bar has been cleared. Few hypotheses survive the rigorous vetting process that scientific claims must undergo, but those that do survive have earned the respect of even the most hard-bitten skeptic. Spinners push their "skepticism" far past the point where it is reasonable and to the point where it becomes irresponsible. At one time the smoking/cancer connection was unsure; there were many unanswered questions and doubt was reasonable. No longer. Anyone now questioning that connection is in the same league as the flat-earther or the creationist.

Human-caused climate change is a complex issue that has been much debated in recent years. Climates change over time due to many very complex factors. The Mesozoic Era, the age of the dinosaurs, had a far warmer climate than the earth today. Fossils show that dinosaurs thrived in the high arctic, which had no permanent ice cap and was much milder than today's arctic climate. Even on a small scale there are notable climate vagaries. From about 1300 to 1800 there occurred what climatologists refer to as the "little ice age." Weather worldwide was distinctly cooler than it had been for several hundred years previously or in the two centuries since. Old prints show ice fairs held on the frozen Thames; southern England is almost never that cold these days. Because climate is naturally variable, and because it is subject to complex causes and both positive and negative feedback loops, it is very challenging to single out individual causes, like the human creation of greenhouse gases, and specify their particular effects.

Eventually, though, even when dealing with enormously complex phenomena like climate change, consensus can emerge, and this seems to be the case with human-induced global warming, as the National Academy of Sciences (NAS) reported to the Bush administration in June of 2001.[10] The NAS report concurred with an earlier study from the United Nations Intergovernmental Panel on Climate Change (IPCC) that concluded that global warming is real and that the human production of greenhouse gases is a significant contributory factor.[11] Like all scientific findings, however, the NAS and IPCC reports included qualifications and caveats that mentioned uncertainties in the findings. Such uncertainties are inevitable whenever scientists are required to interpret data that are complex and subject to some degree of imprecision. The Bush administration, because of its ideological opposition to global warming claims, seized on these statements of uncertainty and ignored the broad areas of scientific agreement. While the qualified scientists broadly agreed that climate change is occurring and that humans are contributing, the spokesmen for the Bush administration misleadingly overemphasized the uncertainties in the scientific findings and under-played the degree of consensus.[12] It is true to say, as the Bush spokesmen did, that we do not know with certainty the degree of global warming that will occur or the extent to which humans are responsible. Very little in science is known with certainty. But when scientific consensus warns, with a significant degree of probability, of a looming disaster that timely action can mitigate, it is grossly irresponsible to spin away that warning and opt for inaction.

SMEARING, MISQUOTING, AND MISREPRESENTING CRITICS

As we noted in the last chapter, *ad hominem* smears are common, insidious, and effective. Spinners are especially adept at the clever employment of *ad hominem* techniques. Normally, they do not outright insult their critics (though they sometimes do that too), but couch the insult in what sounds like a high-minded appeal to principle. In wartime we expect people to pull together; each person is to do his or her bit and be a team player. When the Bush administration's handling of the Iraq War drew intensely negative comment, the administration's response was to adopt a self-righteous pose and admonish critics not to "hurt the troops." That is, critics were portrayed as undermining the morale of the troops, and therefore of impairing the fighting strength of our combat soldiers by criticizing their commander in chief. In other words (though this conclusion was left unstated), criticizing the president's conduct of the war is tantamount to treason. You do not have to answer the arguments of your critics if you can tar them as traitors. An apparently high-minded appeal to supporting the troops is in fact a roundabout way of dismissing your critics by calling them names.

Another way of belittling your critics, without calling them names even indirectly, is to misquote them or mischaracterize their claims or positions. That way you can make them look clueless, ridiculous, or hateful without saying anything negative about them. Fritz, Keefer, and Nyhan note that in the 2004 presidential campaign George Bush and his opponent, John Kerry, frequently misquoted and misrepresented each other.[13] For instance, Kerry said that the White House had claimed Saddam Hussein definitely had nuclear weapons.[14] In fact, the repeated claim made by members of the administration was that Iraq was *pursuing* the development of nuclear weapons, not that it already had them.[15] Bush and Vice President Dick Cheney twisted a Kerry quote to claim that he was refusing to call the campaign against terrorism a "war" on terror, and this, they implied, revealed Kerry's lack of resolve in confronting terrorism.[16] In fact, Kerry had employed the phrase "war on terror" on many occasions.

CONCLUSION

This chapter has presented just a few of the spinners' tricks of the trade. No such list can be exhaustive, and they are constantly looking for new angles and techniques. There may be a sucker born every minute, but the spinners are always looking for better ways to make him bite. So we can't cover all the bases, but, perhaps we can list a few rules that will save us most of the time from being victimized by spinners. Here are my seven rules:

(1) *Never* trust figures or statistics given out by politicians, advertisers, or special interest groups. *Always* check them out with authoritative sources, like the FactCheck.org Web site.

(2) Read Darrell Huff's *How to Lie with Statistics* or some other good book on statistical reasoning (read one dealing with statistical concepts rather than just number crunching). Spinners can use even accurate statistics to mislead, and you need to know the tricks.

(3) *Never* trust controversial factual claims made by politicians, advertisers, or special interest groups. Be especially skeptical

of any claims they make about their opponents or competitors. *Always* check them out before trusting them.

(4) Be careful with language. Get in the habit of using precise, clear, and direct language yourself and you will be better able to catch the spinners when they equivocate or obfuscate.

(5) Give science the benefit of the doubt. Science is not perfect and it is not always right. Some scientific "truths" are proven wrong in every generation. But be *very* suspicious when you hear attacks on established science, as when pundits or politicians dismiss scientific results, even though those results are backed by strong scientific consensus. Check the Web sites of the major scientific bodies, like the National Academy of Sciences, or the American Association for Advancement of Science, or the National Institutes of Health, or the sites of major museums like the American Museum of Natural History to get guidance to legitimate scientific information.

(6) If you find an image particularly moving, inspiring, or infuriating or if it motivates you to any strong emotion, ask yourself whether you are being manipulated. Does the image represent reality or is it a distortion? Did it even happen as depicted? These days computers can use special software to create all sorts of misleading images, so beware when, for instance, e-mail attachments seem to show a political candidate hanging around with Jane Fonda or shaking hands with bin Laden.

(7) Don't ever let popular catchphrases, buzzwords, or sayings do your thinking for you. When you hear lots of people saying the same thing, stop and ask if it really makes sense or if it is really true. When politicians use the same words or phrases repeatedly, like "change" or "hope," or if they say that they are "compassionate conservatives" or "reformers with results," ask what, if anything, those words and phrases really mean.

Don't be a sucker.

NOTES

1. Ben Fritz, Bryan Keefer, and Brendan Nyhan, *All the President's Spin: George W. Bush, the Media, and the Truth* (New York: Simon & Schuster, 2004), p. 64.

2. Ibid., p. 81.

3. Ibid., pp. 23–24.

4. Ibid., p. 44.

5. Ibid., p. 24.

6. Ibid., pp. 57–58

7. Ibid., pp. 84–85.

8. Ibid., pp. 81–82.

9. Ibid., p. 82.

10. Ibid., pp. 90–91.

11. Ibid., p. 91.

12. Ibid., p. 92.

13. Ibid., pp. 228–230.

14. Ibid., p. 229.

15. Ibid., p. 229

16. Ibid., p. 228.

SUGGESTIONS FOR FURTHER READING

Obviously, the Fritz, Keefer, and Nyhan book leads the list here. Anyone not already alarmed by the power of propaganda will be after reading this book. Spinners are predators, and your mind is their hunting ground. They know the turf well. The only hope for rationality is that people who love the truth will be equally diligent. For an understanding of dirty tricks using statistics, the all-time classic is Darrell Huff's *How to Lie with Statistics* (New York: Norton, 1993), which is over fifty years old and still the champ. The book is often hilarious, with delightful illustrations by Irving Geis. There are innumerable books on statistics that teach you how to do the math, but only a few that really teach you how to *think* about statistical concepts. One of the latter is John L. Phillips's *How to Think about Statistics*, rev. ed. (New York: W. H. Freeman, 1992), which actually tells you what all those confusing terms and formulas are about. Some knowledge of statistics is essential if you want to avoid being a sucker.

Chapter Fifteen

EVERYTHING YOU KNOW IS WRONG!

Pseudoscience and Bogus Scholarship

WHAT DO WE MEAN BY "PSEUDOSCIENCE" AND "BOGUS SCHOLARSHIP"?

If you have not yet, someday you will run into someone who tells you that everything you know is wrong. Here are some of the things they might tell you:

Evolution is a lie, the earth is only a few thousand years old, and living dinosaurs were on the Ark with Noah. The Adam and Eve story happened exactly as told in the book of Genesis.

The Egyptian pyramids were not built by the ancient Egyptians but by friendly extraterrestrials who used advanced technology to build the pyramids and other notable ancient monuments.

The "Holocaust" allegedly perpetrated by the Nazis against the Jews and other peoples never occurred. In fact, there were no gas chambers or death camps and the German government had no policy of extermination. The story about a "Holocaust" is the invention of Hollywood propagandists and others who have a vested interest in defaming the German people.

At one time Europeans lived in peaceful, nurturing, egalitarian societies where women were revered, benevolent matriarchs ruled, and everyone worshipped the Mother Goddess. Warfare and strife began when men took over and established patriarchy.

You didn't know any of these things? No, as a matter of fact, you did not know any of these things. You cannot know what isn't true. The last dinosaur went extinct over 60 million years before anything vaguely human (say *Australopithecus*) was around. The Egyptians built the pyramids, not space aliens. The Nazis did pursue, and largely accomplish, a policy of genocide. There was no time when Europeans were peaceful goddess-worshippers ruled by wise matriarchs. These things *are* known. Yet millions of your fellow citizens reject this knowledge and cling to bizarre, fraudulent fantasies.

In this chapter we look at **pseudoscience** and **bogus scholarship**— weird, irrational theories that try to camouflage their weirdness and irrationality by adopting the trappings of scientifically and academically respectable disciplines. Thus creationists emphasize their scientific credentials and Holocaust deniers write dense academic prose with footnotes and extensive bibliographies. Creationists, Holocaust deniers, and the like express outrage that their "scientific" or "scholarly" endeavors are not treated with respect. Snubbed by the established scientific and scholarly bodies and journals, they organize their own conferences and publish their own journals. They have their own, sometimes lavishly endowed, think tanks and institutes. Some occupy respectable professorships at legitimate universities. Some, such as the creationists, petition legislatures and school boards to require that public schools present their views on an equal footing with established science.

Why would somebody reject some of the best-established scientific and historical results and opt instead for castles built on the clouds? Sometimes the answer is easy. Sometimes people promote bogus science or scholarship just to make a buck. Other times the answer is more complicated, and involves people's deepest hopes and anxieties. Many cannot bear the thought that their most cherished convictions could be wrong. Some fear that any backtracking or concession will imperil their whole worldview. They fear that if they permit any crack in their creed, however tiny, soon the whole bastion of their beliefs will tumble down. Christian fundamentalists, for example, cannot let go of even the most obviously mythological or legendary elements of scripture. As some of them have admitted to me, if you start to doubt that in the Garden of Eden, circa 4004 BCE, a naked woman was accosted by a talking snake who urged her to eat a piece of fruit, then soon you will have to deny that Christ died to save us from our sins. To save the talking-snake story, creationists are willing to reject much of modern science. It is also easy to see the motivation behind proponents of fake history, like the Holocaust deniers. As Deborah Lipstadt shows in her book *Denying the Holocaust*, Holocaust denial is a tool for the promotion of extreme right-wing ideologies.

"Well, so what?" you might ask. What is the harm if some people choose to live in their own bizarre fantasy worlds? Are they hurting anybody but themselves? Isn't it a bit self-righteous and puritanical to chastise people for harboring out-of-the-mainstream beliefs? Why not practice "live and let live?" Indeed, hasn't it often happened that the "crackpots" of one era were hailed as far-seeing prophets by people of a later age? Didn't they laugh at Galileo, Newton, Darwin, and Einstein?

These questions deserve an answer. Answering the last question first, yes they laughed at Galileo, but, as a wise person—I think it was Martin Gardner—once observed, they also laughed at Bozo the Clown, and there were ten thousand Bozos for each Galileo. Just because a few former "crackpots" turned out to be right—while tens of thousands of others turned out just to be crackpots—there is no reason to ignore doctrines that, so far as we can now tell, are blatantly contrary to reason.

What harm do irrational beliefs cause? Untold amounts. The dissemination of irrational doctrines does terrible harm by making us lazier, stupider, more gullible, and easier to manipulate. It is often tempting to believe pleasing delusions rather than face up to hard truths. Evolution is one such hard truth. It is easy to sympathize with the outraged Victorian matron who heard of Darwin's theory and expostulated to her husband: "Oh! My dear! Descended from apes! Let us hope that it is not true, and if it is true, that it does not become generally known." But if the chimps *are* our cousins, then wishing will not change that fact. Thinking is hard work and it takes courage to face the facts. It is easy to be lazy, to follow the path of least resistance, to give your brain a rest and indulge in groundless beliefs because they comfort you, amuse you, or reinforce your prejudices.

It does matter what people think. Thoughts have consequences; "As he thinketh in his heart, so is he," says scripture (Proverbs 23:7). The philosopher W. V. O. Quine pointed out that our beliefs do not exist in isolation, but form an intricate web of interconnections. In other words, what you think about one thing can ultimately affect what you think about everything else. Buy into creationist claims about evolution, and soon you will be throwing out, not just evolution, but much that science has learned since 1600. An irrational belief is mental poison that can spread toxins through your whole system of beliefs. Worse, it is fatally easy for gullible, lazy, and irresponsible thinking to become a habit. When you cling to a belief that is plainly against evidence and reason, it will be a little easier to swallow the next irrational belief, and even easier to gulp down the next one, until, finally, your mind leaves its perch in reality and flies away to cloud-cuckoo-land.

Still, if creationism, Holocaust denial, and other like doctrines were practiced only among consenting adults, then the damage that they do would be limited and not such a matter of concern. The fact is, however, that advocates of pseudoscience and fake history are often very aggressive in promoting their doctrines, especially in schools and colleges. As noted earlier, creationists push their agenda to school boards around the country. Holocaust "revisionists" have taken out full-page ads in college newspapers to promote their claims. When irrationality is no longer privately practiced, but is pursued with missionary zeal, then it has to be opposed. All legitimate intellectual inquiry is based upon a set of essential values. Those values require that ideas undergo a rigorous and dispassionate evaluation in the light of the strictest methods and the best available evidence. The vetting of claims entails much hard thinking, stringent testing, careful scrutiny, and painstaking and infinitely patient accumulation and sifting of evidence. Ideas that do not measure up must be rejected, even if they are expedient, comforting, congenial, safe, or "politically correct." Pretending that creationism or Holocaust "revisionism" are legitimate theories is tantamount to saying that the intellectual values that underlie scientific and scholarly inquiry don't matter. But they do.

So the theories of pseudoscientists and bogus scholars are not harmless, and they should be opposed. Effective opposition to irrational doctrines requires first that we understand exactly what is going wrong with them. Let's focus on pseudoscience and how it is to be identified. What logical or methodological foibles or errors make a theory pseudoscientific? To say that a theory is pseudoscience is not merely to say that it is wrong. Much of the best science has turned out wrong—or at least not 100 percent right. Indeed, many of today's best theories are regarded not as literally and exactly true accounts, but as models that give an idealized or schematic representation of reality. Even some of the best-known natural laws are recognized as idealizations, that is, as representing what *would* happen in certain ideal situations that are, in reality, only approximated. For instance, Galileo's famous law of falling bodies, s = ½ gt², states that the distance that an object in free fall near the earth's surface will travel in a given period of time is equal to one-half times the rate of acceleration due to gravity, 9.8 m/sec² or 32 ft/sec², multiplied by the square of the time elapsed. Yet this rule, found in every elementary physics text, is only an approximation. It holds precisely only for a body falling in a perfect vacuum and no such perfect vacuum exists.

So to say that a theory is pseudoscience is not to say merely that it is in error, but that it is fraudulent, that is, that it can be maintained only by flouting the norms that guide and regulate good scientific practice. What are the norms that good science respects and pseudoscience violates? Philosophers of science used to think that question was easy to answer, and formulated various **demarcation criteria**, simple, universal rules, which, they held, distinguished scientific theories from nonscientific ones. Sir Karl Popper, one of the leading philosophers of science of the twentieth century, held that every legitimate scientific theory is "falsifiable," that is, some experiment, observation, or measurement should be able to discredit the theory. Pseudoscientific theories on the other hand, said Popper, are expounded by their followers in such a way that they cannot be refuted by any evidence, that is, they are unfalsifiable. Popper therefore held that all legitimate science is falsifiable and all pseudoscience is not. So if we want to see whether a theory is pseudoscience, we simply ask if any observation, experiment, or measurement would falsify it, and, if not, into the trash heap of pseudoscience it goes.

Falsifiability is an appealing and intuitive criterion. Surely, we do not accept a theory as scientific if it is compatible with all conceivable observations or data. For instance, it cannot be scientific to "explain" an odd occurrence by saying that it was done by magical, undetectable fairies. But as a proposed criterion of demarcation, falsifiability has many problems, some of which are too technical to get into here. Perhaps the most serious problem is that falsifiability is far too *permissive*, that is, it is too easy to meet the required condition. To meet Popper's demarcation criterion a theory only has to be falsifiable *in principle*, that is, we only have to propose *some* circumstance, however improbable, that would get us to give up our theory. Therefore, if creationists and other pseudoscientists are willing to name *any* possible observation, however far-fetched, as incompatible with their claims, then the criterion of falsifiability cannot rule out their claims. For instance, creationists could say that if we ever find in the fossil record a creature that is exactly midway between humans and apes in all of its anatomical features, then they will accept evolution. It is very unlikely that there ever existed a creature that in every anatomical feature was exactly half ape and half human; no evolutionist predicts that such a creature did exist. Distinctively human traits (bipedalism, large brain, less hair, etc.) were acquired piecemeal, and did not all evolve at the same rate. Nevertheless, such a stipulation would save creationism from the charge that it is unfalsifiable.

The same holds for all other sets of supposed demarcation criteria. No simple, universal, one-size-fits-all set of rules can be used to distinguish science from nonscience. Each such set of proposed criteria has turned out either to be too strict or too permissive. That is, it either excludes much of legitimate science along with the nonsense, or it lets in a lot of nonsense along with the good science. So far, nobody has found that set of criteria which—like Goldilocks's porridge—is just right, that is, it stamps the "scientific" label on *all* and *only* those theories that deserve it. There is no cardinal sin committed by all and only those theories that deserve the "pseudoscience" label. For instance, there is no *one* thing wrong with creationism; thick books have been written just to point out *some* of the main things wrong with it (see Strahler, 1987, for instance). Just as there are many different kinds of bad bosses (the sadistic monster, the nitpicking micromanager, the smiling manipulator, etc.), so there are many different ways that pseudosciences can pervert good scientific practice (see examples below).

We probably cannot define "pseudoscience" with enough precision to satisfy all philosophers, but this is no reason to say, as some philosophers do, that the term "pseudoscience" is merely a rhetorical grenade to toss at doctrines we do not like. When we call a theory "pseudoscientific," we are not merely making a verbal put-down; we are making a principled judgment, like a doctor making a diagnosis. Medical diagnosis is a tricky art (as we see in the TV medical show *House*). Different diseases sometimes have very similar symptoms and sometimes patients with the same disease will show different symptoms. With some diseases demarcation criteria are not available, that is, there is no simple, highly reliable test to determine whether a patient does or does not have a disease. Still, a skilled diagnostician can look at all the patient's signs and symptoms, and, drawing on a wealth of experience and by making careful comparisons and observations, he or she can make an accurate diagnosis.

Identifying pseudoscience is similar to diagnosing a disease. There is no simple test, no demarcation criterion. Still, there are identifiable norms of good science and symptoms of pseudoscience, just as medicine recognizes signs of health and symptoms of disease. The term "pseudoscience" is the label we reserve for theories that aspire to scientific status, but fail egregiously when judged according to the recognized norms of good science. The judgment that a theory deserves to be classified as "pseudo" is a *holistic* judgment, that is, we have to look at the theory *as a whole* and fairly consider its strengths along with its weaknesses. A good theory can be flawed just as a good person can be flawed, but the good theory or person must have strong virtues to compensate for the vices. If a theory is rotten to the core with error and illogic, and if it has no redeeming virtues—except to serve the ideological (or pecuniary) demands of a special interest—then, in the immortal words from David Hume's *Enquiry Concerning Human Understanding*, "Commit it then to the flames: for it can contain nothing but sophistry and illusion."

Just as medical texts give symptoms of disease, so we might point out symptoms of pseudoscience. Some philosophers will object that we can identify a doctrine as pseudoscience only if we can articulate a set of permanent and universal norms and methods of science. But, they will ask, have not historians of science shown that there has been no single, universal, permanent scientific method and that the norms of science change over time? It is true that the norms and methods of science change over time; if they did not, they could never improve. Yet scientific communities at any given time *do* strictly enforce certain standards and demand adherence to recognized rigorous methods and techniques (and I think that there is more historical continuity in scientific norms and methods than some philosophers or historians will admit). Scientists are excruciatingly picky about what they will allow and what they will not. They have to be. In science, as opposed to ordinary life, "good enough" is not good enough. Scientists want to get it *right*.

I have really been far too cautious and reserved in making so many caveats in the last few paragraphs. In reality, diagnosing pseudoscience is not nearly as tricky as identifying some rare disease. The classic pseudosciences—creationism, astrology, UFOlogy, and so on—are so spectacularly defiant of scientific norms, or even of the most basic practices of good reasoning, that putting the "pseudo" label on them is a cinch. Let's take a look at some, really just a few, of the symptoms of pseudoscience. We note that pseudoscientific theories often fail by (a) giving poor explanations, (b) employing arbitrary (*ad hoc*) hypotheses, and (c) using biased or misleading evidence. Also, we note that the bad behavior of pseudoscientists often is a tip-off.

SYMPTOMS OF PSEUDOSCIENCE

(1) Poor Explanations

As noted in an earlier chapter, one of the central aims of science is to explain natural phenomena, that is, to substantiate clear, coherent, and informative answers to our "why" questions about the natural world. Good science offers good explanations; bad science offers poor explanations. One typical feature of pseudoscientific theories is that they fail spectacularly when they purport to offer explanatory hypotheses.* In general, the allegedly explanatory hypotheses of pseudoscience offer (1) either no explanation at all, or, what often amounts to the same thing, (2) explanation by scenario (e.g., the appeal to vague or occult agencies or potencies such as magic, poltergeists, "astrological influences," or "psychic powers"), rather than by a specifiable, scrutable causal process or mechanism, or (3) explanations that are demonstrably wrong or are given for phenomena that have much more likely and familiar explanations.

---

*Usage note: Most philosophers use the terms "theory" and "hypothesis" interchangeably, treating them as synonymous. Both terms are used to refer to something postulated as true, particularly a proposed explanation of natural phenomena. Here I use "theory" to mean a comprehensive, overarching model, like the theory of evolution, and by "hypothesis," I mean a particular or restricted explanatory account encompassed within such a broader theory. Thus, evolution would be the theory, and the evolutionary explanation of the origin of birds would be a hypothesis of that theory.

Let's give some examples:

(a) Astrology claims that your character, personality, and personal fate are strongly influenced by mysterious astrological influences determined by the positions of the stars, sun, and planets relative to the earth at the exact time that you were born. For instance, they might claim that people born under the sun sign Aries (i.e., the sun is in the constellation Aries on a person's day of birth) will have a probability significantly greater than chance of having an extroverted personality. Careful testing has failed to establish such correlations. For instance, the number of extroverts born under Aries is no greater than would be expected on the basis of chance. Worse, astrology has never offered any candidate for a reasonable explanation of how astrological influence is supposed to work, that is, how the astronomical bodies could possibly influence human personality and fate. Known physical forces such as gravity, electromagnetism, or charged particles are far too weak in their influence upon the earthly environment to have such a strong effect on human infants. When a baby is born, for instance, an attending nurse exerts a greater gravitational attraction on the newborn than the planet Jupiter. Jupiter is far more massive, but it is also immensely farther away. No other plausible candidates have been offered to account for the supposed astrological influences. So astrology offers no semblance of a possible explanation of its supposed effects.

(b) One of the most exciting hypotheses in paleontology is that birds are the evolutionary descendants of dinosaurs. Most, but not all, vertebrate paleontologists now appear to agree that birds are the evolutionary offspring of theropod dinosaurs, that is, bipedal carnivorous dinosaurs of the type made famous by movie monsters like *Velociraptor* and *Tyrannosaurus*. Close skeletal affinities between early birds and small theropod dinosaurs have been recognized since the first discoveries of bird fossils. Recent discoveries of feathered dinosaurs strongly support the dinosaur/bird connection. By contrast, how do creationists explain birds? young-earth creationists, those who accept a literal interpretation of the Book of Genesis, have to say that, as it tells in Genesis 1:21, God directly created the birds on the fifth day of creation. That is, God, said "Let there be birds!" and POOF! The air was full of birds! One problem with such an "explanation" is that we do not, and in principle cannot, have any idea about how supposed supernatural agents like gods and ghosts bring about their alleged effects. Saying "God did it" only introduces a scenario, a shadowy image—perhaps something like a cartoonish rendering of Michelangelo's paintings in the Sistine Chapel—but tells us nothing intelligible about the creative process. God just says "Let there be," and it is so. End of story. Saying "God did it" is no more informative than attributing effects to magic, poltergeists, astrological influences, or psychic powers. In other words, saying "God did it," is just a less candid way of saying "we don't know how it happened." By contrast, the causal processes invoked by evolutionary theory, such as natural selection and genetic drift, are very well known and can be described in precise detail.

(c) In the 1970s, at the height of the "New Age" movement, an Israeli "psychic" named Uri Geller became a media sensation and the darling of parapsychologists when he appeared on numerous television programs to demonstrate his "psychic" powers. Geller apparently could bend solid objects, like spoons or car keys, with the power of his mind. He could also seemingly read other people's minds and tell the contents of a sealed envelope. Two Stanford University physicists tested Geller and, concluding that his supposed paranormal powers were real, published their results in the highly prestigious science journal *Nature*. Yet, in a variation of the saying "It takes a thief to catch a thief," it took a stage magician, one skilled at fooling audiences into thinking that something truly magical has occurred, to expose Geller. Professional magician James Randi demonstrated that all of Geller's "psychic" stunts could be performed by the techniques of stage magic—simple trickery, that is, nothing paranormal. Therefore, all those tricks that Geller "explained" by "psychic power," in fact, had much more likely and familiar explanations in terms of trickery and the gullibility of audiences, including Stanford University physicists.

So when a hypothesis is supposed to give a causal explanation, but that "explanation" is nonexistent, incomprehensible, patently false, or "explains" something that has a much better, mundane explanation, this is a good sign that a hypothesis is part of a pseudoscientific theory.

(2) Ad Hoc *Hypotheses*

A second symptom indicating that a theory is pseudoscientific is that it employs *ad hoc* hypotheses. An *ad hoc* hypothesis is an arbitrary assumption that is made for the sole purpose of protecting a pet theory from refutation by observation or experiment. There is no independent evidence for an *ad hoc* hypothesis (and often much evidence *against* it); it is invented purely to insulate a favored theory from criticism. Good scientific theories are expected to be free of *ad hoc* hypotheses. Pseudoscientific theories tend to surround themselves with a bodyguard of *ad hoc* hypotheses; these assumptions have the job of screening those theories from unpleasant encounters with pesky contrary evidence. Here are two examples:

(a) Fundamentalist creationists are committed to the actual occurrence of Noah's Flood, a worldwide deluge that supposedly literally inundated the entire earth's surface a few thousand years ago. One problem (of many) with this proposal is that there has to be a source for such an inconceivable amount of water as a worldwide flood would require. To deal with this problem—which has to be dealt with, since there could have been no flood if there was no source of the water—creationists postulate a "water canopy" that, they say, existed in pre-Flood times and contributed much of the flood's water. This "water canopy" is supposed to have been a vast envelope of water vapor that encompassed the earth and was allegedly suspended in the upper atmosphere. At the time of the Flood, God caused the water vapor in the canopy to condense and fall as vast amounts of rain. The problem is that there is absolutely no evidence for, and, in fact, much against, the existence of any such "water canopy." It is a sheer figment of creationists' imagination. The "water canopy" story is one of very many *ad hoc* hypotheses that creationists invent to prop up their claims.

(b) Many psychics, including the Mr. Geller mentioned above, will often demonstrate their paranormal "abilities" before gullible audiences. However, when skeptical magicians or other experts in the arts of deception are present, the psychics' marvelous "powers" will mysteriously vanish. Why do these marvelous "powers" vanish just when somebody is present who can detect any tricks that might deceive people into thinking that something paranormal was going on? The alleged psychics say that when skeptics are present they give off "bad vibes," that is, their very skepticism causes them to emanate a sort of negative psychic energy that prevents the psychics from being able to employ their true powers. Now, needless to say, there is no independent evidence whatsoever that skeptics emit "bad vibes" that can interfere with others' psychic abilities. This supposition is a purely *ad hoc* claim that serves no purpose except to lend spurious protection to the psychics' claims to paranormal "powers."

So when you see that a theory is clearly about to collapse under the evidence and resorts to desperate *ad hoc* crutches to prop itself up, you should be suspicious that the theory is pseudoscience.

(3) Biased Evidence

A third symptom of a bad theory is when it is based on biased evidence. Just about any theory can be made to look good if we present only the evidence in its favor and ignore the evidence against it. A good theory has to be good in the light of *all* the available evidence, the cons as well as the pros. When the advocates of a theory consider only the evidence in its favor and ignore the evidence against, they are guilty of the fallacy of **confirmation bias**. Here are two examples of bad theories based on highly selectively gathered and presented data:

(a) The ancient astronaut theory was developed by author Erich von Däniken in his 1970 book, *Chariots of the Gods?* In this book von Däniken presents pictures and descriptions of many ancient monuments and artifacts which, considered just by themselves, might be taken to support the claim that technologically advanced aliens visited the earth in ancient times. Some of the drawings and sculptures he presents could, looked at in a certain way, seem to indicate that our ancestors had contact with beings that were capable of space travel. The problem is that when we consider other evidence, much of which has long been known, that licenses other and much more plausible interpretations of those artifacts, the supposed evidence for ancient astronauts simply melts away. Further, the ancient monuments which, according to von Däniken, could only have been built with the help of advanced alien technology can be shown to have been constructed by ancient peoples using the techniques and knowledge then available.

(b) The evidence that space aliens are visiting our planet in the present day is superficially impressive. UFO proponents point to photographs, numerous sightings, "crashed saucers," animal mutilations, and "close encounters." If you looked only at the weird events and talked only to those who had seen strange things in the sky or who had "abduction" experiences, you could pretty soon be convinced that something extraterrestrial was going on. After all, many of the people reporting sightings and "close encounters" are sane, intelligent, and honest people who often are reluctant to come forward with their stories. On the other hand, if you take a look at the psychological research into the nature of anomalous experiences and see how easy it is for people to think that they have seen or experienced something when they have not, you will have second thoughts. In fact, people, even adults, can sometimes fail to distinguish their own dreams and fabrications from reality. Hypnotic "regression" is sometimes used to help "abductees" draw out their "repressed" memories of abduction, but it is demonstrably easy to implant false memories under hypnosis. Also, there are various forms of hallucinations that are experienced by psychologically normal persons that are very "lifelike" and are likely the source for many "abduction" experiences. Even seeing is fallible since it is very easy for us to misjudge things we see in the sky. When considering the evidence as a whole, the reality of UFOs is much more dubious.

By the way, confirmation bias can result in bad policy as well as bad science. When people in power only look at intelligence that reinforces their prior convictions and desires, and dismiss evidence that contradicts it, bad things can happen.

What we say about pseudoscience can also be said, *mutatis mutandis*, about bogus scholarship based on skewed "research," like Holocaust "revisionism." History as a discipline has its rigorous scholarly standards just as a natural science does. For instance, just as in the natural sciences, good historical theories cannot be based on biased evidence. As Michael Shermer shows in his devastating critique of the Holocaust deniers, they are biased in their treatment of historical evidence.[1] Typical of their *modus operandi* is to take pieces of evidence one by one and argue vigorously, making *ad hoc* excuses, that each bit of evidence, on its own, is not conclusive and might be explained away. Shermer gives some examples:

We have the account of a survivor [who] says he heard about the gassing of Jews when he was at Auschwitz. The denier says that the survivor exaggerates and that [his or her] memories are unsound. Another survivor tells another story different in details but with the core similarity that Jews were gassed at Auschwitz. The denier claims that rumors were floating throughout the camp and many survivors incorporated them into their memories. An SS guard confesses after the war that he actually saw people being gassed and cremated. The denier claims that these confessions were forced out of the Nazis by the allies. But now a member of the Sonderkommando—a Jew who helped the Nazis move dead bodies from the gas chambers and into the crematoria—says he not only heard about it and not only saw it happening, he actually participated in the process. The denier explains this away by saying that the Sonderkommando accounts make no sense—their figures of number of bodies are exaggerated and their dates incorrect. What about the camp commandant, who confessed after the war that he not only heard, saw, and participated in the process but orchestrated it? He was tortured, says the denier. But what about his autobiography, written after his trial, conviction, and sentencing to death, when he had nothing to gain by lying? No one knows why people confess to ridiculous crimes, says the denier, but they do.[2]

But historical evidence is *cumulative*. When many pieces of independent evidence, none of which by itself is conclusive, fit together into a coherent and mutually supportive body of evidence, then the conclusion can be put beyond a reasonable doubt. A few pieces of evidence might be dismissed or explained away, but when, as with the Holocaust, we have many, many different lines of evidence that converge to the conclusion that the Nazi government did plan and carry out a policy of genocide, the patent flimsiness (and *ad hoc* nature) of the denier's excuses becomes evident. There are photographs, documents (like the minutes of the Wansee Conference where top Nazis planned the "final solution" to the "Jewish problem"), artifacts, and testimony by third parties, surviving victims, and the perpetrators themselves. Also, there is demographic evidence. Millions of people who were there before the Holocaust were simply not there afterward. One very interesting piece of evidence is what the perpetrators of the Holocaust did *not* say when they were held accountable for their crimes after the war. They gave many excuses for their behavior in carrying out these atrocities ("I was only following orders"). One excuse that *nobody* gave was that it didn't happen.

PSEUDOSCIENTISTS BEHAVING BADLY

The behavior of pseudoscientists and bogus scholars often also is a tip-off that should make us suspicious of their doctrines, that is, when you see "scientists" or "scholars" behaving very badly, you need to check their claims very carefully to see if the doctrines they promote are really legitimate. Some of their standard maneuvers include (1) defaming their critics with blatant personal attacks, (2) misrepresenting opponents' arguments or positions, even after having been repeatedly corrected, (3) making greatly exaggerated claims on behalf of their own theories, and (4) appealing to faith, intuition, or "alternative ways of knowing" when the "scientific" evidence falls short. Here are some examples:

1) Defenders of the Goddess theory—those feminist theorists who think that ancient Europeans lived in matriarchal, woman-centered, goddess-worshipping societies that were peaceful, egalitarian, and nonhierarchical—have harsh words for their critics. Those who point out that no credible archaeological evidence supports the Goddess theory are derided as sexist, patriarchal, warmongering, and racist defenders of male dominance (not all critics of the Goddess are male, by the way). At the opposite end of the political spectrum, creationists depict evolution as, literally, a satanic plot, a theory devised by the devil. Likewise, evolutionists are portrayed as rabidly intolerant atheists who hate Christians and the Bible (though a number of leading evolutionary biologists are devout Christians). A creationist cartoon shows a tree with "biological evolution" as the trunk and bearing such dreadful fruits as crime, terrorism, drugs, communism, racism, and sex education. UFO cultists, who claim that the government is in possession of the

bodies of space aliens and perhaps their vehicles, respond to critics by accusing them of being part of the "cover-up."

2) One way to get people to look at your theory more favorably is to deride an opposing theory. For instance, creationists, time and time again, have characterized evolution as "only a theory." By equivocating on the meaning of the word "theory," they intend to imply that, as a mere "theory"—and not fact—evolution cannot lay claim to being established knowledge. This dishonest use of the word "theory" is intended to imply that evolution is merely speculation or conjecture, and not nailed down by the evidence. In ordinary usage, we sometimes say we have a "theory," meaning only an unqualified guess (like the time I was taking a taxi in Albuquerque and the driver told me his "theory" about the "UFO crashes" in Roswell, NM). But when scientists use the word "theory," they mean a general explanatory account or model—which can be extremely well confirmed—not mere speculation or conjecture. Some theories *are* nailed down. When scientists confront apparent anomalies, results that appear to go against theoretical expectations, they do not react by automatically throwing out the theory. They often find that it is the anomalous "facts" that were wrong, not the theory. In science, then, a theory can be established knowledge, and creationists know this, or they should since they have been told many times. Next time, though, there is a flap about the teaching of creationism in your area's schools, be sure to check the "letters to the editor" section of your local paper. Sure enough, every time you will see letters from creationists objecting that evolution is "only a theory."

3) Pseudoscientists and pseudoscholars are prone to utopian thinking and making exaggerated claims. They often see their ideologies as holding the key to human salvation. In the 1970s the New Age movement, as its

name implies, was seen by its advocates as the beginning of a new era, the Age of Aquarius, where, in the words of a song from the 1960s musical *Hair*, "Peace will guide the planets, and love will steer the stars." New Agers thought that by meditating, trance channeling, wearing crystals and pyramids, consulting Tarot and horoscopes, and so on, they could find inner peace and even transform the world into an extended hippie commune. Goddess worshippers think that if we repudiate patriarchy and male dominance and embrace the Goddess, we will have a world with no warfare, oppression, poverty, exploitation, or drug abuse. Proponents of many types of "alternative medicine," such as homeopathy, holistic medicine, chelation therapy, chiropractic, reflexology, iridology, and so on, make very big claims about the near-miraculous powers of their "cures." They abuse medical doctors and the "medical establishment," and tout their treatments as the keys to perfect health. Numerous tests have failed to confirm any of these grandiose claims, not that this has any effect on the boosters of "alternative medicine." Purveyors of bogus claims also often make greatly exaggerated claims about how "irrefutable" their arguments are or how "unquestionable" their evidence is. Some religious apologists, who style themselves as biblical "scholars," claim that they present such an overwhelming case that any skeptic who fairly considers their arguments and evidence will become a convert. One such apologist has proclaimed that it takes more faith to be an atheist than a believer in the face of the supposedly incontrovertible arguments he has offered. Such hyperinflated claims (and egos) are typical of bogus "scholars."

4) English philosopher John Locke observed long ago that every cult or sect pursues reasonable arguments as far as it can, but then, when reason fails, it resorts to faith. The same holds for pseudoscientists and bogus scholars. They

will appeal to legitimate evidence, or, at least, what looks like legitimate evidence, so long as they can. Eventually, it will be plain that some of the things they say cannot be supported by anything that even looks like legitimate scientific or scholarly methods. They then appeal to faith, intuition, or to some other "alternative way of knowing." When the weakness of their "objective" evidence is pointed out, Goddess worshippers don't miss a beat; they simply appeal to women's allegedly superior intuition and insight. Men, blinded by their notions of "objectivity" ("objectivity is what a man calls his subjectivity," a feminist philosopher once proclaimed), "rationality," and the cold, impersonal strictures of "linear" and "masculine" scientific thinking, simply will not have eyes to see the truth about the Goddess.

CONCLUSION

We have, then, a variety of symptoms of pseudoscience and bogus scholarship. Some of these indicators are problems with the theories or claims themselves. For instance, some theories do not offer legitimate explanations of what they are supposed to explain. Others make free use of *ad hoc* hypotheses to avoid potentially falsifying counterevidence, and some are based on biased evidence. Other indications arise from the practitioners of pseudoscience and bogus scholarship; their sneaky and shady behavior suggests that they have something to hide. There is no need to abuse your opponents or mischaracterize their positions if your claim is supported by evidence and logic. There is no need to appeal to faith, mystical insight, or intuition if you can substantiate your theory with data and solid scientific reasoning.

The pursuit of science and scholarship is one of the highest and noblest of human endeavors. Those with the intelligence and dedication to conduct these arduous studies deserve our deepest gratitude and respect. By contrast, those who pervert the ideals of science and scholarship for narrow ideological or pecuniary aims deserve censure and disgrace.

NOTES

1. Michael Shermer, *Why People Believe Weird Things* (New York: W. H. Freeman, 1997), pp. 173–241.
2. Ibid., p. 215.

SUGGESTIONS FOR FURTHER READING

There have been many good books debunking pseudoscience, many of the best printed by the publisher of this book, Prometheus Books. An older book but still one of the best is Terence Hines's *Pseudoscience and the Paranormal: A Critical Examination of the Evidence* (Amherst, NY: Prometheus Books, 1988). It is always pleasurable to see the bright light of critical reason penetrate into the murky depths of pseudoscience, and Hines shines a searchlight on some of the murkiest ideas and doctrines. Two periodicals are devoted to exposing pseudoscience, bogus scholarship, and other weird claims. The *Skeptical Inquirer* has been around since 1976 and is still going strong. Michael Shermer's *Skeptic* is also good. Shermer's book *Why People Believe Weird Things* (cited in the notes) is, like all of his books, fun to read and devastatingly logical. When the proponents of nonsense are not only unreasonable but obnoxious, like the creationists and the Holocaust "revisionists," it is even more fun to see them deflated. The standard guide to the bizarre world of the holocaust deniers is Deborah Lipstadt's *Denying the Holocaust: The Growing Assault on Truth and Memory* (New York: Plume, 1993). There are many good books out debunking creationism. Philip Kitcher's two books on creationism, *Abusing Science* (Cambridge, MA: MIT Press, 1982) from 1982 and *Living with Darwin* (Oxford: Oxford University Press, 2007), are both highly recommended. Kitcher is one of the leading philosophers of science and has diligently fought the good fight against creationist obscurantism. On the trials and tribulations of Karl Popper's falsifiability criterion, see A. F. Chalmers's *What Is This Thing Called Science?* 3rd ed. (Indianapolis, IN: Hackett, 1999). The mother goddess and primitive matriarchy myth is thoroughly debunked by Bruce S. Thornton in *Plagues of the Mind: The New Epidemic of False Knowledge* (Wilmington, DE: ISI Books, 1999).

GLOSSARY

Abductive Argument: An **inference to the best explanation**.

Ad Hominem: A **fallacy of relevance** that attempts to undermine a **conclusion** by turning our attention away from the **argument** and toward the arguer. For instance, characterizing an opponent as a "feminazi" or a "pinhead" is an attempt to discredit an argument by discrediting the person making the argument.

Ad Misericordiam: A **fallacy of relevance** that attempts to support a **conclusion** by manipulating our feelings of sympathy or pity. Infomercials that insist that we will be starving children if we do not make a large pledge to their charity *right now* are employing the *ad misericordiam*.

Ad Populum: A **fallacy of relevance** that appeals to popularity or popular feeling to support a **conclusion**. Saying that a brand is best because it is most popular is often fallacious, because the best brand might cost considerably more than the most popular brand.

Ad Verecundiam: A **fallacy of relevance** that attempts to support a **conclusion** by making an illicit appeal to authority. Citing Einstein's political convictions as authoritative would be fallacious because Einstein's expertise as a physicist did not make him an authority on politics.

Ambiguity: This is said to occur when **expression** could have two or more meanings, that is, when correctly punctuated, that expression could form any of two or more sentences. For instance, the expression H v M → L could mean (H v M) → L or H v (M → L).

Ampliative Argument: An **argument** is ampliative if its **conclusion** adds to the information contained within the **premises**. **Inductive** and **abductive** arguments are ampliative, but **Deductive** arguments are not.

Antecedent: The sentence in a **conditional** that follows the "if" and comes before the "then." "It rains" is the antecedent of "If it rains, then it pours." When a **conditional sentence form** is represented as p → q, the p is the antecedent.

Argument: Any discourse, composed of declarative sentences, which offers reasons, called **premises**, for accepting a given **conclusion**.

Argument Form: The abstract form that any number of particular **arguments** might share. For instance, the argument

$$p \rightarrow q$$
$$p$$
$$\overline{}$$
$$q$$

is the form of every argument that you can get by uniformly substituting any sentences whatsoever for p and q.

Background Knowledge: All knowledge relevant to the evaluation of the probability of a hypothesis apart from the particular evidence being considered on a given occasion. For instance, if someone says that she saw the Loch Ness Monster, we would not only consider her testimony, but how likely, apart from that testimony, we think it is that the monster was seen.

Base Rate Fallacy: Misestimating a **probability** because you overlook a background frequency, the "base rate" that something occurs within a population. For instance, you may be committing the base rate fallacy if you conclude on the basis of a single positive test that you have a rare disease (see chapter 9).

Bayes's Theorem: A theorem of the probability calculus proven in the eighteenth century by the Reverend Dr. Thomas Bayes. Bayes's theorem is used to calculate inverse probabilities. The formula for Bayes's theorem is:

$$p(b \mid a) = \frac{p(b) \times p(a \mid b)}{p(b) \times p(a \mid b) + p(\sim b) \times p(a \mid \sim b)}$$

Bayes's theorem is most often used by philosophers to model rational belief change.

Begging the Question: The fallacy of assuming as a **premise** something that needs to be proven in the **conclusion**. For instance, if you assume that all speech should be free in arguing that there should be no limits on free speech, you beg the question.

Biconditional: The sentence formed by putting together two sentences with the **sentence connective** "if and only if," symbolized by "$\leftrightarrow$"

Binary Connectives: A binary connective connects two sentences (simple or compound) to form a **compound sentence**. "And" (**conjunction**), and "if . . . then" (**conditional**), are examples of binary connectives.

Bogus Scholarship: Any body of work that pretends to meet scholarly standards of objectivity and rigor, but is, in fact, tendentious and unprincipled subterfuge.

Bound Variable: In **predicate logic** a **subject variable** that is quantified by a particular **quantifier**. For instance, in the formula $(\forall x)(Fx \rightarrow Mx)$ & Gx, the two x's inside the parentheses are bound by the universal quantifier. Every variable within the **scope** of a quantifier for that variable is bound by that quantifier. The x following the G is outside of the scope of the **universal quantifier** and so is not bound by the quantifier and is therefore a **free variable**.

Categorical Sentence: A sentence that expresses a relationship between categories or classes of things. "All whales are mammals" and "Some snakes are not poisonous" are examples of categorical sentences.

Causal Factor: When certain members of a population exhibit a complexly caused effect, a causal factor is *one* of the factors contributing to that effect. For instance, a hereditary disposition can be one causal factor, among many, affecting the rates of breast cancer among American women.

Causal Hypothesis: A hypothesis that postulates a causal relationship, such as between smoking habits and the incidence of lung cancer.

Causal Mechanism: A physical process that determines the occurrence of an **event** or changes its **probability** of occurrence. An example would be the biochemical processes involving carcinogens from cigarette smoke that make the development of cancerous tumors certain or more probable in certain individuals.

Causal Model: A **theoretical model** of a possible causal relationship.

Circumstantial *Ad Hominem*: A form of the *ad hominem* fallacy where some circumstance pertaining to the arguer is taken to discredit the **argument**. For instance, attempting to discredit a person's argument by pointing out that he is a paid lobbyist for the organization he is supporting by his argument is an instance of the circumstantial *ad hominem*.

Code Words: Words employed deceptively so that both a speaker and his intended audience know that the real subject is something else. For instance, if the mayor of an all-white suburban town opposes the extension of rail lines from downtown into his community, he may speak of "undesirable elements" or "increased crime rates" as alleged consequences of the rail extension. However, both the mayor and his constituents know that these terms are code for people of color.

Compound Sentence: A sentence that can be broken down into one or more **simple sentences** and one or more **sentence connectives**.

Conclusion: The claim that an **argument** attempts to support or establish with its **premises**.

Conditional: A **compound sentence** formed by putting together two sentences with the **sentence connective** "if . . . then," symbolized by "→."

Conditional Proof: **Proof** that works by assuming the **antecedent** of a **conditional**, proving the **consequent** of the **conditional**, and then discharging the assumption.

Confirmation Bias: The human psychological tendency to notice instances that confirm a presupposition and ignore those that disconfirm it. For instance, you notice when your "lucky rabbit's foot" seems to bring you good luck and ignore all the times it does not.

Conjunct: Either of the two sentences put together by the **sentence connective** "and" to form a **conjunction**.

Conjunction: A **compound sentence** formed by putting together two sentences with the **sentence connective** "and," symbolized by "&."

Connotation: What a term suggests beyond its literal, denotative definition. For instance, when people of Japanese ancestry were called "Japs" during World War II, this term had many negative connotations.

Consequent: The sentence in a **conditional** that follows the "then." "It pours" is the consequent of "If it rains, then it pours." When a **conditional** sentence form is represented as p → q, the q is the consequent.

Contingent Sentence: A sentence that can be true or false, depending on the circumstances. That is, a sentence that is not required to be true or false by its form. For instance, any sentence with the form p v q is contingent, because whether it is true or false depends upon which sentences we substitute for p and q. Any sentence of the form p v ~p, on the other hand, is not conditional, but rather is a **tautology**, because every sentence that has that form is true.

Control Group: The subgroup in a study that represents the hypothetical population not exposed to a certain suspected cause (see chapter 10 for details).

Contradiction: A sentence that is false in every conceivable circumstance. It is **logically impossible** that a contradiction be true. In **sentential logic**, a contradiction is any sentence that is a **substitution instance** of a **contradictory sentence form**.

Contradictory Sentence Form: A **sentence form** such that every substitution instance of that form is false.

Deductive Argument: An **argument** that presents itself as **valid**, that is, as one where the truth of the **premises** is supposed to guarantee the truth of the **conclusion**. A good deductive argument is one that actually is valid; a poor deductive argument is invalid.

Demarcation Criteria: Criteria alleged to distinguish science from nonscience. Philosophers of science have consistently failed to produce a list of such criteria.

Denotation: The literal or "dictionary" definition of a word, apart from its **connotations** or emotional associations.

Disjunct: Either of the two sentences put together by the **sentence connective** "or" to form a **disjunction**.

Disjunction: The **compound sentence** formed by connecting two sentences with the **sentence connective** "or," symbolized by "v."

Entail (noun: **Entailment**): Any **conclusion** that follows by a **valid argument** from a set of **premises** is said to be entailed by those premises.

Likewise, the premises are said to entail that conclusion. Entailment should be carefully distinguished from **material implication**.

Event: Anything that occurs in a definite, discernable way so that we can say without any vagueness or **ambiguity** that it definitely did or did not take place.

Existential Quantifier: In **predicate logic** the existential quantifier, symbolized (∃) is used to state that some x is P, where x is any **subject variable** and P is any **predicate constant**. For instance, (∃x) Fx tells us that some (at least one) x is F.

Experimental Group: The subgroup in a study intended to represent the hypothetical population where all are exposed to the suspected cause (see chapter 10 for details).

Expression: Any symbol or collection of symbols of SL or PL, whether or not that symbol or collection constitutes a sentence in SL or a formula in PL.

Fallacies of Meaning: Fallacies that attempt to persuade by playing upon the **ambiguity**, vagueness, or **connotation** of terms.

Fallacies of Relevance: Fallacies that present considerations irrelevant to the **conclusion** as though they were relevant. For instance, *ad hominem* is a fallacy of relevance, because it shifts attention away from the **argument** and to the arguer.

Fallacies of Unjustified Assumptions: Fallacies that make an assumption that the arguer has no right to make. **Begging the question** is an example of such a fallacy.

Fallacy of Equivocation: A fallacy that works by switching between two **ambiguous** meanings. For instance, creationists frequently say that evolution is "only a theory." In doing so, they equivocate between two meanings of "theory"—one meaning a speculation and the other meaning an established and confirmed scientific account.

Falsifiability: An attempt to demarcate science from nonscience in by saying that a theory is scientific if and only if it can, in principle, be falsified. Falsifiability, though intuitive, is incapable of being phrased so that it is not too exclusive or too inclusive.

Framing: Presenting information about probabilities phrased in such a way to make a positive and perhaps misleading psychological impact. For instance, a beer touted as "most popular in the USA!" might really have only a modest share of the market and be only incrementally more popular than the second-most popular brand.

Free Variable: In **predicate logic**, a **subject variable** that is not **bound** by any **quantifier**. In the formula $(\exists x)(Gx \,\&\, Fy) \lor Mx$ the y is free because here the **existential quantifier** only binds x's, and the x after the M is free because it is not within the **existential quantifier's** **scope**.

Independent Events: Two **events** are independent if the occurrence of one does not affect the **probability** of the occurrence of the other. If you roll a six on a die and then toss a coin, the event of getting the six does not affect the outcome of the coin toss.

Indirect Proof: **Proof** that relies on *reductio ad absurdum* reasoning to prove the **conclusion**. That is, you prove the **argument valid** by showing that the **conjunction** of the **premises** and the **conclusion** **entails** a **contradiction**.

Inference: **(a)** A logical **conclusion** that is drawn from the consideration of a certain body of evidence or a set of **premises**. **(b)** The act of drawing such a logical conclusion.

Inference to the Best Explanation: An **inference** to a **conclusion** where the conclusion states the best explanation of a certain body of data or evidence.

Inverse Probability: For example, the inverse probability of $p(a\,|\,b)$ is $p(b\,|\,a)$.

Law of Non-Contradiction: The fundamental law of logic that says that a statement and its denial cannot both be true.

Loaded Question: A question that, taken straightforwardly, cannot be answered "yes" or "no" without thereby tacitly accepting an unjustified assumption. The classic example of the loaded question is, "Do you still beat your wife?" You confess to being a wife beater with either a yes or no answer.

Loaded Term: A term with a negative **connotation**, intended to bias the listener. For instance, characterizing an opponent in an election as an "extremist" or a "radical" is to use loaded terms.

Logical Impossibility: The impossibility involved in attempting to violate the **law of non-contradiction**, that is, the impossibility involved in trying to assert two contradictory statements.

Main Connective: The **sentence connective** in a **compound sentence** with the broadest **scope**. The connective that joins all of the component sentences together into a single sentence.

Margin of Error: The range of values above and below a certain statistical measure within which there is a degree of **probability** (usually 95 percent) that the real value lies. For instance, if I poll 500 Americans of Scottish descent and find that 29 percent dislike bagpipe music, I would conclude that the actual percentage of Caledonian Americans who dislike bagpipe music would probably be between 25 percent and 33 percent with a margin of error of ± 4 percent.

Material Implication: The relationship between two sentences symbolized by "→" and read as "if . . . then." The "if . . . then" relationship of material implication only says that it is not the case that the **antecedent** is true and the **consequent** false. There is no implication that the consequent *must* be true if the antecedent is or that the consequent can be deduced from the antecedent.

Multiple Place Predicates: Predicates that apply to more than one sub-ject. The T in Taf is a multiple-place predicate that applies to subjects a and f.

Mutually Exclusive Events: Two **events** are mutually exclusive if the occurrence of one excludes or prevents the occurrence of the other. For instance, getting a six on one roll of a die excludes getting a two on the same roll.

Negation: The **compound sentence** formed by attaching the **sentence connective** "and" to another sentence. Negation is symbolized by "~."

Negative Correlation: Two **variables** are negatively correlated if their values tend to vary inversely. That is, as the value of one goes up, the values of the other tend to go down and vice versa.

One-Place Predicate: Predicates that apply only to a single subject. The P in Pa is a one-place predicate.

Personal Probability: Our subjective level of confidence or degree of belief that something is so or will occur. For instance, my belief that on a given occasion a particular politician is telling the truth might be very low, say, .01, or, in other words, I have only a 1 percent con-fidence that he is telling the truth.

Positive Correlation: Two **variables** are positively correlated if their values tend to go up or down together, that is, as the value of one increases, so the other tends to increase also; as the value of one goes down, the other tends to decrease also.

Predicate Constant: The capital letters used in **predicate logic** to des-ignate predicates. For instance P is the predicate constant in the expression $(\forall x)Px$ that says that every x is P.

Predicate Logic (PL): That branch of **symbolic logic** that deals with the logic of subjects and their predicates and the **quantifiers** that govern such **expressions**.

Predicate Term: The term that names the predicate of a **categorical sentence**. "Mammals" is the predicate term of "All whales are mammals."

Premise(s): The reason(s) given for accepting the **conclusion** of an **argument**.

Probability: In this book we consider probability in two senses: (a) the probability of an **event**, that is, how likely that a given physical event will occur given what we know about the world. For instance, the probability that a single toss of a fair coin will be heads is 1/2; (b) a measure of our subjective degree of confidence that something is so or will occur. Both types of probability are measured on a scale from 0 to 1, inclusive.

Proof: A formal demonstration of a **conclusion** that presents the **premises** of the **argument**, the conclusion, the steps leading to the conclusion, and the justifications for each of the steps.

Prospective Experimental Design: A "natural experiment" in which people select themselves into two distinct groups, say, smokers and nonsmokers, who then can be studied, as in a **randomized experimental design**, to test a **causal model**. You put those who have abstained from or have not been exposed to the suspected cause into the **control group** and those who have had the appropriate level of exposure in the **experimental group**. You must carefully screen the members of the control and experimental groups to make sure that none already exhibits the suspected effect. You also try to make the groups as alike as possible with respect to all other possible causal factors for the suspected effect. A prospective design is not as reliable an experimental design as a **randomized design**.

Pseudoscience: Any doctrine, theory, or practice presented as possessing scientific credentials, but really woefully lacking them.

Quantifier: In a **categorical sentence**, the quantifiers are "all," "no," and "some," and tell us how many of a given category we are talking about. For instance, "No whales are fish" says of all the whales there are that none of them is a fish. In **predicate logic** there are two kinds of quantifiers, **existential quantifiers** and **universal quantifiers**.

Randomized Experimental Design: The optimal design for a study. In a randomized design, a group of test subjects is selected at random from a population. From this group of test subjects a second random selection is made to divide the test subjects into two subgroups and assign one subgroup to the **experimental group** and the other to the **control group** (see chapter 10 for details).

Relational predicate: A relational property like "taller than."

Rhetoric: The art of persuading or motivating people through the effective use of spoken or written communication.

Scope (of an assumption): The steps of a **proof** between the step where the assumption is made and the step where the assumption is discharged.

(of a connective): The scope of a **sentence connective** is the connective itself and whatever it connects.

(of a quantifier): The range of symbols to which a **quantifier** is intended to apply. That range is indicated by parentheses, brackets, and braces. Just because a **subject variable** is within the scope of a **quantifier** does not mean that it is **bound** by that quantifier. For instance, in the formula $(\forall x)(Fx \rightarrow Gy)$, the y is within the scope of the quantifier, as the parentheses indicate, but it is not bound by that quantifier.

Sentence Connective: Words or phrases, like "and," "or," and "if . . . then," used to connect sentences in SL. "Not" is also considered a sentence connective, though it applies to a sentence directly and does not join sentences. In PL we still use these connectives, though there they need not join sentences, but may connect other **expressions**, for example, Fx v Gx.

Sentence Constant: A capital letter that stands for a complete **simple sentence**.

Sentence Form: The abstract form that can be shared by any number of different sentences in SL. For instance, the sentence form p v ~q is shared by A v ~B and J v ~(M &l).

Sentence Variable: A **variable** that can stand for any sentence constant.

Sentential Logic (SL): The branch of **symbolic logic** that deals with the logic of whole sentences and their connectives.

Simple Predicate: a nonrelational property, like "is tall."

Simple Sentence: A declarative sentence that cannot be broken down into simpler sentences. Examples: "It is raining." "The cat is on the mat." "Atlanta is the capital of Georgia."

Statistical Hypothesis: A hypothesis that claims that a particular numerical relationship exists between the values of certain variables.

Statistical Significance: Informally, a numerical statement of our degree of confidence in a statistical measure or in the results of a study. It is generally assumed that a study is statistically significant if we have a 95 percent degree of confidence in the results.

Strength of a Correlation: Informally, it is the measure of how closely the values of two correlated variables are related. A perfect correlation is one where any change in one value means a corresponding change in the other value. A zero correlation means that there is no correlation, no connection between the values of two variables. If the correlation is less than perfect, then there is only some tendency, from very strong to very slight, for a change in one variable to correspond to a change in the value of the other.

Subject Constant: The small letters used in **predicate logic** to denote particular persons, places, things, or concepts. Subject constants are never used to designate general properties.

Subject Term: The term that names the subject of a **categorical sentence**. For instance, "whales" is the subject term of "All whales are mammals."

Subject Variable: The small letters in **predicate logic** that stand for any subject. Subject variables are used with **predicate constants** and **quantifiers** to express sentences in PL. For instance, $(\forall x)(Gx \rightarrow Fx)$ says that for all x, where x can be any subject whatsoever, if x is G, then x is F.

Substitution Instance: A sentence that has a particular **sentence form** or an **argument** that has a particular **argument form**.

Syllogism: A form of **deductive argument** employing **categorical sentences** devised by Aristotle (384–322 BCE) consisting of two **premises** and a **conclusion**.

Symbolic Logic: Broadly, all logic that is done with special logical symbols (e.g., **quantifiers** and **sentence connectives**). Here symbolic logic encompasses **sentential logic** and **predicate logic**.

Tautologous Sentence Form: A **sentence form** such that every **substitution instance** of that form is true.

Tautology: A sentence that is true in every conceivable circumstance. A tautology is necessarily true, that is, its negation is a **contradiction**. In **sentential logic**, a tautology is any sentence that is a **substitution instance** of a **tautologous sentence form**.

Theoretical Model: An imaginary representation of possible states of affairs, thought to approximate aspects of physical reality and intended to be a part of a theoretical account of some body of natural phenomena.

Truth Functional: **Sentential logic** is said to be truth functional because the truth-value of its **compound sentences** is determined strictly by the truth-values of its **simple sentences** and the **connectives** joining those sentences.

Truth Table: A visual representation of all the possible truth-values that can be taken by a set of simple or **compound sentences**. *Tu quoque*: A form of *ad hominem* **argument** that works by taking an argument that makes an accusation and turning the accusation, or another just as bad, back on the accuser. For instance, if an opponent is charging you with dishonesty, you attempt to show that he has been similarly or even more dishonest.

Unary Connective: A "**connective**" that really only applies to one sentence, simple or compound, to make a new **compound sentence**. The only unary connective is "not" (negation).

Universal Quantifier: In **predicate logic** the **universal quantifier**, symbolized (∀) is used to state that all x's are P, where x is any **subject variable**, and P is any **predicate constant**. For instance, (∀x)Fx tells us that every x is F

Valid (noun: **validity**): A valid **argument** is one where the **conclusion** must be true if the **premises** are all true. That is, if you assert the truth of the **premises** of a **valid argument** but deny the **conclusion**, you contradict yourself. An argument that presents itself as valid but fails to be is called an invalid argument.

Valid Argument Form: An **argument form** such that every **argument** that is a **substitution instance** of that form is a **valid** argument.

Variable: A general property possessed by members of some population such that the property can take a range of possible values. The IQs of the population of candidates for election to Congress in 2008 would be an example of a variable.

Weasel Words: Words or phrases that seem to promise something but do not. Ads that say "up to 50 percent off" are weasely.

INDEX